The Definitive Guide to Building Java Robots

■ ■ ■

Scott Preston

Apress®

The Definitive Guide to Building Java Robots

Copyright © 2006 by Scott Preston

ISBN: 1-59059-556-4

Printed and bound in the United States of America 9 8 7 6 5 4 3 2 1

Coke®, Pepsi®, and 7 UP® are registered trademarks of The Coca Cola Company, PepsiCo Beverages of North America Inc., and Cadbury Beverages North America, respectively.

Trademarked names may appear in this book. Rather than use a trademark symbol with every occurrence of a trademarked name, we use the names only in an editorial fashion and to the benefit of the trademark owner, with no intention of infringement of the trademark.

Lead Editor: Steve Anglin
Technical Reviewer: Simon Ritter
Editorial Board: Steve Anglin, Dan Appleman, Ewan Buckingham, Gary Cornell, Tony Davis, Jason Gilmore, Jonathan Hassell, Chris Mills, Dominic Shakeshaft, Jim Sumser
Project Manager: Sofia Marchant
Copy Edit Manager: Nicole LeClerc
Copy Editor: Mike McGee
Assistant Production Director: Kari Brooks-Copony
Production Editor: Katie Stence
Compositor: Susan Glinert
Proofreader: April Eddy
Indexer: Carol Burbo
Artist: April Milne
Cover Designer: Kurt Krames
Manufacturing Director: Tom Debolski

Distributed to the book trade worldwide by Springer-Verlag New York, Inc., 233 Spring Street, 6th Floor, New York, NY 10013. Phone 1-800-SPRINGER, fax 201-348-4505, e-mail orders-ny@springer-sbm.com, or visit http://www.springeronline.com.

For information on translations, please contact Apress directly at 2560 Ninth Street, Suite 219, Berkeley, CA 94710. Phone 510-549-5930, fax 510-549-5939, e-mail info@apress.com, or visit http://www.apress.com.

The source code for this book is available to readers at http://www.apress.com in the Source Code section.

Contents at a Glance

Contents

About the Author

SCOTT PRESTON works as a Java architect in Columbus, Ohio, where he resides with his wife, Emily, and dog, Castle. Scott has over 20 years of software and electrical experience, including positions with the U.S. Navy, Bank One, CompuServe, UUNET, and Covansys Inc., in addition to running his own robotics company, Preston Research LLC. Scott also gives lectures about robotics at COSI (Center of Science and Industry) and manufactures small Java-enabled robots called CubeBots®. Scott is a member of the Java Community Process and an alumnus of The Ohio State University.

About the Technical Reviewer

SIMON RITTER is a Java technology evangelist at Sun Microsystems. Simon has been in the IT business since 1984 and holds a bachelor of science degree in physics from Brunel University in the UK. Originally working in the area of UNIX development for AT&T UNIX System Labs and then Novell, Simon moved to Sun in 1996. At that time, he began working with Java technology and has since divided his time between Java technology development and consultancy. He now specializes in emerging technologies, including grid computing, RFID, robotics, and smart sensor networks. Simon and his performing Java-powered LEGO robots have appeared before audiences worldwide.

Acknowledgments

I would like to especially thank my loving wife, Emily, for putting up with me while I wrote this book and for all the hours I spent at the PC and downstairs with the robots when I could have been spending it with her.

Second, I would like to thank Steve Anglin, Simon Ritter, Sofia Marchant, Michael McGee, and Katie Stence for helping me write this book, and to readers and others at Apress who have been a joy to work with.

Third, I would like to thank Ken Gracey from Parallax, Inc., and Jim Frye from Lynxmotion, Inc., for supplying me with various parts, components, and advice during the writing of this book.

Fourth, I would like to thank my mother for passing on her common sense and buying me an Atari 400 in 1980, and my father for passing on his engineering smarts and helping me build the original Feynman in 2002.

Fifth, I would like to thank my in-laws, Frikkie and Karen Roets, for their hospitality last Christmas (and always), and for the use of their office to contact Apress about writing this book.

Sixth, I would like to thank my high-school science teacher, Jan Greissinger, for inspiring me to love science as much as I do today, and also Guy Kawasaki for his books and e-mails, which inspired me to write this book.

Finally, I could not end without mentioning my friends Harry and Crissy, Ron and Sophia, Mark and Maria, Bard and Ann, Mark and Tracy, and John and Kristi. I was meaning to spend more time with you this summer, and even come out and visit those who are a little more than a drive away. Plan on that in 2006.

Scott Preston

Introduction

Notes on Style

I admit I was a programmer before I started building robots. So my perspective may be somewhat skewed in the direction of a programmer. However, I also didn't want this book to be from a purely software engineering perspective. I wanted to keep the text balanced between robotics and programming and not get too cute with either discipline, though from time to time I'm afraid I may have indulged myself.

Who Should Read This Book

If you want off-the-shelf robot components, free software, and development tools, this is the book for you. You can download all the software—it's GPL (General Public License) or Apache License—and you can purchase the components from your favorite robot supplier and/or hobby shop. The following sections outline the experience you should have to get the most out of the book.

Your Programming/Java Experience

I *could* say that you should have a good understanding of object-oriented techniques and Java before getting started with this book, but if you're like most roboticists, you'll likely learn as you go, and by following the various examples I've included within these pages.

Of course, if you don't have a background in Java, you will undoubtedly experience a learning curve before things begin to click. If you start getting lost due to the vocabulary or the complexity of the examples, just purchase one of the beginning Java books from Apress. They're excellent. If things still don't make sense, send me an e-mail or visit my web site and post a question.

Your Robot Building Experience

For those picking up this book, you should hopefully be an intermediate robot builder already; be familiar with microcontroller concepts, servo controllers, electronic speed controls, and sensors; and have either built a robot from scratch or from a kit. I can recommend a few robots from Lynxmotion, Inc., or if you want to build one from scratch, take a look at some of the Apress books penned by David Cook.

How This Book Is Structured

I've structured this book as if I were sitting down to build a Java robot. I start out by reviewing the basics of communication, and then discuss how to get the robot to move, hear, see, and navigate, before exploring how to optimize code and create shortcuts.

I've divided each chapter into subtopics that progress from easy to difficult. Each subtopic includes the following:

- An introduction to the topic

- A detailed discussion of the code example

- A code example demonstrating the topic

- A section or chapter summary, if needed

What You Will Need

While you can use this book quite effectively without every item named in the following table, the required and optional items shown will help you facilitate the examples in this book. I also provide a list of what you need in each chapter's introduction.

Table 1. *Items Needed for Book Examples*

Required	Optional
Java 1.4 SDK	DLink DBT-120 or other Bluetooth adapter
Java APIs (comm, advanced imaging, speech, etc.)	EB500 Bluetooth Transceiver from Parallax
Parallax Javelin or BASIC Stamp	Pan and Tilt Camera Kit from Lynxmotion
MiniSSC-II Servo controller	Lynxmotion SSC-32 Servo controller
Parallax Board of Education (BOE) or other carrier board	Lynxmotion Extreme Hexapod 2
Web camera	
Sound card and microphone	
Small mobile robot	
Miscellaneous robot sensors (sonar, infrared, bump, etc.)	

Platform and Version Notes

I developed this book and its examples with the Sun Java Standard Edition 1.4.2 SDK, using the Eclipse 3.02 IDE running on Microsoft Windows XP. However, if you don't have a Microsoft operating system, you can easily port the examples in this book to Linux, Macintosh, or any OS running a JVM.

You can download the latest SDK from http://java.sun.com/j2se/1.4.2/download.html and the latest version of Eclipse at www.eclipse.org/downloads/index.php.

While you can use J2SE 5.0 or Eclipse 3.1, both were not ready at the time this book was written, so the programs have not been tested with those versions.

Book Road Map

The chapters of this book build upon each other, with the primary goal being robot navigation, which we tackle in Chapter 7. However, you can really expand the capability of your robot by using speech as explored in Chapter 5, or by using some of the items discussed in Chapter 9. I draw on topics from all of the previous chapters in Chapter 9, while simultaneously introducing some fun and powerful programs. See Figure 1.

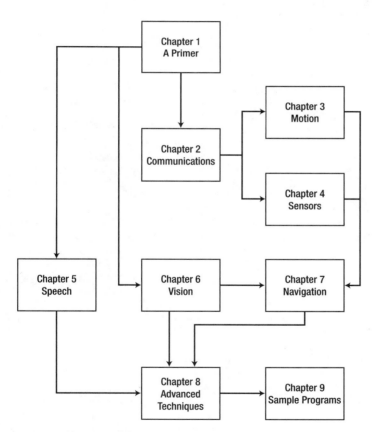

Figure 1. *Book road map*

Updates and Software

I will constantly be updating my site at www.scottsbots.com/definitiveguide. Please stop by to visit, download new source code and examples, and get links to Internet resources. I have also included a special section for purchasing robots or parts needed for this book.

■ ■ ■

CHAPTER 1

A Primer

"Everything should be made as simple as possible, but not simpler."

— Albert Einstein

1.0 Introduction

Before you begin programming your robot with Java, you should consider some things that will make your Java robot experience much more enjoyable. They include the following:

- A configured personal computer and various software*
- A serial link
- A microcontroller
- A robot

Note Be sure your PC has a fast Internet connection as I will often refer to links from the Internet for download or reference.

To begin, I'll walk you through a setup similar to mine. Forgive me non-Windows users, all screen captures are from Windows XP. When the occasion arises, I'll mention an alternative way of achieving the same thing with a UNIX-based operating system.

Personal Computer Setup

To facilitate use of your personal computer for this book, you should do the following. Download and install the Java Standard Edition 1.4.2 from:

- http://java.sun.com/j2se/1.4.2/download.html

Download and install Eclipse 3.02 from:

- http://download.eclipse.org/eclipse/downloads/index.php

If you have any other Java Runtimes installed on your machine, make sure you set your Eclipse preferences to this path, as shown in Figure 1-1.

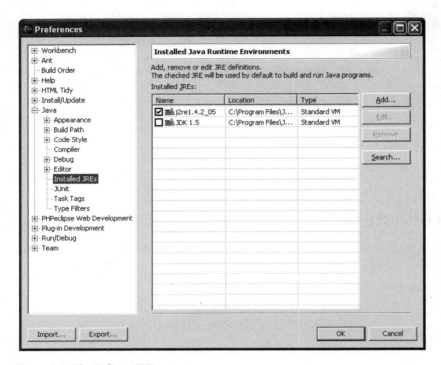

Figure 1-1. *The Eclipse JRE setup*

Download the latest source code for this book at:

- www.scottsbots.com/definitiveguide

You can add this JAR to your project. This way you should be able to call the classes from your own project with your own programs.

Serial Link Setup

If you don't have a serial port (some new computers only come with USB connectors), I recommend you get a USB nine-pin serial adapter, shown next in Figure 1-2.

Figure 1-2. *The IOGear USB Serial Adapter (GUC232A)*

The Microcontroller Setup

You should have a microcontroller you can program in PBASIC. I used the BASIC Stamp 2 for all the examples in this book because it does the job well. It was my first microcontroller, and it cost the least.

The BASIC Stamp 2 (shown in Figure 1-3) operates at 20MHz and can execute approximately 4,000 instructions per second. It has 16 I/O pins, plus two dedicated serial pins, one for transmit, and one for receive.

Figure 1-3. *The Parallax BASIC Stamp 2*

You can purchase one from www.parallax.com for $49.

The Microcontroller Programmer Setup

All examples in this book are in PBASIC because it's the most popular Microcontroller language at the moment. You can also find many examples and sample code on the Internet and at the Parallax site. At the back of the book, I've included a quick reference for PBASIC as well as a Javelin Stamp version of the examples.

You can download the latest version of the programmer from www.parallax.com. Figure 1-4 shows a picture of a sample program loaded into the BASIC Stamp Windows editor.

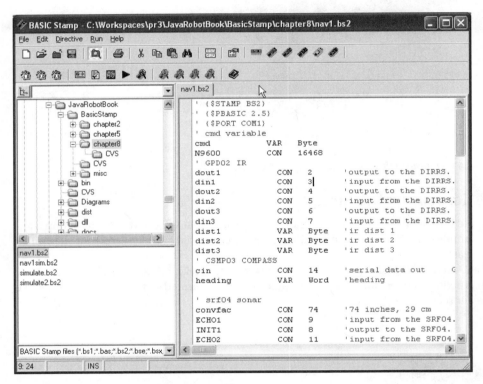

Figure 1-4. *The BASIC Stamp Windows editor*

The Robot Setup

If you do not have a robot and would like one in a kit, several fine specimens can be found at www.lynxmotion.com, www.parallax.com, or www.prestonresearch.com. For most of the examples in this book, I use a differential drive robot or CubeBot (as shown in Figure 1-5).

Figure 1-5. *A CubeBot*

Summary

Hopefully you have everything you need to get started. I'm now going to start by explaining the thought process behind robotics programming (in other words, getting your robot to do stuff). Then I'll talk about some concepts in Java you should know about before embarking on a robotics project. Finally, I'll show you an example of how to begin modeling your software in a way that's both easy to use and effective.

1.1 Organizing Your Behavior

What does your robot do? This is the number one question people ask when I tell them I have a robot. My answer five years ago would be something like, "It moves around a room and avoids the furniture." Then people would say "Oh...," and I would afterward talk about the technology or the software, which never kept their attention.

Thus, I wanted something for my robot to do besides these basic things. I wanted it to do something that would be cool, something like a simple human task, something I could tell people about and not get blank stares in return. So, I picked the chore of getting a beverage from the refrigerator.

I thought that moving to the refrigerator would not be that difficult, but as I started to compile a list of tasks, then subtasks, and then detailed steps, I realized that I had better start by organizing my thoughts around what I wanted to program (see Figure 1-6). How I organized them (my thoughts) requires a little explanation, so here's the definition of those terms:

- **Events:** These are the things that cause a robot to do something. Does it hear a word, see something, or get a request from the network, or is there a scheduled task, or something like that.

- **Tasks:** These are the things that events trigger. So if the robot gets a request to move someplace, the top level task would be to move. The move task would then have to call a subtask or another task to help.

- **Subtasks:** These are the things that help the task. So, if the task is to move from position A to position B, a robot must know what direction it's facing or consequently turn and face that direction. Subtasks may call other subtasks or send or receive data packets from the robot's subsystems.

- **Data packets:** These are the final level of granularity in our task organization. A data packet sends information to a controller to command the robot's motor controls, or sensors, whose sole purpose is to get and receive data from the robot's subsystems or peripherals.

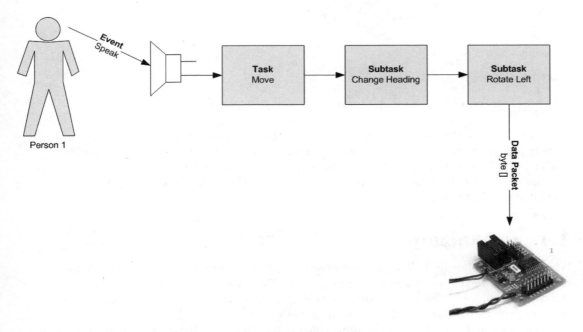

Figure 1-6. *A behavioral model of events, tasks, subtasks, and data packets*

In Table 1-1, shown next, I've listed some examples of each.

Table 1-1. *Sample Events, Tasks, Subtasks, and Data Packets*

Events	Tasks	Subtasks	Data Packets
Verbal command	Diagnostic	Change heading	RGB image stream
Vision (motion)	Move	Calculate start position	Byte[] serial output
Vision (landmark detection)	Follow object	Calculate shortest path	Byte[] serial input
Remote control command	Determine object location	Create motion vector	Speech synthesis to speakers
Battery low		Calculate a hough transform	
Scheduled event		Sleep	

There could be even more tasks or subtasks. The amount you add will depend on the noise in your environment. Once you're able to come up with the task and subtask that defines what you want your robot to do, you're ready to start handling some of the technical problems associated with robotics, like motion and perception.

Motion

How you make your robot move will depend on the answers to the following questions:

- How much money do you have to spend?

- How fast do you want your robot to move?

- What surface will your robot move on?

- How much will your robot weigh?

- How long will the power source last?

Let's say you have a budget of $200, you don't want your robot to move particularly fast, it will move on concrete or some other smooth surface, it will weigh about 150 pounds and need to stay alive about two hours before recharging. If this is the case, your options are limited. If the terrain changes to desert or the budget increases to $2,000, your list of possible technical solutions will change drastically. However, just having a drive system is not going to allow you to solve the main objective of getting a robot to navigate to the fridge. To do that, the robot will have to *perceive*.

Perception

To illustrate what the world of robot perception is, I'm going to ask you to do a few experiments. You'll really have to do these experiments to fully understand the problem.

To start with, go to your living room and shut your eyes. Hold your hands in front of you and try to make it to the kitchen so that you are in front of your refrigerator. If /when you hit something, that's fine, it was your bump sensor. So, back up, follow the wall, or do whatever you need to do to navigate until you're in front of the fridge and at a spot where you can raise your arm and open its door.

Now you were cheating in this example because you knew what direction you were facing when you started. So go back to the living room, spin around about ten times (don't fall down) and then repeat this experiment.

Oops, you were cheating again since you had a map of the room from memory and you knew where you were starting from. So now have someone spin you around, or take you to a new room, and then repeat the experiment.

Starting to understand the difficulty? Maybe you might be able to do better if you had a compass or someone to tell you the direction you were facing. Maybe you'd do better if you knew how far you were from a wall. You might do better if you kept track of how many steps you took and you knew how far each step was.

The point of this experiment is that after a few tries at getting to the refrigerator with the sensors you can purchase for your robot, you'll understand just how difficult robot perception is.

Navigation

From the last experiment you know just how difficult it is with a human brain to get around in a simple environment even when you have a map and a number of sensors and a good memory. Nevertheless, if you've ever been late to an appointment or gotten lost on the way to a new address, you know that sometimes even eyesight and a brain are not enough because there are so many unforeseen obstacles or the information that you have to work with is not "perfect."

Currently one of the holy grails of robotics and artificial intelligence is consistent, accurate navigation. You'd think this would be easier given GPS and complex military navigation systems, yet it remains an elusive goal and the U.S. government is willing to pay two million dollars to the first group that comes up with a vehicle that can navigate across the desert 175 miles within a 12-hour time limit. You can find more information on this challenge at www.darpa.mil/grandchallenge/.

1.2   Java Concepts

Java is an object-oriented programming language developed at Sun Microsystems in 1991. In this section, I'll describe some important concepts you'll see in this book that might not be obvious to a beginner (see Table 1-2).

Table 1-2. *Important Java Concepts*

Concept	Description
Constructors	A constructor is a method in a Java class that defines how it's instantiated. Keep a close eye on how you want your objects to be created. If you're too flexible, you could run into timing or other exceptions. If you're too rigid, your class will be too hard to use.
Exceptions	Errors in your robot programs will happen. Make sure you handle exceptions; they'll provide you with valuable debugging information for your code.

Table 1-2. *Important Java Concepts*

Concept	Description
Events	Usually done for graphical user interfaces, events are ways to send a class a notification of a state change. For example, when you receive data on a serial port, it will throw an event, informing the listening class that there's data in a buffer that must be read.
Interfaces	I'm going to keep the use of interfaces simple. They'll define patterns of behavior for similar classes.
Super Classes	I'm going to create super classes for all classes that have a "type-of" relationship. For example, a Parallax Stamp, a Scott Edwards, and a MiniSSC-II servo controller are types of controllers that communicate to a serial port. I would create a super class to handle common types of functionality.
Delegate Class	A delegate is a class that shares some common functionality but does not share a "type-of" relationship. For example, a controller isn't a type of sensor, but there might be common functionality I want to add to both. I would then create a delegate class to handle the functionality similarly for both classes.
Proxy Class	This is a class that has the functionality of many classes or components which are combined to act as a single class. I would use two types of proxy classes: a physical proxy representing a robotic device like a sensor, and an abstract proxy representing a behavior like navigation.
Server	A Java program that will not interact with a user interface or command line.
Client	A Java program that will interact with a user interface or a command line and a server.
Threads	If you want to do more than one thing at a time, you should use multiple threads.
Thread Safe Concurrent Access	Let's say you have multiple threads trying to access a single serial port on a PC. You need to find a way to limit access in a thread-safe way so you don't create dead-lock conditions.

Pausing Your Programs

I was at a conference when I heard a talk on state machines and thought it would be a good way to introduce timing and synchronization. A state machine is a model composed of three things: states, transitions, and actions. To illustrate an example of a state machine, I will use a retractable pen. It's a very simple state machine. The pen is either extended and ready to write, or it's retracted so you can put it in your pocket. To change its state, you click its top, or twist it if it's a fancy pen.

Let's define some terms as such: a state is some information about the model. A transition is an indicator of a change in state caused by some action. The simple state machine shown in Figure 1-7 shows how they are typically drawn. Starting at the top circle (called the initial state) the pen tip is retracted. Click the top of the pen and it's at a new state, extended and ready to write, which is now represented by the bottom circle. Click it again, and you're at your original state. Pretty simple, huh?

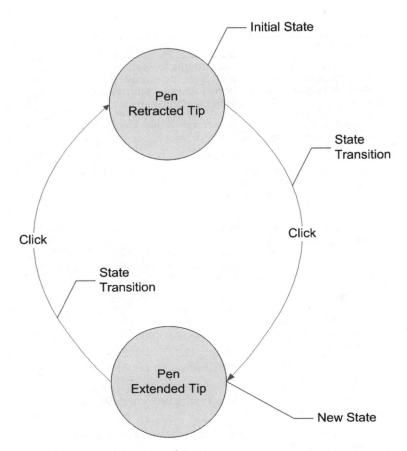

Figure 1-7. *A simple state machine*

So when you have a set of subtasks that you need to perform to get your robot to move, you should have a state diagram that transitions your robot from one state or subtask to another state or subtask.

However, doing this programmatically in Java with robots is a bit harder than dealing with the theory or picture just discussed, but the idea of a state machine does help in organizing what you want your robot to do, how you want your robot to do it, and most importantly: when you want your robot to do it. Finally, in order for your program to transition properly, when it's ready you'll need to be able to "pause" your program to allow these new states to materialize.

To pause your program with Java, use the following four ways defined in Table 1-3.

Table 1-3. *Ways to Pause a Java Program*

Pause Method	Description
Thread.sleep(ms)	This is a static method and will tell the current Java thread to sleep for a certain number of milliseconds. Keep in mind that this will put all Java programs using this thread to sleep, so if you're doing multiple things like waiting for a serial event and checking a parallel port reading, you'll have to create a new thread.
Timer Task	Another way of getting something to occur on a certain interval is to create a new timer task that will occur at a fixed time in milliseconds from when it was invoked.
Loop Until Finished	If you don't know how long something will take to complete, but don't want to do anything until it's finished, you can just put a program in a loop. Make sure you insert a Thread.sleep(1); in the loop so that way your PC does not have 100-percent CPU utilization while waiting. It could prevent what you are waiting for (like an image capture, voice command, and so on) from getting enough cycles to do anything.
wait() and notify()	If you have two cooperating threads—say, one thread for a serial port, and another reading an image from your webcam—you could use the wait() on your serial port and then notify() on the webcam class. The wait() method will cause the current thread of the serial port to wait until the webcam thread invokes the notify() or notifyAll() method.

Now that we're done with some of the important concepts in Java and we know how to pause our programs, our final step is to organize our hardware in a way that makes modeling our behavior easy.

1.3 Organizing Your Hardware

Both PCs and microcontrollers have their place in robotics. Each is good at some things and poor at others, but with both you get more than you would from using each separately.

Microcontrollers are very good at talking to smaller electronics. So if you have sensors, servos, or motor controllers, then use a microcontroller for this. Usually, they have many I/O ports, anywhere from 8–40 depending on the type of microcontroller you use, where PCs are limited to their communication ports. You'll discover later how you can use a PC parallel port to do some basic digital I/O, but when you start doing pulse width modulation (PWM) with a PC parallel port, you'll find yourself running into limitations.

PCs are very good at controlling decisions, storing data, interfacing with people, and using multimedia. Though there are some chips out there that can do speech synthesis, and cameras are available that can handle some basic color and object recognition, you'll find they have limited ability. Plus, your microcontroller's ability to interface with people, store data, and make decisions may leave a lot to be desired.

Organizing Your Components

The first thing I did was model the physical connections between my PC and my robot. I found that having three layers simplified the grouping. You can choose another arrangement for your robot, but this is what worked for me. An outline of the layering is shown in Table 1-4.

Table 1-4. *Layers in Robotics Programming*

PC Layer	Control Layer	Device Layer
This is the layer you are most familiar with. It will contain your interfaces to your peripherals like your serial port, parallel port, webcam, sound output or input devices, etc.	This layer represents the third-party controllers. These controllers allow you to communicate in both the language of a robot and the language of a computer.	This is the layer that represents the hardware devices you've connected.
Serial Port	Parallax Stamp	Robot Arm
Webcam	MiniSSC-II Servo Controller	Sonar
Sound Card	Microcontroller	Compass
Database		Differential Drive
Logic		Robot Leg

Modeling Your Hardware and Behavior

Once you organize the components you have to work with, it's time to create some "soft" models of those hardware components.

- Pick a name (for example, PanTiltCamera).

- Model what you want it to do (move up/down, move left/right, take a picture, and so on).

- Stub out your class.

- Plan what can go wrong and how you want to deal with it.

After you've modeled your hardware and behavior, you should be ready to calculate the synchronization between the two.

Timing

Timing in life is important; timing in robotics is mandatory. If you have a larger microcontroller, I would suggest using flow control (for example, having your PC and microcontroller negotiate when each are ready to talk). But since I only have 16 I/O ports with my BASIC Stamp 2, I'll manually synchronize the serial communication. You should be aware of how long things take though.

For example, a 9600-baud communication rate with your microcontroller takes about 3 feet per character. If you have three characters to transmit, like the bearing of your compass, it could take less time to execute the command than it would to get the data back from your serial connection.

But timing is not just important for synchronization. It also defines the resolution at which your robot can get data from its environment. For example, if you have a sensor that reads sonar every 200 milliseconds, then you have a maximum number of readings per second of 5. If your robot travels 1 meter per second (a slow walking pace), then the resolution of your robot will be 7 inches.

Summary

By now, you should be ready to start using Java with your robotics. Your PC should have its software installed and you should have a working serial connection and microcontroller. While you don't need a robot for the next chapter, make sure to order one soon so that when you're ready for Chapter 3, you can hook up your robot and get it moving with some of your own Java programs.

Hopefully, your programs will do more than just avoid the sofa or move in circles. So take some time to figure out what you want your robot to do. Then, to make it easier follow these steps: First, organize what you want your robot to do. Second, choose events that trigger action. Third, create tasks that organize behavior. Fourth, create subtasks that perform the details. Finally, model data packets that represent the information moving from your hardware and PC.

It might also help to arrange your programs in such a way that when you move from subtask to subtask or task to task you create a state transition diagram like Figure 1-2 shown earlier. I would not worry too much about the Java concepts right now, but come back to them if you get stuck at some point later in the book. What you don't find listed here can be uncovered in numerous Apress books which do an excellent job explaining these concepts.

Finally, once your behavioral model is defined, you should start modeling your hardware. So starting from your PC and moving to your peripherals, if needed create simple models of your hardware that map easily to the behavior you want your robot to perform.

For example, if I want my robot to move, I would map a serial port to a servo controller and that would be it. But if I want it to face a specific direction, I would have a serial port mapped to a servo controller as well as a microcontroller, which would be mapped to a compass.

Just one tip before proceeding: start simple, and then increase the complexity of your model only after you have tested a simple version of it. You will run into many problems along the way and nothing is worse than troubleshooting your own complicated do-everything code.

■ ■ ■

CHAPTER 2

Serial Communication

"The problem with communication is the illusion that it has been accomplished."

— George Bernard Shaw

2.0   Introduction

In this book, all communications used with your microcontroller will use RS-232 serial communication at 9600 baud, eight data bits, one stop bit, and no flow control. There are other methods of communicating with microcontrollers, notably I2C (Inter-Integrated Communication), parallel communications, Ethernet, WiFi, and Bluetooth just to name a few. But I have chosen to use serial communications for its popularity and its extensibility with other software and devices.

I will show and describe 12 Java classes and 2 BASIC Stamp programs. All of the classes are in package com.scottpreston.javarobot.chapter2. All of the Stamp programs are in the folder / BasicStamp/chapter2.

In this chapter, I will introduce you to the Java Communications API by explaining some of its more important classes, and then test it using some simple programs. Later, I will simplify it for your use with robotics and then extend serial communications over a network using Java Server Pages and a web client.

Once I have discussed and simplified serial communications, I will model a microcontroller program in a Java class. By modeling the microcontroller program in Java, it should simplify the programming of your robot.

The chapter will conclude with an example that uses a Bluetooth serial adapter in conjunction with a BASIC Stamp to demonstrate wireless serial communications.

Configuring Your Serial Port

Again, configure the serial port to the following: 9600 baud, eight data bits, no parity, one stop bit, and no flow control. To configure this for Windows, open the Control Panel, choose System ➤ Hardware ➤ Device Manager, and then click Ports. Make sure to note the (*COMx*) port number. You can see the windows for these in Figures 2-1 and 2-2 shown next.

■**Note** UNIX users, the ports here are numbered ttyS0, ttyS1, and so on. Replace all references to COMx with ttySx.

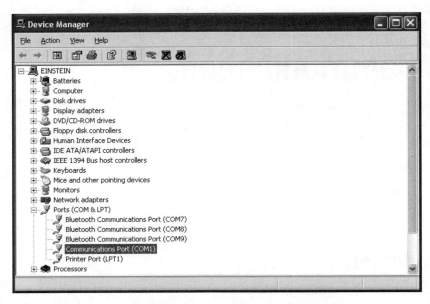

Figure 2-1. *The Device Manager window*

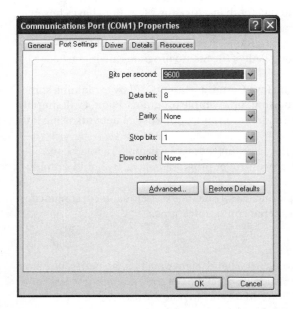

Figure 2-2. *The Communications Port Properties window*

The Java Communications API

I will use the following classes from the Java Communications API for port access. Table 2-1 summarizes the class names and class descriptions.

Table 2-1. *Important Classes in Java Communications API*

Java Class	Description
javax.comm.CommPortIdentifer	This is the main class for controlling access to communications ports. It provides a list of communications ports made available by the driver, assists with the opening of communications ports, and assists with port ownership.
javax.comm.SerialPort	This is the standard RS-232 communications port provided by the comm.jar. Per the Java documentation, this class defines the minimum required functionality for serial communications ports.

Code Objectives

The objective for this example is to list all available communications ports.

■Tip Make this the first program you run since it will test the installation of the Java communications API.

Code Discussion

The fields in this class are ComPortIdentifer, portId, and an enumeration of all ports called portsList. Next, I'll create an empty constructor where I initialize the enumeration of the ports. This will be the list of all ports identified by the driver.

The second method in the class is the list() method. The first line in the method is a while loop that iterates through the enumeration of ports. Upon getting the next element from the enumeration, it receives the portType (serial or parallel), and then prints the name of the port. Upon outputting the name to the console, I'll make an attempt to open the port, pause 250 milliseconds, and then close the port. This will be repeated until the enumeration has no more elements.

This class throws two exception types. The first, InterruptedException, is thrown by the static Thread.sleep() method, while the PortInUseException is thrown by the portId.open() method. (See Example 2-1.)

Example 2-1. *ListOpenPorts.java*

```java
package com.scottpreston.javarobot.chapter2;

import java.util.Enumeration;

import javax.comm.CommPort;
import javax.comm.CommPortIdentifier;
import javax.comm.PortInUseException;

public class ListOpenPorts {

    private CommPortIdentifier portId;
    private Enumeration portList;

    public ListOpenPorts() {
        portList = CommPortIdentifier.getPortIdentifiers();
    }

    public void list() throws InterruptedException, PortInUseException {
        while (portList.hasMoreElements()) {
            portId = (CommPortIdentifier) portList.nextElement();
            if (portId.getPortType() == CommPortIdentifier.PORT_SERIAL) {
                System.out.print("Serial Port = ");
            }
            if (portId.getPortType() == CommPortIdentifier.PORT_PARALLEL) {
                System.out.print("Parallel Port = ");
            }
            System.out.print(portId.getName() + ", ");

            CommPort port = portId.open("OpenTest", 20);
            Thread.sleep(250);
            System.out.println("Opened." + portId.getCurrentOwner());
            port.close();
        }
    }

    public static void main(String[] args) {
        try {
            ListOpenPorts openPorts = new ListOpenPorts();
            openPorts.list();
        } catch (InterruptedException ie) {
            System.out.println("Unable to sleep.");
        } catch (PortInUseException pe) {
            System.out.println("Failed. Port In Use.");
        }

    }
}
```

For later classes, it will be useful to not use the Thread.sleep() method, but to instead add a single static method that you can call, and which handles the InterruptedException. For this, I am going to create a Utils class to store these static utility methods. (See Example 2-2.)

Example 2-2. *The Utils.pause() method*

```
public static void pause(long ms) {
      try {
            Thread.sleep(ms);
      } catch (Exception e) {
            e.printStackTrace();
      }
}
```

Section Summary

All communications used throughout this book with your microcontroller will employ RS-232 serial communication at 9600 baud, eight data bits, one stop bit, and no flow control. Once this is configured on your PC using a combination of the classes CommPortIdentifier and SerialPort from Java Communications API for serial communication, you should be able to get access that let's you both read and write to and from your PC's serial port with Java.

The classes I created in this section were

- ListOpenPorts.java: This class showed how to iterate through the enumeration provided by the Java API CommPortIdentifier class to select a serial port.

- Utils.pause(): This class is going to be just a utility class that currently has a pause method which will cause the current thread to sleep and trap its exception.

While you can use the API directly, I've found it more helpful to write a wrapper class that simplifies access. This is what I will talk about in the next section.

2.1   A Simple Serial Port

In the ListOpenPorts class, we were able to access and open the serial ports, but using this technique presents three problems. First, it's cumbersome to create and use the serial port by iterating through all those that are available, and then when the one that's available matches the one you want, you can use it. Second, using the input streams and output streams from the serial port is difficult if you want to send and receive data packets as defined in Chapter 1. Third, the usage of this port is not generic enough.

Code Objectives

To compensate for these shortcomings I am going to create the following:

- A serial port interface so that I can create multiple serial port implantation classes, but won't have to modify the code using the interface.

- A simpler constructor so that I can specify a serial port with baud and identifier.

- Methods that work well for sending and receiving data packets to and from the microcontroller.

Code Discussion

The first item to create is a serial port interface. The Java interface is a means of hiding different implementations with the same behavior. For now I'll create serial port access to a local port, but later I'll want to provide the same behavior over a network.

The first thing you notice from the interface is that it contains no logic, just method stubs. This is because an interface is only there to define behavior, not to implement any of the behavior. The actual work will be implemented by another class that *implements* this interface.

The second thing you notice are the names of the methods. For instance, the read() method will return a byte array. The readString() method will return a String. The write method will return nothing and will take a byte array since it's only an input parameter. There is also a close() method for freeing resources and resending ownership so that other classes or programs can access the implementing object.

I have added two serial port accessor methods: setDTR for use with the Parallax Stamp carrier boards, and setTimeout as a means to assist in the data packet synchronization with the connected microcontroller.

The three static strings are for use with the WebSerialClient defined later in this chapter. The read() and readString() have methods with input parameters because (depending on the timeout value) sometimes it's better to wait for the response within the serial port class rather than calling Thread.sleep() externally and then calling two separate write() and read() methods. (See Example 2-3.)

Example 2-3. *JSerialPort.java*

```
package com.scottpreston.javarobot.chapter2;

public interface JSerialPort{

    public byte[] read();
    public String readString();
    public void write(byte[] b) throws Exception;
    public void close();
    public void setDTR(boolean dtr);
    public void setTimeout(int tOut);
    public static final String READ_COMMAND = "r";
    public static final String WRITE_COMMAND = "w";
    public static final String WRITE_READ_COMMAND = "wr";
    public byte[] read(byte[] b) throws Exception;
    public String readString(byte[] b) throws Exception;

}
```

Now that I have created the generic interface for all the serial ports I am going to use in this book, it's time to write our first implementation class, StandardSerialPort. Figure 2-3 shows the class diagram for JSerialPort and StandardSerialPort.

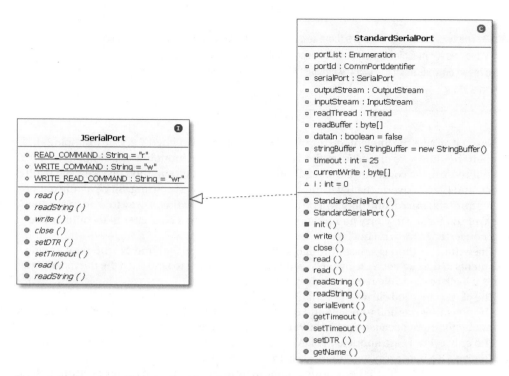

Figure 2-3. *The class diagram for JSerialPort and StandardSerialPort*

To begin let's look at the class-level variables. The Enumeration portList is a returned list of ports by the Driver. The ComPortIdentifier, portId, is the actual port we're interested in working with, while SerialPort is the actual java.comm.SerialPort we'll be use to read and write data packets with our microcontroller. InputStream and OutputStream, with variable names of the same name, are the returned streams from our working SerialPort.

The byte[] readBuffer will be a temporary buffer used while reading our serial port's input stream. The Boolean, dataIn, is an indicator flag that lets the class know how long to read the input stream into the readBuffer. Finally, the last two variables currentWrite and i are used in conjunction with read-write behavior implemented in the WebSerialClient.

Moving to the class constructors, I created two constructors for this class simplifying the input parameter creation to just baud and id. Because I'm just checking to see if the port ends with a specific number (for instance, 1,2,3,…,n), this class will work with either Windows- or UNIX-based serial ports. In the case where the baud is not set, I decided on a default baud rate of 9600. Each constructor also calls a common init method. Inside this method you'll find the same logic used in Example 2-1, ListOpenPorts. Once an enumeration is created, I iterate through this enumeration until I find the serial ports (specifically the one that ends with the int passed in as an input parameter). I then open a named instance of this port and set the default parameters to be eight data bits, one stop bit, no parity, and no flow control. Next, I set the input stream and output stream of the port to be equal to two class variables of the same name, followed by adding the event listener and notifyOnDataAvailable flag.

■**Note** The two pause methods are there to wait for the driver to set the values of the ports. I have found on my Windows XP machine that if I don't pause a little, the drivers sometimes return exceptions. You can remove these on your machine if you wish, just be sure to stress test them by trying many port open and closes in a loop.

Next, I'll discuss the implementation classes of the JSerialPort interface. (See Example 2-4.) The read() method is really just a method that sleeps until the input buffer is empty. Once empty, it returns the contents of the readBuffer. The readString() method just calls the read() method and then converts the bytes into a tilde-delimited list as a String. Since all the data coming from the microcontroller will be a stream of bytes, I wanted a way to read individual bytes without having to worry about them being changed into a character that could not be easily converted back to an int.

The write() method is a pass-through to the output stream with the exception of adding the contents to the currentWrite byte[]. I keep this because I want to ignore it if the microcontroller echoes it back to me while reading the input stream.

The close() method closes the SerialPort.

The two other methods—read() and readString() with input parameters—are not used but are once again there because the jSerialPort interface requires them.

The only event I care about is the DATA_AVAILABLE event. When this event is triggered, I'll initialize a 32-byte array, and then while the inputStream is available, I'll read the input stream into the readBuffer. I then perform some logic to make sure that the data returned is not equal to the data sent, and if that's the case, I set the dataIn Boolean to true.

Of the last three methods, setTimeout() is not used, and setDTR() and getName() are there to provide limited access to their corresponding SerialPort variables.

An example sequence of events for a typical write/pause/read action would be the following:

1. byte[] is written to a serial port.

2. The microcontroller reads byte[].

3. The external program calls pause(x).

4. Time passes.

5. Time is up.

6. The microcontroller returns byte[].

7. The standard serial port event DATA_AVAILABLE is triggered.

8. The external program calls read().

9. All data is read; dataIn is set to true.

10. The read returns byte[] of data from microcontroller.

Example 2-4. *StandardSerialPort.Java*

```java
package com.scottpreston.javarobot.chapter2;

import java.io.IOException;
import java.io.InputStream;
import java.io.OutputStream;
import java.util.Enumeration;

import javax.comm.CommPortIdentifier;
import javax.comm.SerialPort;
import javax.comm.SerialPortEvent;
import javax.comm.SerialPortEventListener;

public class StandardSerialPort implements SerialPortEventListener,
        JSerialPort {

    private Enumeration portList;
    private CommPortIdentifier portId;
    private SerialPort serialPort;
    private OutputStream outputStream;
    private InputStream inputStream;
    private byte[] readBuffer;
    private boolean dataIn = false;
    private byte[] currentWrite;
    private int i = 0;

    public StandardSerialPort(int id) throws Exception {
        init(id, 9600);
    }

    public StandardSerialPort(int id, int baud) throws Exception {
        init(id, baud);
    }

    private void init(int comID, int baud) {
        String comIdAsString = new Integer(comID).toString();
        try {
            portList = CommPortIdentifier.getPortIdentifiers();
            while (portList.hasMoreElements()) {
                portId = (CommPortIdentifier) portList.nextElement();
                if (portId.getPortType() == CommPortIdentifier.PORT_SERIAL) {
                    if (portId.getName().endsWith(comIdAsString)) {
                        // create serial port
                        serialPort = (SerialPort) portId.open(
                                "StandardSerialPort", 3000);
```

```java
                    // set config parms
                    serialPort.setSerialPortParams(baud,
                            SerialPort.DATABITS_8, SerialPort.STOPBITS_1,
                            SerialPort.PARITY_NONE);
                    serialPort
                            .setFlowControlMode(SerialPort.FLOWCONTROL_NONE);
                    Utils.pause(50);
                    // config output stream
                    outputStream = serialPort.getOutputStream();
                    // config input stream
                    inputStream = serialPort.getInputStream();
                    // add events listener
                    serialPort.addEventListener(this);
                    serialPort.notifyOnDataAvailable(true);
                    Thread.sleep(50); // waits till ports change state.
                }
            }
        }
    } catch (Exception e) {
        e.printStackTrace();
    }

}

public byte[] read() {
    while (!dataIn) {
        try {
            Thread.sleep(1);
        } catch (Exception e) {
        }
    }
    dataIn = false;
    return readBuffer;
}

public String readString() {
    byte[] b = read();
    StringBuffer s = new StringBuffer();
    for (int i = 0; i < b.length; i++) {
        if (b[i] != 0) {
            int in = (int) b[i];
            if (in < 0) {
                in = in + 256;
            }
            s.append(in);
            s.append("~");
        }
    }
```

```java
        s.deleteCharAt(s.length() - 1);
        return s.toString();
    }

    public void write(byte[] b) throws Exception {
        currentWrite = b;
        outputStream.write(b);
    }

    public void close() {
        serialPort.close();
    }

    public byte[] read(byte[] b) throws Exception {
        // not used
        return null;
    }

    public String readString(byte[] b) throws Exception {
        //      not used
        return null;

    }

    public void serialEvent(SerialPortEvent event) {

        if (event.getEventType() == SerialPortEvent.DATA_AVAILABLE) {
            readBuffer = new byte[32];
            i = 0;
            try {
                while (inputStream.available() > 0) {
                    int numBytes = inputStream.read(readBuffer);
                }
                int byteCount = 0;
                for (int i = 0; i < currentWrite.length; i++) {
                    if (currentWrite[i] == readBuffer[i]) {
                        byteCount++;
                    }
                }
                if (byteCount != currentWrite.length) {
                    dataIn = true;
                }
            } catch (IOException e) {
                e.printStackTrace();
            }
        }
    }

}
```

```
public void setTimeout(int timeout) {
    // not used
}

public void setDTR(boolean dtr) {
    serialPort.setDTR(dtr);
}

public String getName() {
    return serialPort.getName();
}

}
```

Section Summary

For this section, I created a simpler-to-use serial port. I did this by simplifying the construction of the port to take parameters of just the serial port id (1,2,3,…,n) and a baud rate as an int. Second, I modified the input and output streams to take parameters and return data useful to me in robotics: byte[] and strings. Finally, I created an interface to the serial port called the JSerialPort, which can be used in later sections to force the same behavior for multiple serial port implementations.

The interface and class I created in this section were

- JSerialPort.java: This is the interface that will specify behavior for all serial ports.

- StandardSerialPort.java: This class is the simpler version of the Java API SerialPort.

The only thing that the StandardSerialPort does not do is handle concurrent serial port usage. That will be the topic of the next section.

2.2 Concurrent Serial Port Usage

If we connect more than one thing to a serial port, we'll run into many PortInUseExceptions. We want to avoid that, otherwise our programs will be exiting when we don't want them to. (See Table 2-2.)

Table 2-2. *Pros and Cons of Concurrent Usage*

Solution	Pro	Con
Create serial port inside each dependent object.	Each class is self-contained.	Concurrent use likely; plus, application will throw PortInUseException. Closing of serial port has to be done via method call to invoking object.
Create serial port outside of consuming objects.	Concurrent use limited to current thread. Closing of serial port can be done outside of individual objects.	Each class requires SerialPort to be sent in constructor. Not thread-safe.
Create single class that has control of all required actions of serial port.	Self-contained. Thread Safe. Closing of port managed inside of class.	Poor reuse.
Use a singleton of serial port inside each dependent object.	Class is self-contained. Concurrent use is limited to JVM and is thread-safe. Closing of objects is done outside of individual objects.	Limited to single serial port regardless of com ID.
Use a singleton of serial ports inside a resource pool of all available serial ports.	Class is self-contained. Concurrent use is limited to JVM and is thread-safe. The closing of objects can be done outside of individual objects. Can request any available serial port system it can find.	None.

Code Objective

The objective of this example is to show how to create a resource pool of serial ports without getting conflicts if multiple objects want to access them at once.

Code Discussion

The only field in SingleSerialPort class is a vector: portsInUse. This vector is a collection of the currently initialized serialPorts. Because a vector is synchronized, this ensures that the ports are accessed in a thread-safe manner.

I created a private constructor to prevent initialization. All StandardSerialPorts will be returned via the getInstanceMethods.

The getInstance method uses the name of the SerialPort (COM1 or stty1) to identify itself and either create a new one or return a port already in the pool.

Finally, the close() method removes the ports from the pool and closes them. (See Example 2-5.)

Example 2-5. *SingleSerialPort.Java*

```java
package com.scottpreston.javarobot.chapter2;

import java.util.Vector;


    private static Vector portsInUse = new Vector();

    private SingleSerialPort() {
        // prevents initialization
    }

    public static StandardSerialPort getInstance(int comid) throws Exception {
        return getInstance(comid,9600);
    }

    public static StandardSerialPort getInstance(int comid, int baud) ➥
throws Exception {

        StandardSerialPort instance = null;
        String tmpComID = new Integer(comid).toString();

        // return a port in use if it exist.
        for (int i=0; i< portsInUse.size(); i++) {
            StandardSerialPort aPort = (StandardSerialPort)portsInUse.get(i);
            if (aPort.getName().endsWith(tmpComID)) {
                return aPort;
            }
        }
        // otherwise create the port if its in the list
        if (instance == null) {
            instance = new StandardSerialPort(comid,baud);
            portsInUse.add(instance);
        }
        return instance;
    }

    public static void close(int comid) {

        String tmpComID = new Integer(comid).toString();
```

```
        // return a port in use if it exist.
        for (int i=0; i< portsInUse.size(); i++) {
            StandardSerialPort aPort = (StandardSerialPort)portsInUse.get(i);
            if (aPort.getName().endsWith(tmpComID)) {
                aPort.close();
                portsInUse.remove(i);
            }
        }
    }

    public static void closeAll() {
        // cycle through all and close
        for (int i=0; i< portsInUse.size(); i++) {
            StandardSerialPort aPort = (StandardSerialPort)portsInUse.get(i);
            aPort.close();
            portsInUse.remove(i);
        }
    }
}
```

Section Summary

In this section, I discussed and compared five different ways to handle serial port concurrency. By placing a serial port in a resource pool that is thread-safe, I ensure that the serial port will be accessed in a synchronized fashion and I will never get a PortInUseException when accessing the serial port while programming my robot.

The class I created in this section was

- SingleSerialPort.java: This class showed how to create a resource pool of serial ports that provide concurrent access for multiple threads.

You may not have a need for this functionality if you are always working from your PC with a single program accessing the serial port; however, as you will see in the next section, we can have multiple threads accessing the same serial port. In such cases, strings or images serial port comes in very handy.

2.3 Creating a Web Serial Port

I've found that working on a serial port at my desk using my PC is fine, but as soon as I start debugging the code with my robot, I find that working on a remote machine via terminal services is much slower. So, I need another option. I want to work from the Eclipse IDE at my desk, but I also want to do serial communication with a microcontroller connected to my robot's serial port. I also want an easy way to test this remotely and do not want to write software for handling multiple connections or managing data packets of strings or images that might be going back and forth between my desktop and the robot.

To remedy these problems, I'll create a web serial port. This is a serial port I can access over the Internet, send commands to, get data from, and then employ web clients to do remote control for diagnostics and so on.

■**Note** More about the setup of Tomcat can be found in Chapter 8: Advanced Topics.

Setup

The following setup represents my PC with my Java IDE (Eclipse). I have a wireless connection to the Tomcat Servlet Engine running on my robot's computer. (See Figure 2-4.)

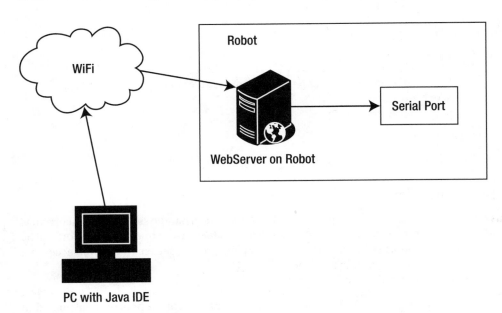

Figure 2-4. *Wireless WebSerialPort setup*

Code Objective

The code objective is to extend the serial port so I can connect to it over my home's wireless connection using HTTP.

Code Discussion

The following example will be utilized in a Java Server Page residing on the web server.

The string, CMD_ACK, will be the acknowledge string returned from the webcom.jsp if everything goes as planned and there are no errors.

The string, COMM_JSP, is the name of the JSP that will take the input and output request from the client.

The READ_ONLY and DEFAULT_TIMEOUT variables are used to best calculate whether the client should wait for the web server to respond with output from the serial port or make a separate request for the output.

Because Tomcat is a multithreaded web server, any two calls from a web browser or web client could happen on different threads. This is not a desired effect, so to avoid the PortInUseException I will use the SingleSerialPort.getIntance() method in the constructor of the WebSerialPort.

The only other public method in this class is execute(), which takes the parameters and actions corresponding to read, write, or write-read. The string, cmds, will be a comma-delimited string of bytes, while the string, timeout, will tell the class to wait around for the result. In this method, I will also throw exceptions if any of the constructor elements are null.

The other methods that get called depend upon the action. The private read() method returns the com.readString() value. This will be a tilde-delimited list of numbers. The write() method will convert the comma-delimited string to a byte[] and send that to the serial port's output stream. Finally, the read() method with input parameters will call the write() method, wait until the timeout, and then call the read() method. (See Example 2-6.)

Example 2-6. *WebSerialPort.java*

```
package com.scottpreston.javarobot.chapter2;
public class WebSerialPort{

    JSerialPort com;

    public static final String CMD_ACK = "ok";
    public static final String COMM_JSP = "webcom.jsp";
    public static final byte[] READ_ONLY = new byte[] { (byte) 0 };
    public static final int DEFAULT_TIMEOUT = 0;
    private int timeout;

    public WebSerialPort(String comId) throws Exception {
        int pId = new Integer(comId).intValue();
        com = SingleSerialPort.getInstance(pId);
    }

    public String execute(String action, String cmds, String timeout,String dtr) ➥
throws Exception{
        if (action == null) {
            throw new Exception("Action is null");
        }
        if (cmds == null) {
            throw new Exception("Commands are null");
        }
        if (timeout == null) {
            throw new Exception("Timeout is null");
        }
        if (dtr == null) {
            throw new Exception("DTR is null");
        }
```

```java
        int tOut = new Integer(timeout).intValue();
        this.timeout = tOut;
        //if (tOut != 0) {
        //    com.setTimeout(tOut);
        //}
        if (dtr.equalsIgnoreCase("true")) {
            com.setDTR(true);
        }
        if (dtr.equalsIgnoreCase("false")) {
            com.setDTR(false);
        }
        if (action.equalsIgnoreCase(JSerialPort.READ_COMMAND)) {
            return read();
        } else if (action.equalsIgnoreCase(JSerialPort.WRITE_READ_COMMAND)) {
            return read(cmds);
        } else if (action.equalsIgnoreCase(JSerialPort.WRITE_COMMAND)) {
            return write(cmds);
        } else {
            return null;
        }
    }
    /**
     *
     * @param cmd
     *             this will be comma delimited seq of cmds
     */
    private String write(String cmd) throws Exception {
        com.write(urlCmdsToBytes(cmd));
        return CMD_ACK;
    }

    private String read(String cmd) throws Exception {
        write(cmd);
        Utils.pause(timeout);
        return read();
    }

    private String read() {
        return com.readString();
    }

    public void close() {
        com.close();
    }
    private byte[] urlCmdsToBytes(String command) {
        String[] commands = command.split(",");
        byte[] cmds = new byte[commands.length];
```

```
        for (int x = 0; x < commands.length; x++) {
            int i = new Integer(commands[x]).intValue();
            cmds[x] = (byte) i;
        }
        return cmds;
    }



}
```

The next part of our serial port extension to the web is webcom.jsp. This JSP will import the classes from Chapter 2, and then parse the parameters on the URL, sending those strings to the constructor of the previous class, WebSerialPort.

Because the constructor throws an exception, I'll wrap the constructor and execute methods in a try-catch block with an example of how to use the JSP. Outside of construction, and invoking the execute method, all functionality and logic for the webcom.jsp is located in the WebSerialPort class. (See Example 2-7.)

Example 2-7. *webcom.jsp*

```
<%@ page import="com.scottpreston.javarobot.chapter2.*" %><%

// WebClient class will throw exception if these are not set
String portId = request.getParameter("portid");
String action = request.getParameter("action");
String cmdInput = request.getParameter("commands");
String timeout = request.getParameter("timeout");
String dtr = request.getParameter("dtr");
try {

WebSerialPort com = new WebSerialPort(portId);
out.println(com.execute(action,cmdInput,timeout,dtr));

} catch (Exception e) {
out.println(e);
int term = '!';
%>

usage: /webcom.jsp?portid=[1,2,..]&action=[r,w,wr]➥
&commands=[100,120,222,..]&timeout=[0,50,..]&dtr=true
<p>sample:
<a href="/webcom.jsp?portid=1&action=wr&commands=100,<%=term%>➥
&timeout=0&dtr=true">sample 1</a>

<% }%>
```

If you did not notice, the WebSerialPort did not implement the JSerialPort interface. Why is that? Well, for two reasons. One, it did not need to since the behavior was slightly different than the standard serial port, and two, all of our implementing classes would not use this port—they would instead need to use the connector to the WebSerialPort: the WebSerialClient.

The class WebSerialClient implements the interface JSerialPort, so now anything I write can just use this interface and I can interchange the WebSerialClient, the StandardSerialPort, or my own implementation and I will not have to modify any of the code that uses these. Pretty slick, huh?

The first field in this class is a formatter object. I use this for debugging the milliseconds of an operation. You will need to debug and experiment with different timeout values for items connected to your microcontroller. Too long and you'll be wasting performance, too little and you'll get nothing back or only junk. I'll discuss more of this in Chapter 4, but it's probably best to make a note of it for now.

The string URL and the URL object will be used to connect to the webcom.jsp on my robot. The dtr variable is set to false if I am connecting to a BASIC Stamp carrier board. The timeout and MAX_DELAY are ints that will determine whether the client should wait for a return from webcom.jsp, or whether it should just make two calls: one write and one read. I've found that depending on your WiFi connection, you might want to increase or decrease this value.

Next, the construction of this client will take the string server that represents the server name or IP address of the web server hosting the webcom.jsp. The string, tcpPort, represents the port where the web server hosting the webcom.jsp is listening. (See Example 2-8.)

Example 2-8. *WebSerialClient.java*

```java
package com.scottpreston.javarobot.chapter2;

import java.io.BufferedReader;
import java.io.InputStreamReader;
import java.net.URL;
import java.text.SimpleDateFormat;
import java.util.Date;

public class WebSerialClient implements JSerialPort {

    private SimpleDateFormat formatter = new SimpleDateFormat(
            "MM/dd/yy - HH:mm:ss.SSS");
    private String url;
    private URL myUrl;
    private boolean dtr = false;
    private int timeout = 0;
    public static final int MAX_DELAY = 500;

    public WebSerialClient(String server, String tcpPort, String portId) {
        this.url = "http://" + server + ":" + tcpPort
        + "/" + WebSerialPort.COMM_JSP + "?portid=" + portId;
    }
```

```java
public byte[] read() {
    return readString().getBytes();
}

public String readString() {
    return request(WebSerialPort.READ_ONLY, JSerialPort.READ_COMMAND);
}

public void write(byte[] b) throws Exception {
    String out = request(b, JSerialPort.WRITE_COMMAND);
    if (out.equalsIgnoreCase(WebSerialPort.CMD_ACK) == false) {
        throw new Exception("WebClient Write Failure: " + out);
    }
}

// added in case where user wants to read after they send commands
// this is specific to the webcom.jsp
public byte[] read(byte[] b) {
    return readString(b).getBytes();
}

public String readString(byte[] b) {
    return request(b, JSerialPort.WRITE_READ_COMMAND);
}

public void close() {
    // do nothing since having more than one port
}

public void setDTR(boolean dtr) {
    this.dtr = dtr;
}

private String request(byte[] commands, String cmdType) {
    // convert byte to string
    String cmdString = byteArrayToString(commands);

    log("WebClient: cmds=" + cmdString + ", cmdType=" + cmdType
            + ", timeout=" + timeout);

    String out = null;
    try {
        String urlString = url
        + "&action=" + cmdType
        + "&commands=" + cmdString
            + "&timeout=" + timeout
            + "&dtr=" + dtr;
```

```
            URL myurl = new URL(urlString);
            log(urlString);
            BufferedReader in = new BufferedReader(new InputStreamReader(
                    myurl.openStream()));
            String str = null;
            while ((str = in.readLine()) != null) {
                // str is one line of text; readLine() strips the newline
                // character(s)
                if (str != null) {
                    out = str;
                }
            }
            in.close();
        } catch (Exception e) {
            e.printStackTrace();
        }
        out = out.trim();
        log("WebClient: out=" + out);
        return out;
    }

    private String byteArrayToString(byte[] b) {
        String s = "";
        for (int x = 0; x < b.length; x++) {
            s = s + b[x] + ",";
        }
        s = s.substring(0, s.length() - 1);
        return s;
    }

    private void log(String s) {
        Date d = new Date();
        String dt = formatter.format(d);
        System.out.println(dt + " *** " + s);
    }

    public int getTimeout() {
        return timeout;
    }

    public void setTimeout(int timeout) {
        this.timeout = timeout;
    }

    public static void main(String[] args) {
    }

}
```

Section Summary

You should now be able to connect to the serial port on your robot from any place in the world. You can write your programs at your PC and as long as you have network connectivity to the serial port on your robot, all the programs can be run from your PC.

The classes and JSP I introduced in this section were

- WebSerialPort: The class that accesses the serial port on the web server for the JSP.

- Webcom.jsp: The Java Server Page that provides access from the WebSerialPort to the WebSerialClient, or direct access via the browser.

- WebSerialClient: The class that implements the JSerialPort interface which allows access to a serial port on a web server the same way you can access a serial port on your local machine.

Depending on your configuration, you're ready to start accessing your microcontroller via your serial port.

2.4 Serial Communications with a Microcontroller

Once you have thoroughly tested and used some of the classes accessing your PC's serial port, you're ready to send and receive some data with it. To do this, connect the serial cable from your PC to your Parallax Board of Education. You can see in Figure 2-5 that the BOE has a spot for either the BASIC or Javelin Stamp, connectors for a serial cable, battery, and bread board for use in experimentation.

Figure 2-5. *The Parallax Board of Education*

■**Note** If you're just starting out with robotics, it's great to have this bread board for adding sensors or creating circuits.

Once your board is hooked up and you can see the microcontroller you've connected, you're ready to program. Your first goal will be to just send some data to the microcontroller and get some data in return.

Code Objective

The objectives for this example are to:

- Send 2 bytes of data to a microcontroller.

- Receive a specific byte back that confirms the byte sent to it.

Code Discussion

The Stamp program has a byte array of size 3 called serialIn. This byte array will be populated from the SERIN command when it's either full or when it receives a termination command of "!". Then, based on the first byte received from the PC, the program will branch to SEROUT with an "a" or "b". (See Example 2-9.)

■**Note** Adjust the serial port timeout or the time between the write and the delay. Then adjust the pause time in the Stamp code and see how the results vary.

Example 2-9. *SerialEcho.bs2*

```
'{$STAMP BS2}
'{$PORT COM1}

serialIn     VAR    Byte(3)
foo          VAR    Byte

main:
  foo = 255
  serialIn(0) = 0
  serialIn(1) = 0
  serialIn(2) = 0
  SERIN 16,16468,1000,main,[STR serialIn\3\"!"]
  PAUSE 100
  LOOKDOWN serialIn(0),[100,101,102],foo
  BRANCH foo,[test1, test2, getCompass]
  PAUSE 5
  GOTO main
```

```
test1:
  SEROUT 16,16468,["a"]
  GOTO main
test2:
  SEROUT 16,16468,["b"]
  GOTO main
getCompass:
  SEROUT 16,16468,["180"]
  GOTO main
```

The next class will communicate with the BASIC Stamp program we just created. It has a single field, the StandardSerialPort called sPort. In the constructor, we create the port with an int 1 corresponding to COM1 in Windows XP. Then we set the DTR to false because having it true sets the Stamp to program mode, which we don't want. Then we pause for 125 milliseconds to give the port time to respond.

The next method, test(), returns a string. The expected string will either be "a" or "b" depending on what was sent, because the Stamp program in the previous example just knows how to return those two strings.

We will also add the close() method to close the StandardSerialPort, sPort.

In the main method, we will send to the test method bytes 101 and 102. We can also catch any exception that could occur by using the StandardSerialPort. (See Example 2-10.)

Example 2-10. *StampSerialTest.Java*

```java
package com.scottpreston.javarobot.chapter2;

public class StampSerialTest {

    private StandardSerialPort sPort;

    public StampSerialTest() throws Exception {
        sPort = new StandardSerialPort(1);
        sPort.setDTR(false);
        Utils.pause(125);

    }

    public String test(byte something) throws Exception {
        byte[] a = { something };
        sPort.write(a);
        Utils.pause(100);
        return sPort.readString();
    }

    public void close() {
        sPort.close();
    }
```

```
    public static void main(String[] args) {
        try {
            StampSerialTest sst = new StampSerialTest();
            System.out.println("From Stamp:" + sst.test((byte)101));
            System.out.println("From Stamp:" + sst.test((byte)102));
        } catch (Exception e) {
            e.printStackTrace();
            System.exit(1);
        }
        System.out.println("Done.");
    }

}
```

Section Summary

The Stamp program and Java class created in this section were

- SerialEcho.bs2: This program resides in the microcontroller and will echo an "a" and "b" depending on the commands sent to the controller.

- StampSerialTest.java: This class is designed to send and receive specific information to the microcontroller on coordination with SerialEcho.bs2.

Once you have tested basic access to your microcontroller, now it's time to extend on this concept a bit and model your microcontroller, first by creating a generic one that can be used for any type of microcontroller, and then by creating a version that corresponds precisely to your Stamp program.

2.5 Modeling a Microcontroller with Java

While I could use the StandardSerialPort to send and receive data to and from a robot, this makes it more difficult down the road as the robot's capability increases. So, to begin you will need a microcontroller. I choose the Parallax BASIC Stamp because it's easy to program and there are lots of examples and support available for this model.

The first Parallax BASIC Stamp comes in nine different versions, not including the OEM versions. They come with 8, 16, and 32 I/O pins that operate from 4MHz to 50MHz and can be programmed with up to 12,000 instructions. They are quite versatile and there are plenty of examples of software on the Internet, as well as those provided from the manufacturer's web site at www.parallax.com.

The two pictured in Figure 2-6 and Figure 2-7 are the BASIC Stamp 2 and the Javelin Stamp. The Javelin Stamp is the Java version. You can find all the program examples in this book for the Javelin Stamp in Appendix 2. All other examples will be for the BASIC Stamp 2 since it's the most popular and, as I said earlier, there are more examples for this microcontroller at present.

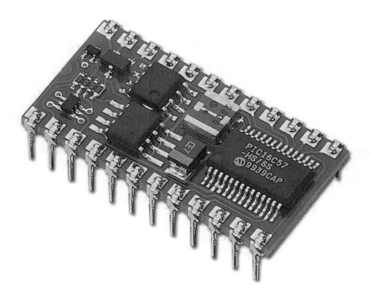

Figure 2-6. *The Parallax BASIC Stamp*

Figure 2-7. *The Parallax Javelin Stamp*

When using either Stamp with your Java programs, I have found it tedious to perform the same serial port and byte management for each class that will access the Stamp. To resolve this problem, I'll create a class that handles all communication with the controller. But like the serial port, I may have different implementations for access, so first I want to create an interface for all controllers, and then I want to write an implementation class specifically for my Stamp.

Code Objective

The objective for this example is to simplify communication for my robot by modeling a Stamp program in Java.

Code Discussion

The first interface I'll create will be called JController. This interface will have three execute() methods and one close() method.

The only difference between the two execute methods will be the return type. In execute(), the return type will be a string. This will call the readString() method from the JSerialPort. In execute2(), the return type will be a byte[]. This will call the read() method from the JSerialPort. (See Example 2-11.)

Example 2-11. *JController.java Interface*

```
package com.scottpreston.javarobot.chapter2;

public interface JController {

    public String execute(byte[] cmd, int delay) throws Exception;
    public byte[] execute2(byte[] cmd, int delay) throws Exception;
    public void close();
}
```

Next, I'll write the implementation for the interface defined in the preceding example. As I began writing implementation classes for the Javelin Stamp, and six versions of the BASIC Stamp, I found myself repeating a lot of the same calls to the execute methods. So, rather than writing them seven times, I decided to create a master controller that would implement the functionality of all of them. It will also be able to handle any new controllers that might come up in later chapters. I'll call this class Controller, and so that the actual implementation classes are created, I will make it generic.

This class has a single field, serialPort of type JSerialPort. The constructor of this class will take the JSerialPort interface so that it can use either the WebSerialClient or the StandardSerialPort. I also set the DTR to false since none of the controllers I use will use this, and for the Stamp Carrier Boards having this set to true will put the Stamp into program mode.

The first method, execute(), will return a string. The first thing that is checked for is the instance of the JSerialPort. If it's of type WebSerialClient, then I want to put the delay in the serial port on the web server. This is due to a timing lag between the executing machine and the web server connection. I set the maximum delay in the WebSerialClient class and if the delay is less than or equal to this number, the delay will be set in the WebSerialClient; otherwise, I will call Utils.pause() and make two calls to the client. Also, in both cases I need to check to see if the delay is zero. If that's the case, I don't want to ready anything; I just want to write. (See Example 2-12.)

Example 2-12. *Controller.java*

```java
package com.scottpreston.javarobot.chapter2;

public abstract class Controller implements JController {
    private JSerialPort serialPort;

        public Controller(JSerialPort sPort) throws Exception {
        serialPort = sPort;
        serialPort.setDTR(false);
    }

    public String execute(byte[] cmd, int delay) throws Exception {
        String out = null;
        if ((serialPort instanceof WebSerialClient)
                && delay <= WebSerialClient.MAX_DELAY) {
            serialPort.setTimeout(delay);
            if (delay == 0) {
                serialPort.write(cmd);
            } else {
                out = serialPort.readString(cmd);
            }
        } else {
            if (delay == 0) {
                serialPort.write(cmd);
            } else {
                serialPort.write(cmd);
                Utils.pause(delay);
                out = serialPort.readString();
            }

        }
        return out;
    }

    public byte[] execute2(byte[] cmd, int delay) throws Exception {
        byte[] out = null;
        if ((serialPort instanceof WebSerialClient)
                && delay <= WebSerialClient.MAX_DELAY) {
            serialPort.setTimeout(delay);
            if (delay == 0) {
                serialPort.write(cmd);
            } else {
                out = serialPort.read(cmd);
            }
```

```
        } else {
            if (delay == 0) {
                serialPort.write(cmd);
            } else {
                serialPort.write(cmd);
                Utils.pause(delay);
                out = serialPort.read();
            }
        }
        return out;
    }

    public void close() {
        serialPort.close();
    }
}
```

To provide an example of how these three classes fit together—StandardSerialPort, JController, and Controller—I have provided the UML class diagram in Figure 2-8.

At the beginning of SimpleStamp, I create three constants. These constants are used in two ways. The first is to make it easier to modify command strings when synchronizing the Stamp program. Second, because the actual commands sent to the Stamp are bytes, I can use these constants as the actual commands for the byte[] sent to the write() method of the serial port.

The constructor of this class will get an instance of a SerialPort from the SingleSerialPort class.

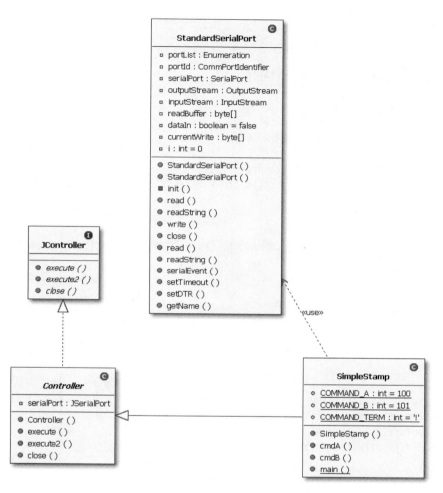

Figure 2-8. *StandardSerialPort, JController, Controller, and SimpleStamp*

The command methods create byte[] with the commands specified via the constants of the class, and then invoke the execute() method on the parent with a time delay of 150 milliseconds for each method. (See Example 2-13.)

Example 2-13. *SimpleStamp.java*

```java
package com.scottpreston.javarobot.chapter2;

public class SimpleStamp extends Controller {

    public static final int COMMAND_A = 'd';
    public static final int COMMAND_B = 'e';
    public static final int COMMAND_TERM = '!';

    public SimpleStamp(int id) throws Exception {
        super(SingleSerialPort.getInstance(id));
    }

    public String cmdA() throws Exception {
        byte[] a = new byte[] { (byte) COMMAND_A, (byte) COMMAND_TERM };
        return execute(a, 150);
    }

    public String cmdB() throws Exception {
        byte[] b = new byte[] { (byte) COMMAND_B, (byte) COMMAND_TERM };
        return execute(b, 150);

    }

    public static void main(String[] args) throws Exception {
        SimpleStamp t = new SimpleStamp(1);
        System.out.println(t.cmdA());
        System.out.println(t.cmdB());
        t.close();
    }
}
```

Section Summary

In this section, we created a controller interface called JController that will specify behavior between all controllers we will use in this book. We also created an abstract class that carries with it two implementation methods for executing communication. With the two just implementing different read methods, execute() will return a string, and execute2() will return a byte[].

Once the generic controller is created we can extend this class for our specific BASIC Stamp program implementations, while just focusing on the bytes they need to send and the method names we want to create that will correspond to commands in the Stamp program.

The classes and interface created in this section were

- JController.java: This is the interface that will specify behavior for all controllers.

- Controller.java: This is the abstract super-class implementing execute() and execute2() for all future controllers.

- SimpleStamp.java: This is an implementation class for the SerialEcho.bs2 program presented in section 2.3.

The only thing left to create is to get wireless communication with the combination of our BASIC Stamp and Bluetooth device.

2.6 Bluetooth Serial Communications

This is so easy once the Bluetooth device is set up. All you need to do is change the com port ID. I used the EB500 from Parallax. This plugs right into the boards they have and it's a great value at under $100 compared with other Bluetooth serial adapters. Make sure you use the com port as specified beneath the Bluetooth Serial Port under the Client Applications tab.

You can find the instructions for setting up the microcontroller and the EB500 adapter at the Parallax site or in the manual under the title "Connecting Between a PC with a DBT-120 and a BOE." Photos of the EB500 and DBT-120 are shown in Figures 2-9 and 2-10.

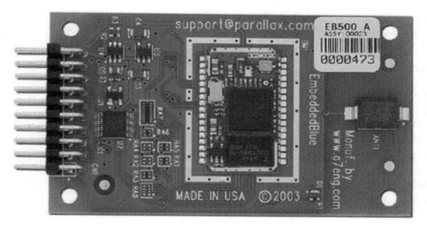

Figure 2-9. *The Parallax EB500 Bluetooth Transceiver Module*

Figure 2-10. *DLink DBT-120 USB Wireless Bluetooth Adapter*

Code Objectives

The objectives for this code are to:

- Demonstrate a wireless serial connection

- Show that a serial connection is the same as a wired one with the proper software installed on the Stamp

Code Discussion

The Bluetooth board connected to our BOE (Board of Education) will communicate directly to our PC via one of its serial connections. While our PC will not notice any difference, there are some slight changes that have to be made on the Stamp side.

First, some initialization commands need to be sent to the EB500, along with the address of our USB Bluetooth adapter on the PC. Once it's connected, our program looks very much like the original with the exception of the SEROUT pin and the SERIN pin: pin 1 versus pin 16.

The Java code is the same code as that used earlier in Example 2-4. Just change the port ID to match the Bluetooth adapter and you are set. (See Example 2-14.)

Example 2-14. *BluetoothStamp.bs2*

```
' {$STAMP BS2}
serialin     VAR    Byte
INPUT 5
PAUSE 1000
SEROUT 1,84, ["con 00:11:95:4F:54:39",CR]
SERIN 0,84,[WAIT("ACK",CR)]
WaitForConnection:
  IF IN5 = 0 THEN WaitForConnection
```

```
main:

  serialIn(0) = 0
  SERIN 0,84,1000,main,[STR serialIn\3\"!"]
  PAUSE 100
  LOOKDOWN serialIn(0),[100,101],serialIn
  BRANCH serialIn,[test1, test2]
  SEROUT 1,84,["none", CR]
  PAUSE 5
  GOTO main

test1:
  SEROUT 1,84,["a"]
  GOTO main
test2:
  SEROUT 1,84,["b"]
  GOTO main
```

By copying this code to your BASIC Stamp, to gain complete access of your now wireless robot, all you need to do is change your serial port ID.

2.7 Chapter Summary

My goal for this chapter was to introduce you to using the Java Communications API to talk with your microcontroller. Hopefully, you now know how to do this and a little bit more.

In section 2.0, I created ListOpenPorts.java. This class showed you how to iterate through all the communications ports to get the serial ports with a specific com ID in the port name. I also added a Utils class that will allow me to call the Thread.sleep function while catching the exception.

In section 2.1, I created the JSerialPort interface and StandardSerialPort. The interface provides a standardized behavior for all serial ports, including the WebSerialClient discussed in section 2.3. The StandardSerialPort class provides for simpler access to the com port API for our usage with robotics.

In section 2.2, I created a resource pool of StandardSerialPorts so that these ports could be accessed concurrently in a multithreaded way.

In section 2.3, I created a way to access the serial port over the Internet with the WebSerialPort, webcom.jsp, and WebSerialClient.

In section 2.4, I connected to the Basic Stamp microcontroller.

In section 2.5, I created the JController interface and Controller. The interface provides standardized behavior for all controllers and the Controller is an abstract superclass that provides functionality for all Parallax controllers being used in this book.

Finally, in section 2.6 I showed you an example BASIC Stamp program that allows for Bluetooth wireless access to your microcontroller from a serial port provided by a Bluetooth adapter.

In the next chapter, we will build on serial communication and model more robot components to get the robot to move. We'll work with legged robots, wheeled robots, robotic arms, and some other types of robotic controllers.

CHAPTER 3

Motion

"Every object in a state of uniform motion tends to remain in that state of motion unless an external force is applied to it."

— Newton's First Law of Motion

3.0   Introduction

Making your robot move is a lot easier these days with the advent of Serial Servo Controllers (SSC) and Electronic Speed Controllers (ESC). They all use the same mechanism to move, a Pulse Width Modulation (PWM) designed to control the position of a servo.

A servo is a small motor that allows the position of its output gear to be precisely positioned by a PWM signal. Figure 3-1 shows a picture of the standard servo, which is the main one I used for differential drives, arms, and legged robots.

Figure 3-1. *The Hitec HS-422 Standard Servo (Lynxmotion Inc.)*

In an SSC, you have anywhere from 8–32 servos you can control. You can digitally position them with byte accuracy (0–255) where 0 would be full Clockwise (CW) and 255 would be full Counter Clockwise (CCW).

In an ESC, the same digital ranges (0–255) represent the speed of a DC motor forward or backward. So, depending on how you have the terminals connected, 0 could represent full speed forward, 255 could be full speed backward, and 127 could signify stopped.

While you can control servos by sending PWM signals via a microcontroller, you are limited in the number of servos you can control at once usually because you will want to take sensor readings, make decisions on what way to go, or which actions to take next, and so on. If you don't have a servo controller, you can write a BASIC Stamp program that will simulate a servo controller, but I strongly recommend you get one for Chapter 7.

In Example 3-1, the program will loop in 10-millisecond intervals if nothing is received from the serial in (SERIN) it moves to old. Because the old values have not been overwritten, the program sends the old pulsout values to the old pin and pos. This example only works for one pin at a time.

Example 3-1. *servo.bs2*

```
'{$STAMP BS2}
'{$PORT COM1}

pin         VAR     Byte
oldPin      VAR     Byte
pos         VAR     Byte
oldPos      VAR     Byte
pulse       VAR     Word

main:
    SERIN 16,16468,old,10,[WAIT(255), pin, pos]
    pulse = (pos/255)*750
    pulsout pin,750+pulse
    oldPin = pin
    oldPos = pos
    GOTO main

old:
    pulse = (oldPos/255)*750
    pulsout oldPin,750+pulse
    GOTO main
```

This chapter contains 21 Java class examples and the previous BASIC Stamp example. The first of these will handle access to servo controllers, followed by examples of wheeled robots, robot arms, and legged robots.

Figure 3-2 shows two continuous rotation servos from Parallax and one Scott Edwards MiniSSC-II servo controller.

Figure 3-2. *A servo controller and a servo with wheels*

You can connect the servo controller to your serial port via the RJ-11 connector (phone jack) or via the jumper on the board. I have not shown the connection of power to the servos. This should be 3.8 to 6.0 volts (sometimes you can go as high as 7.2 volts for high-quality servos). There is also a connector for a 9- to 12-volt battery to power the controller board.

■**Note** There are other controllers out there. See Appendix B for more information.

Once you connect your servo controller to your PC's serial port, you're ready program.

3.1   Servo Controllers

Servo controllers greatly simplify the PC's ability to communicate with servos and electronic speed controls, much like a microcontroller simplifies the PC's ability to communicate with sensors.

Before we actually start programming our controllers, I'd like to make a note about timing. When you move a servo to a position between 0 and 180 degrees, there is a minimum time that it takes to move the servo to that position. For your standard servo, it takes 480 milliseconds to move 180 degrees. Also, since you will be sending this request via a serial port, the time it takes to send a 3-byte command at a 9600-baud rate takes about 3 milliseconds per byte, for a total of 12 milliseconds.

To help out with the discussion, I've included a class diagram (see Figure 3-3) of the three main classes as well as their Chapter 2 counterparts: JSerialPort for serial communications, JController for controller standardization, and Controller, which the SSC extends.

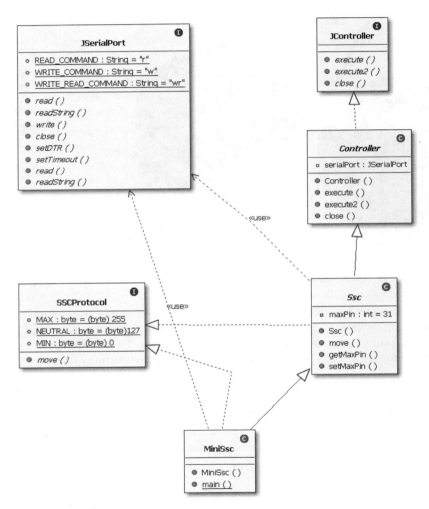

Figure 3-3. *A class diagram of classes in section 3.1*

Figure 3-4 offers a close-up photo of the MiniSSC-II. I started working with this SSC a few years ago and I love it. Currently, there are more powerful controllers out there, but this was the original and I own three, one for Feynman5, one for a robot arm, and one for a spare.

Figure 3-4. *The Scott Edwards MiniSSC-II Servo Controller*

You can connect to it with 2400 or 9600 baud and it has an output for up to 8 servos. For more detailed information please refer to either www.lynxmotion.com or www.seetron.com/ ssc.htm. Make sure you refer to the manual to finalize your connections.

Code Objectives

The objectives for this example code are to:

- Use our serial port to control servo positioning (SerialSsc.java)

- Create a standardized protocol interface for stamp or other class implementations (SSC.java)

Code Discussion

The first example showed how you could get an SSC to work by just using the StandardSerialPort (implementing a JSerialPort) from the last chapter.

The class will move the servo from full CW to full CCW (0 to 255). I paused the servo for 100 milliseconds between positions so that we could see it stop at each position. Once this loop is complete, I close the serial port. (See Example 3-2.)

Example 3-2. *SerialSsc.java*

```java
package com.scottpreston.javarobot.chapter3;

import com.scottpreston.javarobot.chapter2.StandardSerialPort;

public class SerialSsc {

    public static void main(String[] args) {
```

```java
        try {
            // create serial port
            StandardSerialPort serialPort = new StandardSerialPort(1);
            // increment position by 5 each time in loop
            for (int pos = 0; pos < 255; pos = pos + 5) {
                // create byte array for ssc commands
                byte[] sscCmd = new byte[] { (byte) 255, 0, (byte) pos };
                // send byte array to serial port
                serialPort.write(sscCmd);
                // pause between commands
                Thread.sleep(100);
            }
            // close serail port
            serialPort.close();
        } catch (Exception e) {
            // print stack trace and exit.
            e.printStackTrace();
            System.exit(1);
        }
    }
}
```

While the preceding class does just what I want it to, I thought that given all the work in the coming sections and chapters it would be a good idea to standardize communication to the SSC because its communication protocol is fixed. To do this, I created the interface SSCProtocol.java. It has a single method defined, move(pin, pos). The method has the following parameters: pin—the pin position of where the servo is plugged in; and pos—the position of the servo from 0 to 255. I also added a few constants to simplify classes using this protocol. (See Example 3-3.)

Example 3-3. *SSCProtocol.java*

```java
package com.scottpreston.javarobot.chapter3;

public interface SSCProtocol {

    // maximum
    public static final byte MAX = (byte) 255;
    // neutral
    public static final byte NEUTRAL = (byte)127;
    // minimum
    public static final byte MIN = (byte) 0;

    /**
     * @param pin - connector on the MiniSSC 0-7
     * @param pos - byte from 0-255
     */
    public void move(int pin, int pos) throws Exception;

}
```

Now that I have an interface defined for all SSC communication, I'm ready to create the base SSC class. Like Controller.java I made this class abstract because I want to write two implementations that reuse functionality (for example, the move() method).

This class has a single field, maxPin, because I also want to differentiate how many pins each child class of the SSC has. Depending on the servo controller you have, make sure you set this accordingly.

The constructor takes the JSerialPort. In the move method, I add error handling to the input parameters, throwing an exception if the parameters are out of bounds, and then create a byte[] with the parameters before calling the execute method from the Controller parent class. In the byte[] sent via the execute() method, I added the sync byte of 255 each time, because we know we have to send it as part of the SSCProtocol. (See Example 3-4.)

Example 3-4. *SSC.java*

```java
package com.scottpreston.javarobot.chapter3;

import com.scottpreston.javarobot.chapter2.Controller;
import com.scottpreston.javarobot.chapter2.JSerialPort;

public abstract class Ssc extends Controller implements SSCProtocol{

    // maximum possible for LM32
    private int maxPin = 31;

    // takes JSerialPort
    public Ssc(JSerialPort serialPort )throws Exception {
        super(serialPort);
    }

    // move will send signal to pin (0-7) and pos (0-255)
    public void move(int pin, int pos) throws Exception{
        // keep pos in valid range
        if (pos < 0 || pos >255) {
            throw new Exception("Position out of range, must be ➥
between 0 and 255. Value was " + pos + ".");
        }
        // keep pin in valid range
        if (pin < 0 || pin > maxPin) {
            throw new Exception("Pin out of range, must be between 0 and "
                    + maxPin + ". Value was " + pin + ".");
        }
        // create byte[] for commands
        byte [] b = new byte[] {(byte)255,(byte)pin,(byte)pos};
        // send those bytes to controller
        execute(b,0);
    }
```

```
        // accessor
        public int getMaxPin() {
            return maxPin;
        }
        // setter
        public void setMaxPin(int maxPin) {
            this.maxPin = maxPin;
        }

}
```

Now that the general super-class has been created, it's time to create a specific class for the MiniSSC-II. This class has no fields and simply calls the parent constructor and setMaxPin method to limit the total pins to seven.

In the example program in main(), I call the same logic that composed the class SerialSSC in Example 3-2. Move the servo through the range of motion in 5-byte increments. You'll note that its command structure is simpler (no bytes to create or cast), and you have error control built in. (See Example 3-5.)

Example 3-5. *MiniSsc.java*

```
package com.scottpreston.javarobot.chapter3;

import com.scottpreston.javarobot.chapter2.JSerialPort;
import com.scottpreston.javarobot.chapter2.SingleSerialPort;
import com.scottpreston.javarobot.chapter2.Utils;

public class MiniSsc extends Ssc implements SSCProtocol {

    // calls super and sets max pin to 7
    public MiniSsc(JSerialPort serialPort) throws Exception {
        super(serialPort);
        setMaxPin(7);
    }

    // sample program
    public static void main(String[] args) {
        try {
            // get single serial port instance
            JSerialPort sPort = (JSerialPort) SingleSerialPort.getInstance(1);
            // create new miniSSc
            MiniSsc ssc = new MiniSsc(sPort);
```

```
        // move from position 0 to 255, 5 per 100 ms
        for (int pos = 0; pos < 255; pos = pos + 5) {
            // move
            ssc.move(0, pos);
            // wait 100 milliseconds
            Utils.pause(100);
        }
        // close serial port
        sPort.close();
    } catch (Exception e) {
        // print stack trace and exit
        e.printStackTrace();
        System.exit(1);
    }
  }

}
```

Section Summary

In this section, we showed a difficult way and an easy way to model a servo controller. We also added an interface to ensure communication for different controllers and added an implementation for the MiniSSC-II. The classes discussed were the following:

- SerialSsc.java: A serial version of servo control (an example of a hard way)

- SSCProtocol.java: An interface designed to standardize communication to a servo controller

- SSC.java: Super-class used by the MiniSSC and other classes for servo communication

- MiniSSC.java: Implementation class for the Scott Edwards MiniSSC-II

Now that you know how to control servos with your PC, you're ready to get a robot to move. In the next section, I'll talk about differential drive robots (with two wheels) and there I'll use the MiniSSC and your PC's serial port to make it move.

3.2 Wheeled Motion

Using a servo controller connected to an electronic speed controller or a pair of "hacked" or continuous rotation servos is an excellent way to facilitate wheeled motion. Figure 3-5 shows a picture of the differential drive of a CubeBot connected to a MiniSSC-II. Notice that the servo wires are to the rear of the platform. This means the motors are inverted, so I'll have to account for this in the classes in this section.

Figure 3-5. *The differential drive of a CubeBot*

Three classes and one interface will be discussed in this section. Figure 3-6 shows a class diagram that summarizes the classes.

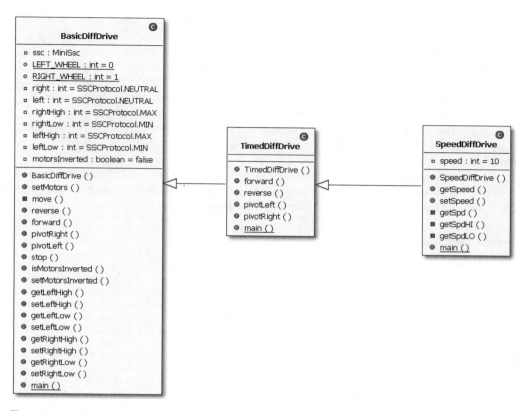

Figure 3-6. *A class diagram of classes in section 3.2*

Code Objectives

The objective in this section is to provide basic movements: forward, reverse, pivotRight, pivotLeft, and stop.

Code Discussion

I'll start off this section by writing a basic differential drive class, called BasicDiffDrive. The fields of this class have a single instance field, ssc, for the MiniSSC class, which controls the servos and provides their functionality. I also have two constants that represent the hardware connections for the left and right wheels. The remaining fields are used to keep state for the servo positions for constant or various speeds.

The constructor for this class takes a JSerialPort, which builds the MiniSSC. The setMotors() method sets parameters regarding the position and movement of the SSC. This method is followed by move(), which calls the MiniSSC method of the same name.

The four directional methods—forward(), reverse(), pivotLeft(), and pivotRight()—have two functions: first, to check to see if the motors are connected in an inverted fashion (like the CubeBot), and then to set the values of the motors, and secondly, to call the move method. While I could have just called the ssc.move(), allowing me to extend and add a speed control later, I could not have reused the method for later subclasses. However, if you don't want speed control, you can simplify this by just inserting the move positions directly in each of the four directional methods.

The setters and accessor methods are included so classes can access the state variables of right and left for the subclass TimedDiffDrive. Finally, in main() I test the class by sending the robot forward for 2 seconds, and then stopping. (See Example 3-6.)

Example 3-6. *BasicDiffDrive.java*

```java
package com.scottpreston.javarobot.chapter3;

import com.scottpreston.javarobot.chapter2.JSerialPort;
import com.scottpreston.javarobot.chapter2.SingleSerialPort;
import com.scottpreston.javarobot.chapter2.Utils;

public class BasicDiffDrive {

    // drive will use MiniSSC
    private MiniSsc ssc;

    // left wheel hooked to pin 0
    public static final int LEFT_WHEEL = 0;
    // right wheel hooked to pin 1
    public static final int RIGHT_WHEEL = 1;
    // set all to neutral values
    private int right = SSCProtocol.NEUTRAL;;
    private int left = SSCProtocol.NEUTRAL;
    private int rightHigh = SSCProtocol.MAX;
    private int rightLow = SSCProtocol.MIN;
    private int leftHigh = SSCProtocol.MAX;
    private int leftLow = SSCProtocol.MIN;

    // right will always be the one inverted can change this
    private boolean motorsInverted = false;

    // constructor takes JSerialPort
    public BasicDiffDrive(JSerialPort serialPort) throws Exception {
        // create MiniSSC
        ssc = new MiniSsc(serialPort);
    }
```

```java
    // setting motor values
    public void setMotors(int left, int right) {
        this.left = left;
        this.right = right;
    }

    // actually moving the motors
    private void move() throws Exception {
        // left wheel
        ssc.move(LEFT_WHEEL, left);
        // right wheel
        ssc.move(RIGHT_WHEEL, right);
    }

    // move in reverse
    public void reverse() throws Exception {
        // if inverted move motors opposite or same.
        if (motorsInverted) {
            // opposite direction
            setMotors(leftHigh, rightLow);
        } else {
            // same direction
            setMotors(leftHigh, rightHigh);
        }
        // move motors
        move();
    }

    // move forward
    public void forward() throws Exception {
        if (motorsInverted) {
            setMotors(leftLow, rightHigh);
        } else {
            setMotors(leftLow, rightLow);
        }

        move();
    }

    // pivot on axis right
    public void pivotRight() throws Exception {
        if (motorsInverted) {
            setMotors(leftLow, rightLow);
        } else {
            setMotors(leftLow, rightHigh);
        }
        move();
    }
```

```java
    // pivot on axis left
    public void pivotLeft() throws Exception {
        if (motorsInverted) {
            setMotors(leftHigh, rightHigh);
        } else {
            setMotors(leftHigh, rightLow);
        }
        move();
    }

    // stop the motion
    public void stop() throws Exception {
        // set both motors to same value
        setMotors(SSCProtocol.NEUTRAL, SSCProtocol.NEUTRAL);
        move();
    }

    // accessor
    public boolean isMotorsInverted() {
        return motorsInverted;
    }

    // setter
    public void setMotorsInverted(boolean motorsInverted) {
        this.motorsInverted = motorsInverted;
    }

    // accessor
    public int getLeftHigh() {
        return leftHigh;
    }

    // setter
    public void setLeftHigh(int leftHigh) {
        this.leftHigh = leftHigh;
    }

    // accessor
    public int getLeftLow() {
        return leftLow;
    }

    // setter
    public void setLeftLow(int leftLow) {
        this.leftLow = leftLow;
    }
```

```java
    // accessor
    public int getRightHigh() {
        return rightHigh;
    }

    // setter
    public void setRightHigh(int rightHigh) {
        this.rightHigh = rightHigh;
    }

    // accessor
    public int getRightLow() {
        return rightLow;
    }

    // setter
    public void setRightLow(int rightLow) {
        this.rightLow = rightLow;
    }

    // sample program
    public static void main(String[] args) {
        try {
            // get instance of SingleSerialPort
            JSerialPort sPort = (JSerialPort) SingleSerialPort.getInstance(1);
            // create instnace of BasicDiffDrive
            BasicDiffDrive diffDrive = new BasicDiffDrive(sPort);
            // move forward
            diffDrive.forward();
            // pause 2 seconds
            Utils.pause(2000);
            // stop
            diffDrive.stop();
            // close serial port
            sPort.close();
        } catch (Exception e) {
            // print stack trace and exit
            e.printStackTrace();
            System.exit(1);
        }
    }

}
```

The next class simplifies movement a bit by adding the pause() and stop() methods for you. By extending the BasicDiffDrive class and creating new methods with parameters to take a millisecond argument, our robot can move in a particular direction during a given unit of time. (See Example 3-7.)

Note   I have found that using millisecond resolution is just as accurate as wheel encoders over short distances (<3 meters or <10 seconds). This is because the wheel slippage and time to stop accuracies are at their low end with these distances and speeds. But even these shortcomings are overcome by distance measurement sensors so as to eliminate the "practical" need for wheel encoders.

Example 3-7. *TimedDiffDrive.java*

```java
package com.scottpreston.javarobot.chapter3;

import com.scottpreston.javarobot.chapter2.JSerialPort;
import com.scottpreston.javarobot.chapter2.SingleSerialPort;
import com.scottpreston.javarobot.chapter2.Utils;

public class TimedDiffDrive extends BasicDiffDrive {

    // construct with JSerialPort
    public TimedDiffDrive(JSerialPort serialPort) throws Exception {
        super(serialPort);
    }

    // forward
    public void forward(long ms) throws Exception {
        // calls super
        forward();
        // pause
        Utils.pause(ms);
        // stop
        stop();
    }

    // reverse
    public void reverse(long ms) throws Exception {
        reverse();
        Utils.pause(ms);
        stop();
    }

    // pivot left
    public void pivotLeft(long ms) throws Exception {
        pivotLeft();
        Utils.pause(ms);
        stop();
    }
```

```
    // pivot right
    public void pivotRight(long ms) throws Exception {
        pivotRight();
        Utils.pause(ms);
        stop();
    }

    // sample program
    public static void main(String[] args) {
        try {
            // get instance of SingleSerialPort
            JSerialPort sPort = (JSerialPort) SingleSerialPort.getInstance(1);
            // create instnace of TimedDiffDrive
            TimedDiffDrive diffDrive = new TimedDiffDrive(sPort);
            // move forwrd 2 seconds
            diffDrive.forward(2000);
            // close serial port
            sPort.close();
        } catch (Exception e) {
            // print stack trace and exit
            e.printStackTrace();
            System.exit(1);
        }
    }
}
```

The final thing I need for the differential drive to be complete is a speed control. However, I won't always have wheeled robots. I might want to implement navigational classes with legged robots or other implementations of the differential drive (maybe even a car with an accelerator, brake, and steering wheel). In this case, because I want to reuse my navigational classes (see Chapter 7), I should create an interface and then use that interface in later classes.

The interface I'll create is JMotion. This class has all the methods of BasicDiffDrive and TimedDiffDrive, plus the methods for speed control. (See Example 3-8.)

Example 3-8. *The JMotion.java Interface*

```
package com.scottpreston.javarobot.chapter3;

public interface JMotion {

    // forward
    public void forward() throws Exception;
    // reverse
    public void reverse() throws Exception;
    // pivot right
    public void pivotRight() throws Exception;
    // picot left
    public void pivotLeft() throws Exception;
```

```
// stop
public void stop() throws Exception;
// forward
public void forward(int ms) throws Exception;
// reverse
public void reverse(int ms) throws Exception;
// pivot right
public void pivotRight(int ms) throws Exception;
// picot left
public void pivotLeft(int ms) throws Exception;
// setting speed of robot
public void setSpeed(int speed)throws Exception ;
// get speed of robot
public int getSpeed();


}
```

Note The speed will not work in a hacked servo because it's either full on or full off. There you will have to delay the on-off cycles of your servo to something very fast. It might be difficult getting this to work and be smooth given our baud rate. However, it will work well for an electronic speed control (ECS), but you might want to adjust the speed to a higher resolution than 10.

In the SpeedDiffDrive class, I implement the JMotion interface and have a single field speed which I defaulted to 5.

The setSpeed() method is the heart of the method as it sets the high values for the servo controller as well as the low values. So, at a speed of 10, the high value would be 255, while at a speed of 9 it would be 255 − 13 (12.7) = 242, and so on.

At the bottom of the class, I have to implement the methods from the interface that already exist in the super-class. Why do we need to just create pass-through? Java does not support multiple inheritance, so the compiler only sees the BasicDiffDrive's method for the interface and not the TimedDiffDrive class. (See Example 3-9.)

Example 3-9. *SpeedDiffDrive.java*

```java
package com.scottpreston.javarobot.chapter3;

import com.scottpreston.javarobot.chapter2.JSerialPort;
import com.scottpreston.javarobot.chapter2.SingleSerialPort;

public class SpeedDiffDrive extends TimedDiffDrive implements JMotion{

    // set initial speed
    private int speed = 5;
```

```java
// construct with JSerialPort
public SpeedDiffDrive(JSerialPort serialPort) throws Exception{
    super(serialPort);
}

// accessor for speed
public int getSpeed() {
    return speed;
}

// setter for speed
public void setSpeed(int speed) throws Exception {
    // keep speed between min and max
    if (speed < 1 || speed > 10) {
        throw new Exception("Speed out of range 1-10.");
    }
    // set speed
    this.speed = speed;
    // get high for left
    setLeftHigh(getSpdHI());
    // get low for left
    setLeftLow(getSpdLO());
    // get high for right
    setRightHigh(getSpdHI());
    // get low for right
    setRightLow(getSpdLO());
}

// get speed as fraction of 127 (half of MiniSSC)
private int getSpd() {
    double s = (double) 127 * (speed / 10.0);
    return (int) s;
}

// return high speed
private int getSpdHI() {
    return getSpd() + 127;
}

// return low speed
private int getSpdLO() {
    return 127 - getSpd();
}

// sample program
public static void main(String[] args) {
    try {
```

```
            // get instance of SingleSerialPort
            JSerialPort sPort = (JSerialPort)SingleSerialPort.getInstance(1);
            // create instance of SpeedDiffDrive
            SpeedDiffDrive diffDrive = new SpeedDiffDrive(sPort);
            // set speed to 5
            diffDrive.setSpeed(5);
            // move forward 2 seconds
            diffDrive.forward(2000);
            // close port
            sPort.close();
        } catch (Exception e) {
            // print stack trace and exit
            e.printStackTrace();
            System.exit(1);
        }
    }

    // for interface passthroughs
    public void forward(int ms) throws Exception{
        super.forward(ms);
    }
    public void reverse(int ms) throws Exception{
        super.reverse(ms);
    }
    public void pivotRight(int ms) throws Exception{
        super.pivotRight(ms);
    }
    public void pivotLeft(int ms) throws Exception{
        super.pivotLeft(ms);
    }
}
```

Section Summary

The three classes in this section will get you through most wheeled motion using a serial servo controller and/or electronic speed control. The classes I discussed were

- BasicDiffDrive.java: The basic differential drive control

- TimedDiffDrive.java: The extended version of BasicDiffDrive that allows motion to occur at specific time intervals

- JMotion.java: The interface that defines the basic movements of all types of motion (for wheeled and legged robots)

- SpeedDiffDrive.java: The extended version of TimedDiffDrive that gives speed control to any motion

The next type of motion is still going to be done with servos, but this time it will move something on your robot rather than the robot itself. It will rely on the same principles discussed here but instead of creating methods like forward() or pivotRight(), it will create methods like lookUp() or lookRight() to move a camera.

3.3   Pan and Tilt Mechanisms

Sometimes you just want to move part of your robot. If you have a camera and are doing some things with machine vision (see Chapter 6), then you definitely want a pan and tilt camera system. The one I use is shown in Figure 3-7 and comprises a few brackets and two servos, which can be purchased from Lynxmotion for less than $35. I will take the same concepts used in our differential drive systems like grouping servos together in a class, and then we will use our MiniSSC class to control the servos.

Figure 3-7. *The Lynxmotion Pan and Tilt Kit*

Figure 3-8 shows a diagram that summarizes the classes.

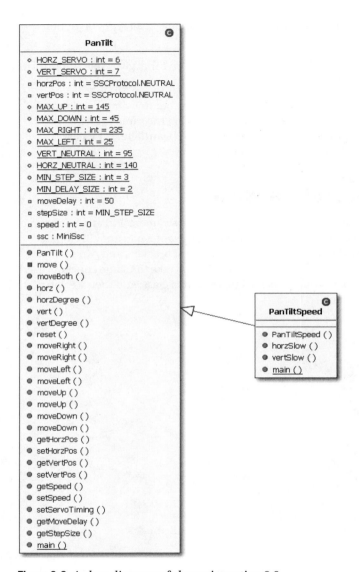

Figure 3-8. *A class diagram of classes in section 3.3*

Code Objectives

The objective in this section is to create a class to control a pan and tilt mechanism from a servo controller.

Code Discussion

The most important part of this class is the preconfigured constants—for example, what pins connect the servos? How far can the servos move? What are the rest positions? These are things you'll have to experiment with to set. The remaining fields are stepSize (how many bytes the system will move per step defaulted to three), speed (how fast the servo will move between steps), and the MiniSSC, which does the work.

The constructor is the JSerialPort and the move method calls separate methods to move the horizontal and vertical control servos. The two methods horz() and vert() will look at the current position values and then send corresponding serial signals to the SSC as long as the positions are within the range of the pan and tilt system.

Rather than always using byte positions from 0 to 255, I added two methods horzDegree() and vertDegree() that will convert angles from 0 to 180, and bytes from 0 to 255.

The other methods are there to move the pan and tilt mechanism in steps. This is useful if you have a camera tracking system and you just want to move a step in a direction but don't know how far left, right, up, or down you want to move.

Because I want the pan and tilt to move smoothly from one position to another in the setServoTiming() method, I perform some error checking to see if the movement rate specified is greater than the maximum speed. For example, if the servo can move from 0 to 90 degrees in 240 milliseconds and I want it to move there in 200 milliseconds, I need to throw an exception because the servo can not move that fast.

Also, if the step size is less than the minimum size, I need to throw an exception because the servo can only respond to signals as fast as the serial controller can send them at a 9600-baud rate.

In the test method main(), I instantiate the PanTilt class with the StandardSerialPort (JSerialPort), and then move left until it's at its left limit, then right, then up, and then down. Although throwing an exception is a rather sloppy way of coding it, I wanted to show you how you can use the exceptions to prevent the system from hurting itself. (See Example 3-10.)

Example 3-10. *PanTilt.java*

```java
package com.scottpreston.javarobot.chapter3;

import com.scottpreston.javarobot.chapter2.JSerialPort;
import com.scottpreston.javarobot.chapter2.SingleSerialPort;

public class PanTilt{

// connected to pin 6 of MinSSC-II
    public static final int HORZ_SERVO = 6;
    // connected to pin 7 of MinSSC-II
    public static final int VERT_SERVO = 7;
    private int horzPos = SSCProtocol.NEUTRAL;
    private int vertPos = SSCProtocol.NEUTRAL;

    // should set these to the best limits of your pan/tilt system
    public static final int MAX_UP = 145;
    public static final int MAX_DOWN = 45;
    public static final int MAX_RIGHT = 235;
    public static final int MAX_LEFT = 25;
    public static final int VERT_NEUTRAL = 95;
    public static final int HORZ_NEUTRAL = 140;
```

```java
    // 3 millieconds at 9600 baud
    public static final int MIN_STEP_SIZE = 3;
    // 2 milliseconds for standard servo
    public static final int MIN_DELAY_SIZE = 2;

    // delay in milliseconds between move
    private int moveDelay = 50;
    // byte size of single step
    private int  stepSize = MIN_STEP_SIZE;
    private int speed = 0;

    // MiniSSC doing work
    private MiniSsc ssc;

    // constructor takes JSerialPort
    public PanTilt(JSerialPort sPort) throws Exception{
        ssc = new MiniSsc(sPort);
    }

    // move both servos to positions
    private void move() throws Exception {
        horz(horzPos);
        vert(vertPos);
    }
    // move both servos with input parameters
    // h = horizontal servo
    // v = vertical servo
    public void moveBoth(int h, int v) throws Exception{
        // set private fields
        horzPos = h;
        vertPos = v;
        // move
        move();
    }
    public void horz(int pos)  throws Exception{
        // check to see if position within limits
        if (pos < MAX_LEFT || pos > MAX_RIGHT ) {
            throw new Exception("Out of horizontal range.");
        }
        // set pos
        horzPos = pos;
        // move
        ssc.move(HORZ_SERVO,pos);
    }
```

```java
public void horzDegree(int angle)  throws Exception{
    // check to see if angle is within limits of 0-180
    if (angle <0 || angle > 180) {
        throw new Exception("Out of range, angle 0-180.");
    }
    // convert fraction of 255
    double theta = ((double)angle/180 ) * 255.0 ;
    // move
    horz((int)theta);

}

public void vert(int pos)  throws Exception{
    if (pos < MAX_DOWN || pos > MAX_UP ) {
        throw new Exception("Out of vertical range.");
    }
    vertPos = pos;
    ssc.move(VERT_SERVO,pos);
}

public void vertDegree(int angle)  throws Exception{
    if (angle <0 || angle > 180) {
        throw new Exception("Out of range, angle 0-180.");
    }
    double theta = ((double)angle/180 ) * 255.0 ;
    vert((int)theta);

}

// reset to neutral position
public void reset( ) throws Exception{
    horzPos = HORZ_NEUTRAL;
    vertPos = VERT_NEUTRAL;
    move();
}

// move right specific step size
public void moveRight(int size) throws Exception{
    horz(horzPos+size);
}
// move right current stepSize
public void moveRight()throws Exception {
    moveRight(stepSize);
}
```

```java
    public void moveLeft(int size) throws Exception{
        horz(horzPos-size);
    }
    public void moveLeft()throws Exception {
        moveLeft(stepSize);
    }

    public void moveUp(int size) throws Exception{
        vert(vertPos+size);
    }
    public void moveUp()throws Exception {
        moveUp(stepSize);
    }
    public void moveDown(int size) throws Exception{
        vert(vertPos-size);
    }
    public void moveDown()throws Exception {
        moveDown(stepSize);
    }

    // accessor
    public int getHorzPos() {
        return horzPos;
    }
    // setter
    public void setHorzPos(int horzPos) {
        this.horzPos = horzPos;
    }
    // accessor
    public int getVertPos() {
        return vertPos;
    }
    // setter
    public void setVertPos(int vertPos) {
        this.vertPos = vertPos;
    }
    // accessor
    public int getSpeed() {
        return speed;
    }
    // setter
    public void setSpeed(int speed) {
        this.speed = speed;
    }
    // servo timing setter
    // stepSize = size of the step as long as it's not minimum step size
    // moveDelay = timing delay between steps
```

```java
    public void setServoTiming(int stepSize, int moveDelay)
throws Exception {
        // ensure will work
        if (stepSize < MIN_STEP_SIZE) {
            throw new Exception("Step size not possible at 9600 baud.");
        }
        if (moveDelay < (stepSize * MIN_DELAY_SIZE)) {
            throw new Exception("Move delay not practical for given step size.");
        }
        this.stepSize = stepSize;
        this.moveDelay = moveDelay;
    }

    public int getMoveDelay() {
        return moveDelay;
    }

    public int getStepSize() {
        return stepSize;
    }

    // sample program
    public static void main(String[] args) {
        try {
            // get instance of SingleSerialPort
            JSerialPort sPort = (JSerialPort)SingleSerialPort.getInstance(1);
            // create instance of PanTilt
            PanTilt pt = new PanTilt(sPort);
            // pan left until exception is thrown
            while (true) {
                try {
                pt.moveLeft();
                } catch (Exception e) {
                    break;
                }
            }
            // pan right
            while (true) {
                try {
                pt.moveRight();
                } catch (Exception e) {
                    break;
                }
            }
            // reset head
            pt.reset();
            // tilt up
```

```
            while (true) {
                try {
                pt.moveUp();
                } catch (Exception e) {
                    break;
                }
            }
            // tilt down
            while (true) {
                try {
                pt.moveDown();
                } catch (Exception e) {
                    break;
                }
            }
            // reset head
            pt.reset();
            // close serial port
            sPort.close();
        } catch (Exception e) {
            // print stack trace and exit
            e.printStackTrace();
            System.exit(1);
        }
    }
}
```

Section Summary

So now you can move your robot and position its camera/eye(s). Moving it gracefully may still take some experimenting, but we created some classes that provide the foundation for panning and tilting and other similar servo configurations.

In this section, I created the following two classes:

- PanTilt.java: The base class for pan and tilt operations

- PanTiltSpeed.java: This is extended from PanTilt to provide smoother movement from one position to another.

While this will function adequately for most tasks, you still might want smoother movement or need more servos to move. In such cases, you may want to try the Lynxmotion SSC-32 and then implement another protocol besides the SSCProtocol so you can move more than one servo with a single serial command. I'll discuss that and more in the next section.

3.4 Advanced Servo Control

From the last example, which showed pan and tilt with speed and error control, you can see that the control of a few servos can get quite complicated. As I get ready to discuss robotic arms and legged robots, I'm going to be working with more than two servos, sometimes up to 12 in the case of the Extreme Hexapod 2. I'll also want to have the same level of speed control as I did with two servos, and also coordinate the moves of more than one servo at the same time.

In this example, I want to focus on making my robot solve higher-level problems like navigation instead of devoting all my code and CPU cycles to managing servo control. Fortunately, there's a new servo control on the market with all of those features: the Lynxmotion SSC-32 (see Figure 3-9). This servo controller allows for speed control and timing. We'll use it when discussing advanced servo controls and group moves.

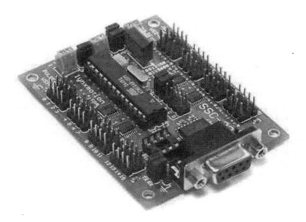

Figure 3-9. *The Lynxmotion SSC-32 Servo Controller*

The Lynxmotion SSC-32 servo controller has 32 output pins compared with the eight pins of the MiniSSC-II. It also allows the same protocol of communication, so if you create some code for the MiniSSC, you can reuse it with the SSC-32 and can increase the baud rate to 115,200. Thus, when we model this controller, we can implement the same SSCProtocol interface, but because it comes with some other built-in features like grouped and timed moves, we'll want to add a new protocol called the GroupMoveProtocol.

Although this protocol is really useful with the LM32, you can also write a class for the MiniSSC to implement the interface. Then you should be able to use Plug N Play (PnP) hardware without changing much software.

Using the GroupMoveProtocol is different than the SSCProtocol for three reasons: one, you can group a number of servos together in a single command instead of sending command strings to each servo; two, you can input the speed at which you want each channel to move; and three, you can set the maximum move for the entire channel.

These three features give the GroupMoveProtocol a lot of advantages over the SSCProtocol and now because we are controlling timing with the controller and not the Thread.sleep() method, our controller program will need to change as well.

In my class, I want three kinds of methods. The first move will just do what the SSCProtocol does, except we'll give the method an extra argument that designates the time to move in milliseconds. The second kind of move will be a group move. This will move all servos in the associated group to the desired position. The third kind of move will determine how to set the groups and pins.

I've included a class diagram of these classes in Figure 3-10.

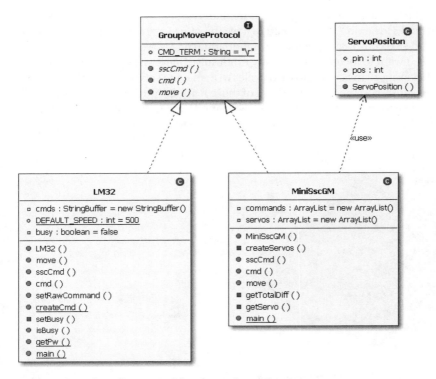

Figure 3-10. *A class diagram of the classes in section 3.4*

Code Objectives

The objective here is to create an interface for managing the GroupMoveProtocol so it can be implemented by the MiniSSC and LM32.

Code Discussion

The interface for group moves is different than that for the SSC because we are embedding timing directly into the command string instead of pausing our program. So the interface should really just be made to accept commands and store them for a final output.

The field in the interface is a constant for command termination as specified by the LM32. The first method, sscCmd(), takes the same inputs as a MiniSSC. The cmd() method will take an additional parameter spd—this will be the speed of the individual move. The final method, move(), will take a single parameter time. This will be the speed of the total move as opposed to the move for the specific servo. (See Example 3-11.)

Example 3-11. *GroupMoveProtocol.java*

```java
package com.scottpreston.javarobot.chapter3;

public interface GroupMoveProtocol {

    public static final String CMD_TERM = "\r";

    /**
     * This is the SSC Constructor Mode w/500 default speed
     * @param ch - channel 0-31
     * @param pos - position 0-255
     */

    public void sscCmd(int ch, int pos) throws Exception;

    /**
     * This is the native constructor mode.
     * @param ch - channel 0-31
     * @param pos - position 0-255
     * @param spd - speed in ms
     * @param tm = time to move in milliseconds
     *
     */
    public void cmd(int ch, int pos, int spd) throws Exception;

    /**
     *
     * @param time - length in milliseconds to move
     * @throws Exception
     */

    public void move(int time) throws Exception;

}
```

Because the LM32 takes commands for timing and we can group servos together, we will have to do much less in our class, and our timings will look smoother and more fluid.

Code Objectives

The objective here is to implement the GroupMoveProtocol for the LM32.

Code Discussion

One of the benefits of a nice object language is code reuse. Notice that I just extend the SSC class, so this class will do the same thing as a standard MiniSSC-II.

The difference seen in the following class is that the interface is the actual format of the command string in the method createCmd(). Also, because we're used to dealing with servo positions between 0–255, I left this in rather than requiring the worker program to keep track of pulse widths between 750 and 2250 milliseconds.

The two fields in the class are cmds—a StringBuffer and a Boolean—to provide status to any class using this object. Because the timing is determined by the LM32, I choose to use a timer to signal the class for state change (busy=false). This is done via the setBusy() method where a single task is set to be run at a specified time in the future (now + milliseconds in future).

The constructor calls the super constructor with the JSerialPort, and sets the maxPins field to 32. The move() method converts the StringBuffer to a byte[] before sending out the serial port via the Controller, execute method.

■**Note** I could have put in a parameter here for a delay in the call to execute(), but I wanted to show you another way to do the same thing without tying up resources during a move.

The construction of the serial command has the following syntax:

```
"#" + channel (0-31)
+ "P" + pulsewidth (750-1500milliseconds)
+ "S" + speed(milliseconds for move)
```

You can string up to 32 commands together before you have to terminate it by appending the following:

```
"T" + time for total move(milliseconds) + "\r"
```

The pulsewidth is the time in milliseconds that I have simplified via the getPw() method. It will return a pulsewidth ranging from 750 to 1500 from a byte between 0 and 255.

Finally, the test program uses only two servos and moves them to positions 100 and 200, respectively, during a 1-second timeframe. (See Example 3-12.)

Example 3-12. *LM32.java*

```
package com.scottpreston.javarobot.chapter3;

import java.util.Date;
import java.util.Timer;
import java.util.TimerTask;

import com.scottpreston.javarobot.chapter2.JSerialPort;
import com.scottpreston.javarobot.chapter2.SingleSerialPort;
import com.scottpreston.javarobot.chapter2.Utils;
```

```java
public class LM32 extends Ssc implements SSCProtocol, GroupMoveProtocol {

    // buffer to store commands
    private StringBuffer cmds = new StringBuffer();
    // default speed in milliseconds
    public static int DEFAULT_SPEED = 500;
    // busy or not
    private boolean busy = false;

    // constructor taking JSerialPort
    public LM32(JSerialPort sPort) throws Exception {
        super(sPort);
        super.setMaxPin(32);

    }

    // move command with parameter of milliseconds
    public void move(int ms) throws Exception {
        // this will pause the current thread for the arm move until
        // it is finished completing its action
        while (busy) {
            Utils.pause(2);
        }
        // set the object status to busy
        setBusy(ms);
        // append final command
        String cmd = cmds.append("T" + ms + CMD_TERM).toString();
        // send bytes to LM32
        execute(cmd.getBytes(), 0);
        // clear command string
        cmds = new StringBuffer(); //resets the string buffer for new set of
                                   // commands
    }

    // override current SSC command
    public void sscCmd(int ch, int pos) throws Exception {
        cmd(ch, pos, DEFAULT_SPEED);
    }

    /**
     * @param ch - channel 0-31
     * @param pos - position 0-255
     * @param spd - speed in milliseconds
     */
```

```java
public void cmd(int ch, int pos, int spd) throws Exception {
    // ensure position is valid
    if (pos < 0 || pos > 255) {
        throw new Exception("position out of bounds");
    }
    // call createCmd then append to string buffer
    cmds.append(createCmd(ch, pos, spd));
}

// allows for raw command string to be sent
public void setRawCommand(String rawCmd) {
    cmds.append(rawCmd);
}

// this is the protocol for the command string for the LM32
public static String createCmd(int ch, int pos, int spd) {

    String out = "#" + ch + "P" + getPw(pos) + "S" + spd;
    return out;
}

// sets the LM32 busy for specific milliseconds
private void setBusy(long ms) {
    // the set busy function
    busy = true;
    // gets time when it should be done
    Date timeToRun = new Date(System.currentTimeMillis() + ms);
    Timer timer = new Timer();
    // schedules time to be run so busy can be set to false
    timer.schedule(new TimerTask() {
        public void run() {
            busy = false;
        }
    }, timeToRun);

}

// accessor
public boolean isBusy() {
    return busy;
}

// static utility method
public static int getPw(int pos) {
    int pulsewidth;
    double percent = (double) pos / 255;
    double pwfactor = percent * 1500;
```

```
        // sets pulsewidth as function of byte size
        pulsewidth = 750 + (int) pwfactor;
        return pulsewidth;

    }

    // same program
    public static void main(String[] args) {
        try {
            // get single serial port instance
            JSerialPort sPort = (JSerialPort) SingleSerialPort.getInstance(1);
            // create new LM32
            LM32 lm32 = new LM32(sPort);
            // sets position for servo at pin 0
            lm32.sscCmd(0, 100);
            // sets position for servo at pin 1
            lm32.sscCmd(1, 200);
            // tells the servos to move there in 1 second.
            lm32.move(1000);
            // close serial port
            sPort.close();
        } catch (Exception e) {
            // print stack trace and exit
            e.printStackTrace();
            System.exit(1);
        }

    }

}
```

Group Move with the MiniSSC-II

This will be more difficult on the MiniSSC-II because we have to control two sets of timing. The first timing will be the move from servo position A to servo position B. The second timing is the step size as limited by 9600 baud. This means that our servo step size for each of our servos is dependent on the number of servos we have hooked up. Since each command is about 3 milliseconds if you have two servos it will take about 6 milliseconds, 9 milliseconds for three servos, and so on.

To make this work, we will have to create a way to process these commands separately for each step, for each servo, and for each time interval.

Code Objectives

Our objective here is to duplicate in a MiniSSC-II what is already done for us in the LM32.

Code Discussion

To make things easier, I'm going to create a data structure called a ServoPosition, which I'll store in a list of commands. Though I could have used a second array, this seemed more readable. (See Example 3-13.)

Example 3-13. *ServoPosition.java*

```
package com.scottpreston.javarobot.chapter3;

public class ServoPosition {

    public int pin;
    public int pos;

    public ServoPosition (int pin, int pos) throws Exception{
        if (pos > 255 || pos < 0) {
            throw new Exception("Position out of range, 0-255 only.");
        }
        this.pin = pin;
        this.pos = pos;
    }
}
```

In MiniSscGM, I have two ArrayLists as fields. The first ArrayList commands will store all the commands as a list of ServoPositions. The second will store all the servos as defined by their current positions.

The constructor takes the JSerialPort and calls createServos(). This method just creates a new ServoPosition and adds it to the ArrayList.

The sscCmd() method, required from the GroupMoveProtocol interface will just call the move method of the same name and parameters.

The cmd() method adds servo positions to the ArrayList until the move() method is called since move() is where all the action takes place.

In move(), the first thing we need to do is get the maximum difference between servo positions in the command. This number will determine the step size for each duration. So if the total move is 1000 milliseconds and the move size is 100 positions, I could tell the servo to move one position every 10 milliseconds if both the protocol and servo were fast enough.

Next in move(), we need to determine the total number of steps based on the minimum step size. Since the minimum size is 3, we would have a total of 33 steps in the command, each of them taking (1000/33) = 30.

The last part of the move() method is incrementing the position, moving the servo, and then pausing the program before it makes it's next step. (See Example 3-14.)

Example 3-14. *MiniSscGM.java*

```java
package com.scottpreston.javarobot.chapter3;

import java.util.ArrayList;

import com.scottpreston.javarobot.chapter2.JSerialPort;
import com.scottpreston.javarobot.chapter2.SingleSerialPort;
import com.scottpreston.javarobot.chapter2.Utils;

public class MiniSscGM extends Ssc implements SSCProtocol, GroupMoveProtocol {

    // store commands in list
    private ArrayList commands = new ArrayList();
    // store servos in list
    private ArrayList servos = new ArrayList();

    // constructor takes JSerialPort as parameter
    public MiniSscGM(JSerialPort jSerialPort) throws Exception {
        super(jSerialPort);
        setMaxPin(7);
        // create servos
        createServos();
    }
    // add servos to list
    private void createServos() throws Exception{
        for (int i = 0; i < getMaxPin() + 1; i++) {
            ServoPosition svo = new ServoPosition(i, SSCProtocol.NEUTRAL);
            // index will be same as id.
            servos.add(svo);
        }
    }

    public void sscCmd(int ch, int pos) throws Exception {
        // calls overridden move method later in this class
        move(ch, pos);
    }

    public void cmd(int ch, int pos, int spd) throws Exception {
        // not going to implement the spd variable for the MiniSSC-II
        ServoPosition svoPos = new ServoPosition(ch, pos);
        commands.add(svoPos);
    }

    public void move(int time) throws Exception {
        // all servo moves will have a minimum step-size of 3
```

```
/*
 * gets maximum difference between current positions and new position
 */
int maxDiff = 0;
for (int i = 0; i < commands.size(); i++) {
    ServoPosition newPos = (ServoPosition) commands.get(i);
    ServoPosition curPos = (ServoPosition) servos.get(newPos.pin);
    int tmpDiff = Math.abs(newPos.pos - curPos.pos);
    if (tmpDiff > maxDiff) {
        maxDiff = tmpDiff;
    }
}
// total steps since 3 is min size.
double totalSteps = ((double) maxDiff / 3.0);
// calculate pause time
// total time of move divded by total steps
int pauseTime = (int) ((double) time / totalSteps);

// loop until total difference between all servos
// current position and goal position is zero
while (getTotalDiff() > 0) {

    for (int i = 0; i < commands.size(); i++) {
        ServoPosition newPos = (ServoPosition) commands.get(i);
        ServoPosition curPos = (ServoPosition) servos.get(newPos.pin);
        int tmpDiff = Math.abs(newPos.pos - curPos.pos);
        if (newPos.pos > curPos.pos) {
            if (tmpDiff > 2) {
                curPos.pos = curPos.pos + 3;
            } else {
                curPos.pos = newPos.pos;
            }
        } else if (newPos.pos < curPos.pos) {
            if (tmpDiff > 2) {
                curPos.pos = curPos.pos - 3;
            } else {
                curPos.pos = newPos.pos;
            }
        }
        // move current servo position plus or minus 3
        move(curPos.pin, curPos.pos);
        Utils.pause(pauseTime);
    }
}
// resets commands list.
commands = new ArrayList();
}
```

```java
        // helper method to get difference
        private int getTotalDiff() {
            int totalDiff = 0;
            for (int i = 0; i < commands.size(); i++) {
                ServoPosition newPos = (ServoPosition) commands.get(i);
                ServoPosition curPos = (ServoPosition) servos.get(newPos.pin);
                int tmpDiff = Math.abs(newPos.pos - curPos.pos);
                totalDiff = totalDiff + tmpDiff;
            }
            return totalDiff;
        }

        private ServoPosition getServo(int id) {
            return (ServoPosition) servos.get(id);
        }

        // sample program same as LM32
        public static void main(String[] args) {
            try {
                // get single serial port instance
                JSerialPort sPort = (JSerialPort) SingleSerialPort.getInstance(1);
                // create new LM32
                MiniSscGM miniSscGM = new MiniSscGM(sPort);
                // sets position for servo at pin 0
                miniSscGM.sscCmd(0, 100);
                // sets position for servo at pin 1
                miniSscGM.sscCmd(1, 200);
                // tells the servos to move there in 1 second.
                miniSscGM.move(1000);
                // close serial port
                sPort.close();
            } catch (Exception e) {
                // print stack trace and exit
                e.printStackTrace();
                System.exit(1);
            }

        }
}
```

Section Summary

You can see from the GroupMoveProtocol that the LM32 has a lot of advantages over the SSCProtocol when you want smoother movement or have a lot of servos you want to command at once.

In this section, I created the following four classes:

- GroupMoveProtocol.java: Similar to the SSCProtocol but used for grouped moves of the LM32.

- LM32.java: The implementation class for the Lynxmotion SSC-32.

- ServoPosition.java: A servo position data structure to assist in implementing the Group-MoveProtocol in the MiniSSC.

- MiniSscGM: The implemented GroupMoveProtocol for the MiniSSC.

In the next section, we'll discuss how to use the LM32 and the GroupMoveProtocol with a robotic arm.

3.5 The Robot Arm

Moving your robot on the ground is just one type of motion. The second type is motion from a fixed position. To demonstrate this, I'm going to use a robot arm. If you don't have a robot arm, you can purchase the components from Lynxmotion, Inc. at www.lynxmotion.com (see Figure 3-11) or make them yourself.

Figure 3-11. *The Lynxmotion Aluminum Arm*

I have included a class diagram of these classes in Figure 3-12.

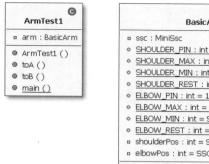
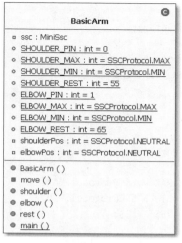
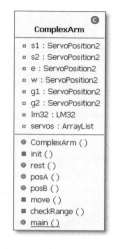

Figure 3-12. *A class diagram of classes in section 3.5*

Code Objectives

The objective in this example is to create a simple model of a robot arm.

Code Discussion

The fields in this class are mostly static constants that will define the range of motion of its two axes: the shoulder and elbow. Of the remaining fields, ssc of type MiniSSC is the worker, and shoulderPos and elbowPos are in the class to maintain state.

The constructor of the class takes the JSerialPort, and the move() method is just a pass-through to the MiniSSC.move() method.

The two methods, shoulder() and elbow(), take input parameters as positions from 0 to 255 for the respective limbs, and the rest() method moves both the shoulder and elbow to their respective rest positions.

■**Note** If you use this class, you may find the movement rather fast and jerky. To slow it down and make it smooth, look ahead to the discussion of the ComplexArm class.

Finally, in main() I just move the arm to its rest position, then to another position, and then close the serial port. (See Example 3-15.)

Example 3-15. *BasicArm.java*

```java
package com.scottpreston.javarobot.chapter3;

import com.scottpreston.javarobot.chapter2.JSerialPort;
import com.scottpreston.javarobot.chapter2.SingleSerialPort;

public class BasicArm {

    private MiniSsc ssc;
    // set shoulder and elbow parameters
    public static final int SHOULDER_PIN = 0;
    public static final int SHOULDER_MAX = SSCProtocol.MAX;
    public static final int SHOULDER_MIN = SSCProtocol.MIN;
    public static final int SHOULDER_REST = 55;
    public static final int ELBOW_PIN = 1;
    public static final int ELBOW_MAX = SSCProtocol.MAX;
    public static final int ELBOW_MIN = SSCProtocol.MIN;
    public static final int ELBOW_REST = 65;
    // instance variables of current position
    private int shoulderPos = SSCProtocol.NEUTRAL;
    private int elbowPos = SSCProtocol.NEUTRAL;

    //constructor taking JSerialPort as parameter
    public BasicArm(JSerialPort sPort) throws Exception {
        ssc = new MiniSsc(sPort);
    }

    // passthrough to ssc
    private void move(int pin, int pos) throws Exception {
        ssc.move(pin, pos);
    }

    // move the shoulder
    public void shoulder(int pos) throws Exception {
        if (pos < SHOULDER_MIN || pos > SHOULDER_MAX) {
            throw new Exception("Out of shoulder range.");
        }
        shoulderPos = pos;
        move(SHOULDER_PIN, pos);
    }

    // move the elbow
    public void elbow(int pos) throws Exception {
        if (pos < ELBOW_MIN || pos > ELBOW_MAX) {
            throw new Exception("Out of elbow range.");
        }
```

```
        elbowPos = pos;
        move(ELBOW_PIN, pos);
    }

    public void rest() throws Exception {
        shoulder(SHOULDER_REST);
        elbow(ELBOW_REST);
    }

    public static void main(String[] args) {
        try {
            // get single serial port instance
            JSerialPort sPort = (JSerialPort) SingleSerialPort.getInstance(1);
            // create new BasicArm
            BasicArm arm = new BasicArm(sPort);
            // move to rest position
            arm.rest();
            // move elbow to 150
            arm.elbow(150);
            // move shoulder to 200
            arm.shoulder(200);
            // close serial port
            sPort.close();
        } catch (Exception e) {
            // print stack trace and exit
            e.printStackTrace();
            System.exit(1);
        }
    }

}
```

The next class will formalize positions a little more than just byte 150 for the elbow and byte 200 for the shoulder.

Code Objectives

The objective here is to make the positions easier to invoke, and to also simplify arm usage.

Code Discussion

The only field I will use in this class will be arm, of type BasicArm.

The constructor takes the JSerialPort and moves the arm to its rest position.

Of the two position methods, toA() and toB() encapsulate the positions of A and B in a method so that you don't have to remember them from within an invoking class. I pause between the methods so that motion can stop since the movement is still jerky. (See Example 3-16.)

Example 3-16. *ArmTest1.java*

```java
package com.scottpreston.javarobot.chapter3;

import com.scottpreston.javarobot.chapter2.JSerialPort;
import com.scottpreston.javarobot.chapter2.SingleSerialPort;
import com.scottpreston.javarobot.chapter2.Utils;

public class ArmTest1 {

    private BasicArm arm;

    public ArmTest1(JSerialPort sPort) throws Exception {
        arm = new BasicArm(sPort);
        arm.rest();
    }

    // to position a
    public void toA() throws Exception {
        arm.shoulder(50);
        Utils.pause(1000);
        arm.elbow(200);
    }

    // to position b
    public void toB() throws Exception {
        arm.shoulder(150);
        Utils.pause(1000);
        arm.elbow(50);

    }

    // sample program
    public static void main(String[] args) {
        try {
            JSerialPort sPort = (JSerialPort) SingleSerialPort.getInstance(1);
            ArmTest1 arm1 = new ArmTest1(sPort);
            arm1.toA();
            arm1.toB();
            arm1.toA();
            sPort.close();
        } catch (Exception e) {
            e.printStackTrace();
            System.exit(1);
        }
    }
}
```

The arm in the next example will have one more servo than the Lynxmotion 5 Axis arm above. This arm will have a total of six servos to control, and because this time I want to eliminate the jerky movement, I will use the LM32 controller and class.

The arm will have the following degrees of freedom shown in Table 3-1.

Table 3-1. *Arm Servos and Descriptions*

Servo Name	Function
Shoulder Rotation Servo	This rotates the arm left and right around its base. (Shoulder left-right)
Shoulder Elevation Servo	This moves the upper arm up and down next to its base. (Shoulder up-down)
Elbow Servo	This move the elbow up and down relative to both its base appendage to wrist appendage. (Bicep - Triceps)
Wrist Servo	This moves the wrist up and down relative to its elbow. (Forearm)
Gripper Rotation Servo	This rotates the gripper left and right the same way that your wrist turns left and right. (Wrist)
Gripper Servo	This opens and closes the gripper. (Fingers)

Code Objectives

The objectives here are the following:

- To model the human arm the best we can so that it's fluid and does not require a lot of coding.

- To write an application class similar to what we did with the basic arm.

Code Discussion

Before I create the ComplexArm class, I need to keep more information available than just the position of an arm and its pin number. To store this information, I extended the ServoPosition class and added three additional fields: min, max, and neutral. This additional information will come in handy when moving six servos since we are moving slowly from one position to another over a certain amount of time. I also need to use these data structures because the LM32 uses a string of servo positions per command rather than sending them out individually. (See Example 3-17.)

Example 3-17. *ServoPosition2.java*

```java
package com.scottpreston.javarobot.chapter3;

public class ServoPosition2 extends ServoPosition {

    // minimum position of arm
    public int min;
    // maximum position of arm
    public int max;
    // neutral position of arm
    public int neutral;

    public ServoPosition2(int pin) throws Exception {
        super(pin,SSCProtocol.NEUTRAL);
        min = SSCProtocol.MIN;
        max = SSCProtocol.MAX;
        neutral = SSCProtocol.NEUTRAL;
    }
    public ServoPosition2(int pin, int pos, int min, int max) throws Exception{
        super(pin,pos);
        if (min > 255 || min < 0) {
            throw new Exception("Minimum out of range, 0-255 only.");
        }
        if (max > 255 || max < 0) {
            throw new Exception("Maximum out of range, 0-255 only.");
        }
        this.min = min;
        this.max = max;
        this.neutral = pos;
    }

}
```

The ComplexArm class in this example uses fields of type ServoPosition2. I named these fields according to the limb they represent (shoulder1, shoulder2, elbow, and so on). In the ArrayList servos I store these servo positions for later use. In lm32, I have an instance of the worker class LM32.

The constructor takes the JSerialPort and calls the init() method. Init() creates new instances of the servo positions and adds them to the ArrayList of servos (in a separate method for a simple constructor).

The rest() method in ComplexArm is similar to BasicArm, except that rather than calling each servo separately, I iterate through the list of servos, create the command, and then call move() over a time of 1 second.

The posA() and posB() methods have specific positions for each servo, but instead of jerking to one position and pausing, the movements are slow over a total time of 1 second.

The move() method checks the range by iteration through the list and checks pin limits. Then it calls the LM32 move() command.

The result is the same as BasicArm, but smoother, and with more axes. (See Example 3-18.)

Example 3-18. *ComplexArm.java*

```java
package com.scottpreston.javarobot.chapter3;

import java.util.ArrayList;

import com.scottpreston.javarobot.chapter2.JSerialPort;
import com.scottpreston.javarobot.chapter2.SingleSerialPort;

public class ComplexArm{

    // servo positions for differnt servos
    // shoulder 1
    private ServoPosition2 s1;
    // shoulder 2
    private ServoPosition2 s2;
    // elbow
    private ServoPosition2 e;
    // wrist
    private ServoPosition2 w;
    // grip 1
    private ServoPosition2 g1;
    // grip 2
    private ServoPosition2 g2;
    // LM32 worker
    private LM32 lm32;
    // list of servos
    private ArrayList servos;

    public ComplexArm(JSerialPort serialPort) throws Exception {
        lm32 = new LM32(serialPort);
        // put in seperate method for cleanliness
        init();
    }

    private void init() throws Exception {

        // note the position pin is not used for the LM32 because it remembers
        // the position
        s1 = new ServoPosition2(0);
        s2 = new ServoPosition2(1);
        e = new ServoPosition2(2);
        w = new ServoPosition2(3);
        g1 = new ServoPosition2(4);
        g2 = new ServoPosition2(5);
```

```java
        // add to collection for easier checks
        servos.add(s1);
        servos.add(s2);
        servos.add(e);
        servos.add(w);
        servos.add(g1);
        servos.add(g2);
    }

    public void rest() throws Exception {
        for (int i = 0; i < servos.size(); i++) {
            ServoPosition2 tmpPos = (ServoPosition2) servos.get(i);
            lm32.sscCmd(tmpPos.pin, tmpPos.neutral);
        }
        lm32.move(1000);
    }

    // move to position A (experimentally determined)
    public void posA() throws Exception {
        lm32.sscCmd(s1.pin, 50);
        lm32.sscCmd(s2.pin, 135);
        lm32.sscCmd(e.pin, 75);
        lm32.sscCmd(w.pin, 200);
        lm32.sscCmd(g1.pin, 150);
        lm32.sscCmd(g2.pin, 255);
        lm32.move(1000); // move in 1 second
    }

    // move to position B (experimentally determined)
    public void posB() throws Exception {

        lm32.sscCmd(s1.pin, 220);
        lm32.sscCmd(s2.pin, 135);
        lm32.sscCmd(e.pin, 100);
        lm32.sscCmd(w.pin, 190);
        lm32.sscCmd(g1.pin, 130);
        lm32.sscCmd(g2.pin, 255);
        lm32.move(1000); // move in 1 second

    }

    private void move(int pin, int pos) throws Exception {
        // check range first
        checkRange(pin, pos);
        // then move
        lm32.move(pin, pos);
    }
```

```
    // will check the servos to see if requested position is
    // within parameters of servo
    private void checkRange(int pin, int pos) throws Exception {
        for (int i = 0; i < servos.size(); i++) {
            ServoPosition2 tmpPos = (ServoPosition2) servos.get(i);
            if (tmpPos.pin == pin) {
                if (pos > tmpPos.max || pos < tmpPos.min) {
                    throw new Exception("Positions out of bounds for pin "
                            + pin + ".");
                }
            }
        }
    }

    public static void main(String[] args) {
        try {
            // get single serial port instance
            JSerialPort sPort = (JSerialPort) SingleSerialPort.getInstance(1);
            // create new ComplexArm
            ComplexArm arm = new ComplexArm(sPort);
            arm.rest();
            arm.posA();
            arm.posB();
            sPort.close();
        } catch (Exception e) {
            // print stack trace and exit
            e.printStackTrace();
            System.exit(1);
        }
    }
}
```

Section Summary

Moving with a complex arm is just about all you will ever need with servo control. We have fine control over position and movement speed as well as coordinated, precise movements.

In this section, I created the following classes:

- BasicArm.java: This class models the basic robot arm with a shoulder and an elbow.

- ArmTest1.java: This class shows how to move the basic arm to two different positions.

- ServoPosition2.java: This class extends the ServoPosition class created earlier for minimum, maximum, and neutral values to be used in the ComplexArm.

- ComplexArm.java: This class uses the ServoPosition2 class and has a total for five axes of movement versus the two in the BasicArm class.

Since we created one limb in this section, two, four, or six should not be that much more difficult. In the next section, I'll show you how to create legs in the same manner that we created arms and then I'll move them all together smoothly using the LM32.

3.6   Legged Robots

Moving a legged robot is very similar to modeling the ComplexArm in section 3.5. It has multiple servos and multiple positions that the legs need. The only thing not included is a gait.

A gait in legged robots is the order and direction of the leg movements. For example, a human has the following gait:

1. Lift left leg up.

2. Move left leg forward.

3. Put left leg down.

4. Shift weight to left leg.

5. Lift right leg up.

6. Move right leg forward.

7. Put right leg down.

8. Shift weight to right leg.

9. Repeat.

That's nine commands for two legs in one direction, which is more complicated than the differential drive classes created in section 3.1. But because the Hexapod implements the JMotion interface if our robot has legs or wheels, navigation will be the same.

A class diagram for this is shown in Figure 3-13.

To get a better idea of what we're going to be moving, look at the photo in Figure 3-14. It has a total of 12 servos, with four degrees of freedom per leg for a total of 48 possible moves.

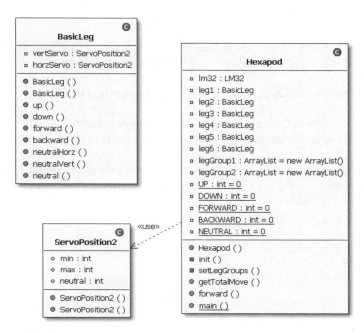

Figure 3-13. *A class diagram of classes in section 3.6*

Figure 3-14. *The Lynxmotion Extreme Hexapod 2*

Code Objectives

The objective here is to implement JMotion for a legged robot.

Code Discussion

I think you'll find that a hexapod robot is nothing more than a few complex arms that have to work together. The class that follows groups the two servos of the hexapod leg and adds some movement methods for the leg.

The two fields are of type ServoPosition2: one for the horizontal motion and one for the vertical.

The constructor does not take a JSerialPort because unlike the ComplexArm, the leg will just be a complicated data structure. It will function to set and get commands to be used with the LM32.

The methods up(), down(), forward(), and backwards() set the commands to the preset positions defined by the servo positions or default values. The neural method does the same for both servos. (See Example 3-19.)

Example 3-19. *BasicLeg.java*

```java
package com.scottpreston.javarobot.chapter3;

public class BasicLeg {

    // each leg has 2 servos
    private ServoPosition2 vertServo;
    private ServoPosition2 horzServo;

    // generic constructor just taking pins
    public BasicLeg(int vPin, int hPin)throws Exception {
        vertServo = new ServoPosition2(vPin);
        horzServo = new ServoPosition2(hPin);
    }
    // constructors with ServoPosition2's
    public BasicLeg(ServoPosition2 vertServo, ServoPosition2 horzServo) {
        this.vertServo = vertServo;
        this.horzServo = horzServo;
    }

    // move leg up
    public String up() {
        return LM32.createCmd(vertServo.pin,vertServo.max,LM32.DEFAULT_SPEED);
    }
    // move leg down
    public String down() {
        return LM32.createCmd(vertServo.pin,vertServo.min,LM32.DEFAULT_SPEED);
    }
    // move leg forward
    public String forward() {
        return LM32.createCmd(horzServo.pin,horzServo.max,LM32.DEFAULT_SPEED);
    }
```

```
// move leg backward
public String backward() {
    return LM32.createCmd(horzServo.pin,horzServo.min,LM32.DEFAULT_SPEED);
}
// reset horz servo
public String neutralHorz() {
    return LM32.createCmd(horzServo.pin,horzServo.neutral,LM32.DEFAULT_SPEED);
}

// reset vert servo
public String neutralVert(){
    return LM32.createCmd(vertServo.pin,vertServo.neutral,LM32.DEFAULT_SPEED);
}

// reset both servos
public String neutral() {
    return neutralVert() + neutralHorz();
}

}
```

The Hexapod class has as fields the LM32 as the worker class and six legs defined as BasicLegs. I also defined two leg groups as ArrayList. Because of the gait I chose, I'll move three legs simultaneously. By placing them in a list, I can move all legs in this group with a single command.

The fields UP, DOWN, and so on are enumerations. The int speed is the speed variable, and MAX_SPEED represents what the minimum time should be for the group move of three legs.

The constructor takes, you guessed it, the JSerialPort and calls two methods init() and setLegGroups(). The init method creates all leg positions for the six BasicLegs. The setLegGroups method adds these to legGroup1 and legGroup2.

The forward() gait is a combination of eight separate commands. The gait commands are created via the getTotalMove() method which comprises a StringBuffer. The method operates by iterating through all the legs and (depending on the command) returns the string from the BasicLeg.motion() method. This is repeated until all the legs are done. Then the group move is executed in the time specified via the getSpeedInMs() method.

The getSpeedInMs() method uses an inverse relationship between the time of the leg move and the speed. This is so that 10 is still fast and 1 is still slow. For example: the speed of the robot at speed 10 is 2500 – 2500 + 250 milliseconds per move of a leg group, and at a speed of 1 the speed of the robot is 2500 – 250 + 250 = 2500 milliseconds per leg.

In the forward() method with a millisecond parameter, it loops through calling forward until the time is up. This is all a function of the speed of the robot and it even throws an exception if the requested move time is less than the minimum time. (See Example 3-20.)

Example 3-20. *Hexapod.java*

```java
package com.scottpreston.javarobot.chapter3;

import java.util.ArrayList;

import com.scottpreston.javarobot.chapter2.JSerialPort;
import com.scottpreston.javarobot.chapter2.SingleSerialPort;
import com.scottpreston.javarobot.chapter2.Utils;

public class Hexapod implements JMotion {

    private LM32 lm32;

    private BasicLeg leg1; // left front
    private BasicLeg leg2; // left middle
    private BasicLeg leg3; // left back
    private BasicLeg leg4; // right front
    private BasicLeg leg5; // right middle
    private BasicLeg leg6; // right back

    private ArrayList legGroup1 = new ArrayList();
    private ArrayList legGroup2 = new ArrayList();

    private static final int UP = 0;
    private static final int DOWN = 1;
    private static final int FORWARD = 2;
    private static final int BACKWARD = 3;
    private static final int NEUTRAL = 4;

    private int speed = 5;
    private static final int MIN_SPEED = 250;

    public Hexapod(JSerialPort serialPort) throws Exception {

        lm32 = new LM32(serialPort);
        // two methods for clean constructor
        init(); // init all legs
        setLegGroups(); // set legs in groups

    }

    // create legs
    private void init() throws Exception {
        // 1st position vertical servo (up/down)
        // 2nd position horzontal servo (forward/backward)
        leg1 = new BasicLeg(new ServoPosition2(0, 127, 50, 200),
                new ServoPosition2(1, 127, 50, 200));
```

```
        leg2 = new BasicLeg(new ServoPosition2(4, 127, 50, 200),
               new ServoPosition2(5, 127, 100, 150));
        leg3 = new BasicLeg(new ServoPosition2(8, 127, 50, 200),
               new ServoPosition2(9, 127, 50, 200));
        leg4 = new BasicLeg(new ServoPosition2(16, 127, 200, 50),
               new ServoPosition2(17, 127, 200, 50));
        leg5 = new BasicLeg(new ServoPosition2(20, 127, 200, 50),
               new ServoPosition2(21, 127, 150, 100));
        leg6 = new BasicLeg(new ServoPosition2(24, 127, 200, 50),
               new ServoPosition2(25, 127, 200, 50));

    }

    // put legs into walking groups
    private void setLegGroups() throws Exception {
        legGroup1.add(leg1);
        legGroup1.add(leg3);
        legGroup1.add(leg5);
        legGroup2.add(leg2);
        legGroup2.add(leg4);
        legGroup2.add(leg6);
    }

    // this will create an entire string of commands for all legs
    public String getTotalMove(ArrayList legs, int cmd) throws Exception {

        StringBuffer cmds = new StringBuffer();
        for (int i = 0; i < legs.size(); i++) {
            BasicLeg tmpLeg = (BasicLeg) legs.get(i);
            if (cmd == UP) {
                cmds.append(tmpLeg.up());
            }
            if (cmd == DOWN) {
                cmds.append(tmpLeg.down());
            }
            if (cmd == FORWARD) {
                cmds.append(tmpLeg.forward());
            }
            if (cmd == BACKWARD) {
                cmds.append(tmpLeg.backward());
            }
            if (cmd == NEUTRAL) {
                cmds.append(tmpLeg.neutral());
            }
        }
        return cmds.toString();
    }
```

```java
    // sample to move forward gate
    public void forward() throws Exception {
        lm32.setRawCommand(getTotalMove(legGroup1, DOWN));
        lm32.move(getSpeedInMs());
        lm32.setRawCommand(getTotalMove(legGroup2, UP));
        lm32.move(getSpeedInMs());
        lm32.setRawCommand(getTotalMove(legGroup2, FORWARD));
        lm32.move(getSpeedInMs());
        lm32.setRawCommand(getTotalMove(legGroup1, BACKWARD));
        lm32.move(getSpeedInMs());
        lm32.setRawCommand(getTotalMove(legGroup2, DOWN));
        lm32.move(getSpeedInMs());
        lm32.setRawCommand(getTotalMove(legGroup1, UP));
        lm32.move(getSpeedInMs());
        lm32.setRawCommand(getTotalMove(legGroup1, FORWARD));
        lm32.move(getSpeedInMs());
        lm32.setRawCommand(getTotalMove(legGroup2, BACKWARD));
        lm32.move(getSpeedInMs());
    }

    public static void main(String[] args) {
        try {
            JSerialPort sPort = (JSerialPort) SingleSerialPort.getInstance(1);
            Hexapod hex = new Hexapod(sPort);
            hex.forward();
            hex.forward();
            sPort.close();
        } catch (Exception e) {
            e.printStackTrace();
            System.exit(1);
        }
    }

    public void forward(int ms) throws Exception {
        if (getSpeedInMs() * 8 < ms) {
            throw new Exception("Speed requested is less than minimum speed.");
        }
        int remaining = ms;
        while (remaining > getSpeedInMs() * 8) {
            forward();
            remaining = remaining - getSpeedInMs() * 8;
        }
        Utils.pause(remaining);
    }
```

```java
    public void stop() throws Exception {
        lm32.setRawCommand(getTotalMove(legGroup1, DOWN));
        lm32.setRawCommand(getTotalMove(legGroup2, DOWN));
        lm32.move(getSpeedInMs());
    }

    public void reverse() throws Exception {
    }

    public void pivotRight() throws Exception {
    }

    public void pivotLeft() throws Exception {
    }

    public void reverse(int ms) throws Exception {
    }

    public void pivotRight(int ms) throws Exception {
    }

    public void pivotLeft(int ms) throws Exception {
    }
    public int getSpeed() {
        return speed;
    }
    public void setSpeed(int speed) {
        this.speed = speed;
    }
    private int getSpeedInMs() {
        return  (MIN_SPEED* 10) - (MIN_SPEED * speed) + MIN_SPEED;
    }
}
```

Section Summary

With the classes created in this section, I encourage you to experiment with your own gaits or different numbers of legs.

In this section, I created the following classes:

- BasicLeg.java: This class is similar to the ComplexArm created in the last section.

- Hexapod.java: This class implements the JMotion interface to move the legged robot the same way you would a wheeled robot.

3.7 Chapter Summary

My goal in this chapter was to introduce you to solving motion problems in robotics. I showed you how to solve three types of motion (wheeled, fixed servo, gaited) with two different types of servo controllers: the Scott Edwards MiniSSC-II and the Lynxmotion SSC-32. Both are great. I use the MiniSSC-II on my main robot Feynman5, and the LM32 on my Hexapod.

In section 3.1, I created the SerialSSC protocol and created a general super-class for both the MiniSSC and LM32 implementation classes. We also created the MiniSSC class that tested our first servo control from the PC.

In section 3.2, I created three differential drive classes for wheeled motion and generated a common motion interface called JMotion.

In section 3.3, I used the MiniSSC class to perform pan and tilt operations for a web camera setup.

In section 3.4, to solve some of the movement problems experienced in section 3.3, I introduced the LM32 servo controller as well as a new protocol for movement called the GroupMoveProtocol. I implemented this protocol with the LM32 and the MiniSscGM implementation class.

In section 3.5, I used the LM32 class to create a fluid motion robotic arm with six servos.

Finally, in section 3.6, I implemented the JMotion interface on a six-legged robot to show that we could use the JMotion class with a differential drive robot or a legged robot interchangeably.

In the next chapter, we'll stop moving for a bit and use the BASIC Stamp to communicate with some of the sensors you might use on your robot. There, we'll discuss digital compasses, logic sensors, and sonar and infrared distance sensors.

CHAPTER 4

Sensors

"The senses collect the surface facts of matter..."

— Ralph Waldo Emerson

4.0 Introduction

You'll find that most of the programming logic for sensors is located inside the microcontroller programs. The reason for this is simple: microcontrollers are much better at communicating with these sensors than PCs. However, using Java programs to initiate and control the "sensing" from these sensors has many advantages that will become more apparent in Chapter 7, which discusses navigation, and Chapter 8, which tackles various advanced topics.

The types of sensors I'll talk about in this chapter are

- Orientation Sensors (Compass): These devices allow your robot to know what orientation it has.

- Switch Sensors: These devices take logical readings of on or off.

- Distance Sensors: These devices allow your robot to measure the distance from itself to the range of the sensor.

In this chapter, I'll talk about three basic Stamp programs and four Java classes. But before we get sensor readings, let's talk about ways to connect your sensors to your microcontroller.

Connecting Your Sensors

Connecting sensors was probably the most difficult part of robotics for me. I started connecting sensors with the typical copper-plated breadboard from Radio Shack ages ago. You can see a few of my first circuits in Figure 4-1.

Figure 4-1. *Some breadboard circuits*

The circuit on the left in Figure 4-1 was connected with 22 AWG hook-up wire. The circuit itself is a Sharp IR detector module, purchased from Radio Shack, which uses two modulated IR LEDs.

The circuit on the right in the figure was standalone and did not require any hook-up except for the five-volt DC battery. It consisted of one IR LED, one IR phototransistor, and a transistor circuit.

In the previous chapter, I used servos for some motion. Early on, before I started making my own connectors, the servo connectors came in quite handy, but they were expensive compared with wire and connectors. To make your own, you'll need the following (pictured in Figure 4-2 from left to right, clockwise):

- Female .100" header: The same hook-up as a servo.

- Make .100" header: The pins you'll need to connect to the Parallax Board of Education.

- 22 AWG hook-up wire (different colors): Fits the pins nicely, and as far as wire, it costs the least.

- .100" header socket: Comes in many different size combinations.

- Crimper (not shown): Necessary for crimping the wires to the headers.

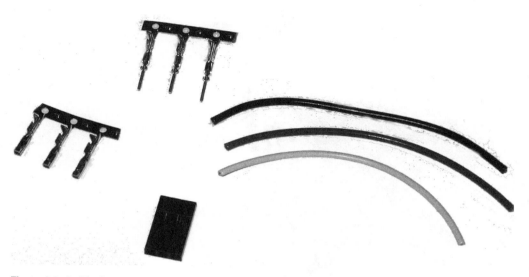

Figure 4-2. *Solderless connectors and .100" headers*

If you have more than one sensor, then the power from the BASIC Stamp or its onboard supplies are probably not sufficient. Also, for some sensors you need to do some additional wiring and circuit construction. To make this easier, you'll need to create your own sensor boards or purchase them from the Internet.

Creating Your Own Sensor Boards

Figure 4-3 shows a Vector 2X compass and a breadboard with hook-up wire. The particular breadboard fits inside a small project enclosure, but it isn't very secure and the solder connections on the bottom of the board (not shown) took a lot of time to make and required a fix or two before it was stable.

I learned that one of the ways to get around this was to create my own PCB (Printed Circuit Board). Figure 4-4 shows a screenshot of the ExpressPCB editor. Here I didn't have to solder; I just created the circuit using some free software and in three days for $59 I was able to get three prototype printed circuit boards that allowed me to connect my Compass to my microcontroller without the quality problems of a DIY breadboard.

Figure 4-3. *A Vector 2x and a breadboard*

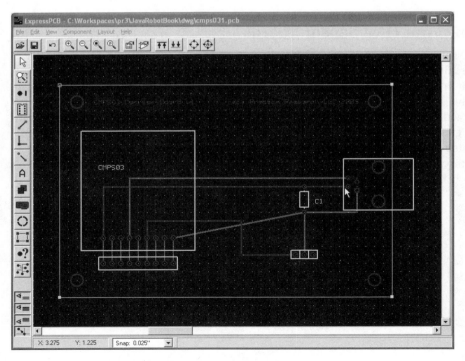

Figure 4-4. *Schematic of CMPS03 board with ExpressPCB software*

The program allows you to order online, and once received you'll have a PCB ready for use (like that shown in Figure 4-5). For more information, visit www.expresspcb.com.

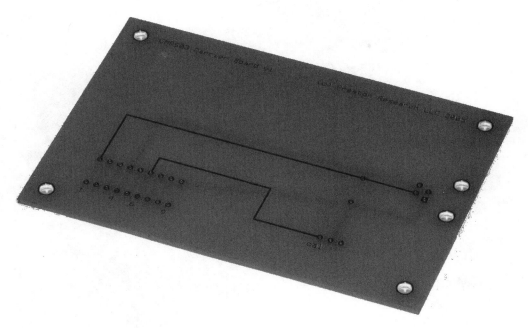

Figure 4-5. *The Preston Research CMPS03 Carrier Board*

Despite this step forward, I still needed something that would connect these sensors to my microcontroller. I wanted something I could connect and disconnect easily without worrying about connectivity or about it coming loose. For this reason, I created a distribution board (shown in Figure 4-6), which could handle the following:

- It could connect ten .100" headers to five RJ11 connectors connected to sensors.

- It could connect four .100 headers to one RJ45 connector.

The secondary purpose of the distribution board is to power the sensors. To eliminate excess wiring and reduce the possibility of connecting a 5V sensor to a 12V source, I added power distribution and regulation, which provided the following:

- Power regulation to sensors from 12VDC down to 5VDC

- An on-off switch and power LED

Figure 4-6. *The Preston Research Sonar Distribution Board*

Using either solder breadboards or PCBs will make your robotic enclosures and sensor connects easier to maintain and more reliable.

4.1 Orientation Sensors (Compass)

The first group of sensors I'll talk about will provide orientation to your robot: the digital compass. The compass gives your robot absolute orientation, which is critical for navigation. In this section, I'll discuss the three types of compasses:

- Dinsmore 1490: A cheap, durable compass with an accuracy of 45 degrees.

- Devantech CMPS03: A single IO compass with two degrees of accuracy.

- PNI Corporation Vector 2X: A four IO compass with two degrees of accuracy.

These three compasses are shown in Figures 4-7, 4-8, and 4-9.

Figure 4-7. *Dinsmore 1490*

Figure 4-8. *Devantech CMPS03*

Figure 4-9. *The PNI Corporation Vector 2X*

Now that you're familiar with the hardware, I'll create some software to get readings from these using a BASIC Stamp. Afterward, I'll create two Java classes.

Code Objective

The objective here is to get compass readings from a robot using one of the three compasses described earlier.

Code Discussion

I'll start with programming the BASIC Stamp. In the first part of this program (see Example 4-1), I connect my three compasses to the different pins on the Stamp (1 and 2) for the Devantech, (8, 9, 10, and 11) for the Vector, and (0, 1, 2, and 3) for the Dinsmore.

Second, I create my main program where I wait for specific commands: 100 to start reading, 101 for the Dinsmore, 102 for the Devantech, and 103 for the Vector.

Third, I create three separate subroutines for the different compasses. For the Devantech compass, I just need to use the PULSIN to get the compass reading, For the Vector, I need to send some signals and wait for a time before I can SHIFTIN the readings. And the Dinsmore reads logic values from the input pins to return one of eight readings (N, E, S, W, NE, NW, SE, SW). (See Figure 4-1.)

Example 4-1. *Compass.bs2*

```
' {$STAMP BS2}
' {$PBASIC 2.5}
' {$PORT COM1}
' cmd variable
cmd             VAR       Byte
N9600           CON       16468

' CMPS03 COMPASS
cin             CON       12 'serial data out      GREEN (a)
headingC        VAR       Word 'heading

' VECTOR COMPASS
sselect         CON       10 'select signal
sdo             CON       09 'serial data out
sclk            CON       11 'clock signal
rst             CON       8  'reset signal
headingV        VAR       Word 'heading

' DINSMORE 1490 COMPASS
north           CON       0
east            CON       1
south           CON       2
west            CON       3
headingD        VAR       Byte
```

```
main:
      cmd = 0
      SERIN 16,16468,main,[WAIT(100), cmd]
      IF cmd = 101 THEN get_dinsmore
      IF cmd = 102 THEN get_devantech
      IF cmd = 103 THEN get_vector
      PAUSE 5
      GOTO main

get_devantech:
    PULSIN cin, 1, headingC ' Get reading
    headingC = (headingC-500)/50 ' BS2(e) - Calculate Bearing in degrees
    SEROUT 16,N9600,[DEC headingC ' out to PC
    GOTO main

get_vector:
    LOW sselect 'start the Vector 2x.
    PAUSE 200 'wait for heading.
    headingV = 0 'clear variable.

    'get the data from Vector 2x.
    SHIFTIN sdo,sclk,MSBPRE,[headingV\16]
    HIGH sclk 'reset pins.
    HIGH sselect

    ' out to PC
    SEROUT 16,16468,[DEC headingV]
    GOTO main

get_dinsmore:
        ' north
      IF north = 1 AND east = 0 AND west = 0 THEN
        headingD = 0
      ENDIF

      ' east
      IF east = 1 AND north = 0  AND south = 0 THEN
        headingD = 90
      ENDIF

      ' south
      IF south = 1 AND east = 0 AND west = 0 THEN
        headingD = 180
      ENDIF
      ' west
      IF west = 1 AND north = 0  AND south = 0 THEN
        headingD = 270
      ENDIF
```

```
' north east
IF east = 1 AND north = 1THEN
  headingD = 45
ENDIF

' north west
IF west = 1 AND north = 1 THEN
  headingD = 315
ENDIF

' south west
IF west = 1 AND south = 1 THEN
  headingD = 225
ENDIF

' south east
IF east = 1 AND south = 1 THEN
  headingD = 135
ENDIF

SEROUT 16,16468,[DEC headingD]
GOTO main
```

■**Note** Make sure you have the directive for PBASIC 2.5 at the top of your Stamp program, otherwise you'll get compile errors on the if-then statements.

Next, I need to create a corresponding Java class that communicates with our compasses. However, before I discuss this class, I'd like to show you a class diagram of how these sensors relate to the classes in Chapter 2 (see Figure 4-10).

The CompassStamp class has four constants and one field. The constants are the actual bytes that correspond to the Compass.bs2 in Example 4-1. Since they're all unique, I can also use them to enumerate the compasses in the class. The instance field, compass, I set defaulted to the Devantech compass. This will be used in the class as the command sent to the BASIC Stamp and used to determine the delay time for getting the reading.

This class has four public methods. The first two, setCompass() and getCompass(), set and get the values for the compass reading. The other two getHeading() methods return the compass heading as an int.

In getHeading(), first I create the byte[] that calls the parent execute() method. Then, because the command string will return a string of tilde-delimited (~) integers, I parse and convert that to an int so it can be returned. This method also uses the private method getCompassDelay() because, depending on the current compass, the delay time to get the reading differs.

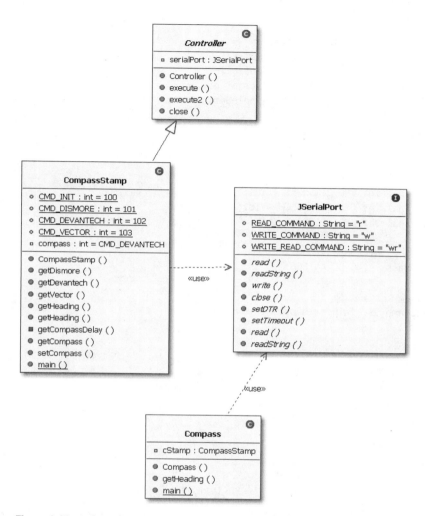

Figure 4-10. *A class diagram relationship to the Chapter 2 classes*

I have also added methods that are more descriptive and take less parameters: getDinsmore(), getDevantech(), and getVector().

Finally, in main(), I test this class by first displaying the heading from the default value, CMD_DEVANTECH, and then CMD_VECTOR. Finally, I set the compass using its setter, setCompass(), and then get the compass reading via getHeading(). (See Example 4-2.)

Example 4-2. *CompassStamp.java*

```java
package com.scottpreston.javarobot.chapter5;

import com.scottpreston.javarobot.chapter2.Controller;
import com.scottpreston.javarobot.chapter2.JSerialPort;
import com.scottpreston.javarobot.chapter2.SingleSerialPort;

public class CompassStamp extends Controller {

    // commands set in basic stamp program
    public static final int CMD_INIT = 100;
    public static final int CMD_DINSMORE = 101;
    public static final int CMD_DEVANTECH = 102;
    public static final int CMD_VECTOR = 103;

    // default reading for compass
    private int compass = CMD_DEVANTECH;

    // constructor
    public CompassStamp(JSerialPort sPort) throws Exception {
        super(sPort);
    }

    public int getHeading(int compass) throws Exception {
        setCompass(compass);
        return getHeading();
    }

    // get heading method
    public int getHeading() throws Exception {
        // calling super execute() method
        String heading = execute(new byte[] { CMD_INIT, (byte) compass },
                getCompassDelay());
        // since returning heading as one, two or three bytes
        String[] h2 = heading.split("~");
        String heading2 = "";
        for (int h = 0; h < h2.length; h++) {
            // convert each byte to char which I append to create single number
            heading2 = heading2 + (char) new Integer(h2[h]).intValue();
        }
        // return 3 chars like '123' which is 123 degrees
        return new Integer(heading2).intValue();
    }

    public int getDinsmore() throws Exception{
        return getHeading(CMD_DINSMORE);
    }
```

```java
    public int getDevantech() throws Exception{
        return getHeading(CMD_DEVANTECH);
    }
    public int getVector() throws Exception{
        return getHeading(CMD_VECTOR);
    }

    // since differnt delay for each compass
    private int getCompassDelay() {
        int delay = 0;
        if (compass == CMD_DINSMORE) {
            delay = 50;
        }
        if (compass == CMD_DEVANTECH) {
            delay = 150;
        }
        if (compass == CMD_VECTOR) {
            delay = 250;
        }
        return delay;
    }

    public int getCompass() {
        return compass;
    }

    public void setCompass(int compass) {
        this.compass = compass;
    }

    public static void main(String[] args) {
        try {
            // since i am testing at my desk and not on my robot
            CompassStamp s = new CompassStamp(SingleSerialPort.getInstance(1));
            // since devantech is default
            System.out.println("Devantech Heading = " + s.getHeading());
            // getting specific heading
            System.out
                    .println("Vector Heading = " + s.getHeading(CMD_VECTOR));
            // using a setter
            s.setCompass(CompassStamp.CMD_DISMORE);
            // getting dinsmore heading
            System.out.println("Dinsmore Heading = " + s.getHeading());
        } catch (Exception e) {
            e.printStackTrace();
            System.exit(1);
        }

    }
}
}
```

Sometimes you may not want to use the stamp class for access but instead create a class you can use to access just the compass by itself. In this case, the final example in this section does just that.

Code Objective

The objective of this example is to model a compass with a separate class.

Code Discussion

The class is very simple. The constructor takes JSerialPort, which is used to construct the CompassClass in Example 4-2. Then the getHeading() method just calls the getHeading() method in the CompassStamp class by passing the CMD_DEVANTECH parameter. (See Example 4-3.)

Example 4-3. *Compass.java*

```
package com.scottpreston.javarobot.chapter5;

import com.scottpreston.javarobot.chapter2.JSerialPort;
import com.scottpreston.javarobot.chapter2.SingleSerialPort;

public class Compass{

    private CompassStamp cStamp;

    public Compass(JSerialPort sPort) throws Exception{
        cStamp = new CompassStamp(sPort);
    }

    public int getHeading() throws Exception{
        return cStamp.getHeading(CompassStamp.CMD_DEVANTECH);
    }

    public static void main(String[] args) throws Exception{
        try {
            // since i am testing at my desk and not on my robot
            Compass compass = new Compass(SingleSerialPort.getInstance(1));
            System.out.println("Compass Heading = " + compass.getHeading());
        } catch (Exception e) {
            e.printStackTrace();
            System.exit(1);

        }

    }
}
```

Section Summary

This section showed three different orientation sensors (compasses) and the software to get those readings to your PC. The three compasses discussed were the Devantech CMPS03 digital compass, the PNI Corporation Vector 2X, and the Dinsmore 1490.

I created two Java classes and one BASIC Stamp program as described in the following bullets:

- Compass.bs2: A BASIC Stamp program to get sensor readings from one of the three compasses

- CompassStamp.java: A Java class that models the BASIC Stamp configuration connected to the three compasses

- Compass.java: A single compass class that's used to connect to the Devantech CMPS03 compass

I would recommend the Devantech compass because of its response time, accuracy, and single I/O pin.

The next type of sensors will return logic data—either a true or a false.

4.2 Switch Sensors

The types of sensors I'll talk about in this section return a logic high (3V to 5V) or low (< 1V) to your microcontroller. The four examples I'll use will be

- Bump Sensors: Great for letting you or your robot know if it's hit something.

- Line Detectors: Excellent for following lines, or for us as encoders or boundary edge detectors.

- Proximity Sensors: Great for letting you or your robot know if it's close to something.

- Combination Switch Sensors: When you have more than one logical sensor you want to return data from at the same time.

The first sensor pictured is the bump sensor, shown in Figure 4-11, in which we see the Lynxmotion Bumper switch assembly kit. These are nice backups to proximity sensors because sometimes nonmechanical sensors can return false readings or the delay time is too large for the speed of your robot. For example, if your robot is traveling at 36 inches per second and you read the sensor five times a second, the sensor resolution is 36/5 or about 7 inches. Double that speed and it's 14 inches.

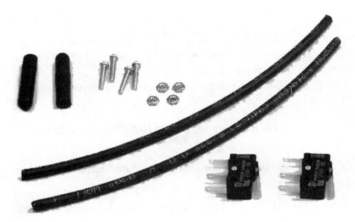

Figure 4-11. *The Lynxmotion Bumper Switch Assembly Kit*

The second type is a single line detector, shown in Figure 4-12. You can use this sensor to read white or black. It also has an adjustable potentiometer that lets you determine its sensitivity.

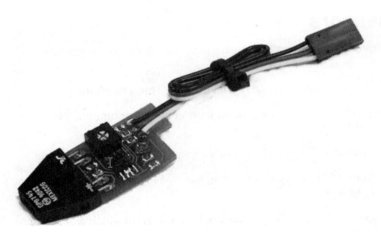

Figure 4-12. *The Lynxmotion Single Line Detector*

The third is the Sharp IR GP2D15 proximity sensor (see Figure 4-13). This is a great sensor, and can detect whether something exists at a specified distance from your robot. You can adjust this sensor to measure from 4 inches to about 24 inches to get an on-off reading.

Figure 4-13. *The Sharp IR Sensor GP2D15*

Now that you've seen some of the sensor types (that return only logical values), I'll describe a BASIC Stamp program that returns single or multiple logic sensor readings, and also explain the Java class that reads it.

Code Objective

The code objective here is to return single or multiple logic readings from the microcontroller, indicating a true or false.

Code Discussion

In the first example, I'll create the BASIC Stamp program (see Example 4-4). For the single switch, I'll either return a "0" for false or a "1" for true. For reading multiple switches at once, it will return a string of ones and zeroes as soon as the readings are made—thus, when reading from multiple switches, the example output from the BASIC Stamp might be "010" or "111," these would then correspond to "false, true, false" and "true, true, true," respectively.

Example 4-4. *switch.bs2*

```
'{$STAMP BS2}
' {$PBASIC 2.5}
'{$PORT COM1}

cmd           VAR   Byte
N9600         CON   16468
switch1       CON   1
m_switch1     CON   2
m_switch2     CON   3
m_switch3     CON   4
```

```
main:
      SERIN 16,16468,main,[WAIT(100), cmd]
   IF cmd = 101 THEN single_switch
   IF cmd = 102 THEN multi_switch
   PAUSE 5
   GOTO main


single_switch:
  IF switch1 = 0 THEN
    SEROUT 16,N9600,["0", CR]
    GOTO main
  ENDIF
  IF switch1 = 1 THEN
    SEROUT 16,N9600,["1", CR]
    GOTO main
  ENDIF

multi_switch:
  IF m_switch1 = 0 THEN
    SEROUT 16,N9600,["0", CR]
  ENDIF
  IF m_switch1 = 1 THEN
    SEROUT 16,N9600,["1", CR]
  ENDIF
  IF m_switch2 = 0 THEN
    SEROUT 16,N9600,["0", CR]
  ENDIF
  IF m_switch2 = 1 THEN
    SEROUT 16,N9600,["1", CR]
  ENDIF
  IF m_switch3 = 0 THEN
    SEROUT 16,N9600,["0", CR]
  ENDIF
  IF m_switch3 = 1 THEN
    SEROUT 16,N9600,["1", CR]
  ENDIF
  GOTO main
```

The corresponding Java class for this BASIC Stamp program is SwitchStamp. The class has static fields for enumeration of the commands and the switches connected to the stamp pins.

The getSingle() method looks for a single character "1" or "0" to be returned from the program. As for the two methods getMulti(): one takes an index parameter that returns a specific reading, and the other returns the entire string of ones or zeroes.

In the main method(), I show the examples of usage of each of these methods (see Example 4-5).

Example 4-5. *SwitchStamp.java*

```java
package com.scottpreston.javarobot.chapter5;

import com.scottpreston.javarobot.chapter2.Controller;
import com.scottpreston.javarobot.chapter2.JSerialPort;
import com.scottpreston.javarobot.chapter2.SingleSerialPort;

public class SwitchStamp extends Controller {

    // commands set in basic stmap program
    public static final int CMD_INIT = 100;
    public static final int CMD_SINGLE = 101;
    public static final int CMD_MULTI = 102;
    // sensors
    public static final int SINGLE_LINE_SENSOR1 = 0;
    public static final int SINGLR_LINE_SENSOR2 = 1;
    public static final int PROXIMITY_SENSOR = 2;


    public SwitchStamp(JSerialPort sPort) throws Exception{
        super(sPort);
    }

    public boolean getSingle() throws Exception{
        // read single reading
        String h = execute(new byte[] {CMD_INIT,CMD_SINGLE},25);
        if (h.equalsIgnoreCase("1")) {
            return true;
        } else {
            return false;
        }
    }

    public String getMulti() throws Exception {
        String r = execute(new byte[] {CMD_INIT,CMD_SINGLE},25);
        String[] r2 = r.split("~");
        String readings = "";
        for (int i = 0; i < r2.length; i++) {
            // convert each byte to char which I append to create single number
            readings = readings + (char) new Integer(r2[i]).intValue();
        }
        return readings;
    }
```

```java
    public boolean getMulti(int index) throws Exception{
        String i = getMulti().substring(index);
        if (i.equalsIgnoreCase("1")) {
            return true;
        } else {
            return false;
        }
    }

    public static void main(String[] args) {
        try {
            // since i am testing at my desk and not on my robot
            SwitchStamp s = new SwitchStamp(SingleSerialPort.getInstance(1));
                // get single switch
            System.out.println("Single Switch = " + s.getSingle());
            // get multiple readings
            System.out.println("Multiple Switches = " + s.getMulti());
            // get proximity switch from multiple readings
            System.out.println("Proximity Sensor = " +
s.getMulti(SwitchStamp.PROXIMITY_SENSOR));

        } catch (Exception e) {
            e.printStackTrace();
            System.exit(1);

        }
    }
}
```

Section Summary

In this section, I discussed a few types of sensors that give logical readings to the microcontroller and ways to access those readings from a Java class. The programs created were

- switch.bs2: The BASIC Stamp program that reads the logic sensor values.

- SwitchStamp.java: Gets the sensor data from the switch.bs2 program.

The next type of sensor I'll discuss are the distance sensors. Like the proximity sensor, which gives a logical reading, these sensors provide an actual distance reading from the sensor to an object it detects.

4.3 Distance Sensors (IR and Sonar)

Distance sensors help your robot navigate and keep from hitting things. Here, I'll discuss two types of range finders: infrared (IR) and sonar. Use Table 4-1 to best identify what sensor you need.

Table 4-1. *Sensor Ranges*

Sensor	Range	Divergence	Best Use
Bump Switch	Few inches	n/a	Fast, fail-safe sensor.
Proximity Switch	Less than 1 foot	20 degrees from center	Proximity for stairs, blind spots.
IR Sensor	4 inches to 31.5 inches	15 degrees from center	Movement in tight quarters where sonar might give false reading.
Devantech SRF04	4 inches to 9 feet	22.5 degrees from center	Obstacle detection.
6500 Sonar	4 inches to 35 feet	15 degrees from center	Large distance ranger with narrow beam width. Good for localization and map building.

The first sensor with the shortest range is the Sharp Infrared GP2D02 distance sensor (see Figure 4-14). It has a range from 4 to 30 inches and costs about $12.

Figure 4-14. *The Sharp Infrared GP2D02*

The second sensor with a medium range is the Devantech SRF04 sonar module (see Figure 4-15). It has a range from 1 to 96 inches, and has a cycle time of about 100 milliseconds. It costs around $24.

Figure 4-15. *The Devantech SRF04 Sonar Module*

The third type is the Polaroid 6500 ranging module with an instrument grade transducer. It has a cycle time of about 200 milliseconds, and the transducer and ranging module together have a range of 1 inch to 35 feet and cost about $49. Figure 4-16 shows three connected at once with DB9 serial connectors to facilitate easy connection with a microcontroller.

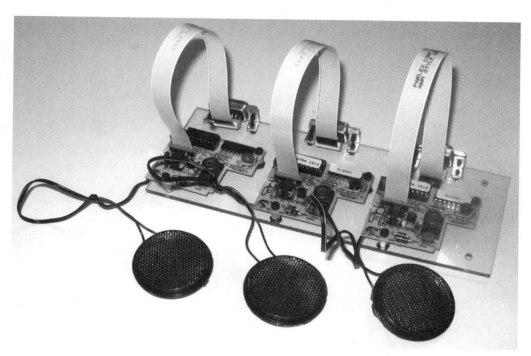

Figure 4-16. *Three Polaroid 6500 Ranging Modules with Transducers*

Code Objective

The objective here is to get range data from a variety of distance sensors.

Code Discussion

The first program I'll discuss is the BASIC Stamp program, will return information from all three distance sensors (see Example 4-6).

The three commands 101, 102, and 103 which will call the three subroutines ping_ir, ping_srf, and ping_6500. Those three subroutines then return data from their respective sensors.

In ping_ir, the sensor uses the SHIFTIN command to get data from the sensor.

In both ping_srf and ping_6500, the sonars use RCTIME to measure the width of the echo returned. The echo pulse width is proportional to the distance.

Example 4-6. *distance.bs2*

```
' {$STAMP BS2}
' {$PBASIC 2.5}
' {$PORT COM1}

' cmd variable
cmd          VAR    Byte
N9600        CON    16468

' IR
dout1        CON    2       'output to the DIRRS.    (green)
din1         CON    3       'input from the DIRRS.   (yellow)
dist1        VAR    Byte    'ir dist 1

' both sonar
convfac      CON    74      '74 inches, 29 cm

' srf04
ECHO1        CON    9       'input from the SRF04.
INIT1        CON    8       'output to the SRF04.
wDist1       VAR    Word     'sonar1

' 6500
ECHO2        CON    11      'input from the 6500.
INIT2        CON    10      'output to the 6500.
wDist2       VAR    Word     'sonar2

main:
  cmd = 0
  SERIN 16,16468,main,[WAIT(100), cmd]
  IF cmd = 101 THEN ping_ir          ' gets compass reading
  IF cmd = 102 THEN ping_srf         ' pings the SRF04
  IF cmd = 103 THEN ping_6500        ' pings the 6500 Sonar Module
  PAUSE 5
  GOTO main

ping_ir:
    LOW dout1
ir1b:
  IF IN3=0 THEN ir1b
  SHIFTIN din1,dout1,2,[dist1\8]
  HIGH dout1
  SEROUT 16,N9600,[DEC dist1,CR]
  GOTO main
```

```
ping_srf:
  PULSOUT INIT1,5              ' 10us init pulse
  OUTPUT INIT1                 ' (delay)
  RCTIME ECHO1,1,wDist1        ' measure echo time
  wDist1=wDist1/convfac        ' convert to inches
  SEROUT 16,N9600,[DEC wDist1,CR]
  GOTO main

ping_6500:
  PULSOUT INIT2,5              ' 10us init pulse
  OUTPUT INIT2                 ' (delay)
  RCTIME ECHO2,1,wDist2        ' measure echo time
  wDist2=wDist2/convfac        ' convert to inches
  SEROUT 16,N9600,[DEC wDist2,CR]
  GOTO main
```

Next is the DistanceStamp class, which reads the data from the distance.bs2 program in Example 4-7. The fields of this class are similar to the CompassStamp with the exception of the command names and the instance field distSensor, which enumerates the distance reading.

Example 4-7. *DistanceStamp.java*

```java
package com.scottpreston.javarobot.chapter5;

import com.scottpreston.javarobot.chapter2.Controller;
import com.scottpreston.javarobot.chapter2.JSerialPort;
import com.scottpreston.javarobot.chapter2.SingleSerialPort;

public class DistanceStamp extends Controller {

    // commands set in basic stmap program
    public static final int CMD_INIT = 100;
    public static final int CMD_IR = 101;
    public static final int CMD_SRF = 102;
    public static final int CMD_6500 = 103;

    private int distSensor = CMD_SRF;

    // constructor
    public DistanceStamp(JSerialPort sPort) throws Exception {
        super(sPort);
    }

    public int ping(int distSensor) throws Exception {
        setDistSensor(distSensor);
        return ping();
    }
```

```java
    // get distance method
    public int ping() throws Exception {
        // calling super execute() method
        String heading = execute(new byte[] { CMD_INIT, (byte) distSensor },
                getSonarDelay());
        // since returning heading as one, two or three bytes
        String[] h2 = heading.split("~");
        String heading2 = "";
        for (int h = 0; h < h2.length; h++) {
            // convert each byte to char which I append to create single number
            heading2 = heading2 + (char) new Integer(h2[h]).intValue();
        }
        // return 3 chars like '123' which is 123 degrees
        return new Integer(heading2).intValue();
    }

    public int getIR() throws Exception {
        return ping(CMD_IR);
    }
    public int getSRF() throws Exception {
        return ping(CMD_IR);
    }
    public int get6500() throws Exception {
        return ping(CMD_IR);
    }

    // since different delay for each compass
    private int getSonarDelay() {
        int delay = 0;
        if (distSensor == CMD_IR) {
            delay = 100;
        }
        if (distSensor == CMD_SRF) {
            delay = 150;
        }
        if (distSensor == CMD_6500) {
            delay = 250;
        }
        return delay;
    }
    public int getDistSensor() {
        return distSensor;
    }
    public void setDistSensor(int distSensor) {
        this.distSensor = distSensor;
    }
```

```
public static void main(String[] args) {
    try {
        // since i am testing at my desk and not on my robot
        DistanceStamp s = new DistanceStamp(SingleSerialPort.getInstance(1));
        System.out.println("Sharp IR Reading = " + s.getIR());
        System.out.println("SRF04 reading = " + s.getSRF());
        System.out.println("6500 reading = " + s.get6500());
    } catch (Exception e) {
        e.printStackTrace();
        System.exit(1);
    }
}
}
```

Section Summary

In this section, I discussed a few types of distance sensors: one infrared and two sonar. The first sensor is the Sharp GP2D02 which is good for short distances. The second, the Devantech SRF04, is a good all-purpose short- to medium-distance sonar, and the third is a Polaroid 6500 ranging module with an instrument grade transducer, which works for up to distances of 35 feet.

The programs created were

- distance.bs2: Which is the BASIC Stamp program getting data from the distance sensors.

- DistanceStamp.java: Which gets this distance data from the distance.bs2 program.

I'd recommend choosing the Devantech SRF04 sensors for three reasons:

1. They use less power than the Polaroid 6500.

2. Their effective range is the same given most indoor conditions.

3. They're more accurate than the Sharp IR sensor, and less prone to noise or floor echo.

4.4 Chapter Summary

In this chapter, our goal was to introduce some of the sensors you'll use in robotics and explain how to connect them with your microcontroller.

If you're building robots with multiple sensors, however, it might be worth your time and money to use a printed circuit board (PCB) for connecting and wiring your sensors to your microcontroller. Two are available at www.prestonresearch.com, and are described in the following bullets.

- CMPS03 Carrier Board: For connecting a Devantech CMPS03 compass to an RJ11 connector.

- Sonar Distribution Board: For connecting up to 14 I/O pins from your microcontroller to your sensors.

If you'd like to create your own PCBs, however, check out www.ExpressPCB.com.

Once the connections to your sensors and microcontrollers are made, use the sensors listed in the following bullets to give your robot some understanding of its environment.

- Dinsmore 1490 Compass: Four I/O; 45-degree accuracy compass.

- Devantech CMPS03 Compass: Single I/O; 2-degree accuracy compass.

- PNI Corporation Vector 2x Compass: Four I/O; 2-degree accuracy compass.

- Lynxmotion Single Line Detector: Good for line following or reading encoders.

- Bump Switches: Emergency stop sensors.

- Sharp GP2D15 infrared proximity sensors: Good for short-range proximity detection.

- Sharp GP2D02 distance infrared sensor: Short-range infrared distance sensor.

- Devantech SRF04 sonar: Good medium-range sonar.

- Polaroid 6500 Ranging Module and Instrument Grade Transducer: Long-range high-power sonar.

The three Stamp programs created were

- compass.bs2: Showed how to connect to the three compasses.

- switch.bs2: Showed how to get readings from one or more logical switches.

- distance.bs2: Showed how to get distance readings from three types of distance sensors.

The four Java classes created were

- CompassStamp.java: This class is designed to work with the compass.bs2 program.

- Compass.java: This class showed how you could model a specific sensor rather than create a CompassStamp for accessing it.

- SwitchStamp.java: This class is designed to work with the switch.bs2 program.

- DistanceStamp.java: This class is designed to work with the distance.bs2 program.

Now that I have discussed the basics of how to get your robot to move and gather basic sensor data it's time to work exclusively with the PC. In the next chapter I will talk about text to speech and voice recognition, but of which are done best with a PC.

CHAPTER 5

■■■

Speech

It usually takes more than three weeks to prepare a good impromptu speech.

— Mark Twain

5.0 Introduction

It won't take you that long to get your PC to speak. Outside of download times, it should only be about ten minutes. I'm also not going to use any microcontrollers in this chapter. This is going to run 100 percent off a PC, so as long as you have a soundcard, speakers, and a microphone, you'll be in good shape.

To get started, follow these steps:

1. Make sure your soundcard is working.

2. Download and install FreeTTS from SourceForge from http://freetts.sourceforge.net. This will install the Java Speech API (JSAPI) and the FreeTTS JARs.

3. Add the following JARs to your class path:

   • jsapi.jar and freetts.jar: Both are available for download from http://freetts. sourceforge.net.

   • sphinx4.jar: Can be downloaded from http://cmusphinx.sourceforge.net.

   • WSJ_8gau_13dCep_16k_40mel_130Hz_6800Hz.jar: Available for download from http://cmusphinx.sourceforge.net/sphinx4/.

4. Download and install the Quadmore DLLs from the Source Code area of the Apress web site (www.apress.com) or from www.quadmore.com.

■**Note** The files from the Apress web site follow the examples in this book. If you download from www.quadmore.com, you will need to modify your examples so they don't include any package structure. Both the QuadmoreTTS.class and QuadmoreSR.class will also need to be in your class path.

5. Install the Microsoft Speech SDK for Windows. This will install the other voices and set up your machine for text to speech, as well as speech recognition using the Microsoft API. You can download these at www.microsoft.com/speech.

6. Once you've downloaded all the files, make sure you spend 15 minutes or so training your system to recognize your voice. You'll also need to buy a headset microphone (about $20), which picks up less noise than external microphones.

To configure Microsoft Speech, see Figures 5-1 and 5-2, shown next.

Figure 5-1. *The Microsoft Speech Recognition tab*

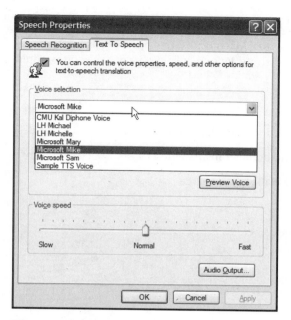

Figure 5-2. *The Microsoft Text To Speech tab*

What Is Speech Technology?

Speech technology consists of speech synthesis and speech recognition. The speech recognition engines are responsible for converting acoustical signals to digital signals, and then to text. Two modes of speech recognition are available:

- Dictation: Users read data directly into a microphone. The range of words the engine can recognize is limited to the recognizers, grammar, or dictionary of recognizable words.

- Command and control: Users speak commands or ask questions. The range of words the engine can recognize in this case is usually defined by a limited grammar. This mode often eliminates the need to "train" the recognizers.

The speech synthesizer engines are responsible for converting text to a spoken language. This process first breaks the words into phonemes, which are then transformed to a digital audio signal for playback.

In this chapter, I'll introduce two types of speech recognition engines: one for continuous dictation using JNI (see the following section), and one using command and control. I'll also introduce three different speech synthesizers: two in Java and one using JNI.

Before I start with speech recognition or synthesis, the following is a quick-start reference to the Java Native Interface or JNI.

The Java Native Interface (JNI)

JNI allows programs that run within the Java Virtual Machine (JVM) to operate with applications and libraries written in other languages. To illustrate, let's create a simple native code example using Visual C++.

1. Open Visual Studio.

2. Select Managed C++ Library. If it's named SimpleJNI, the tool will create the following files:

   • AssemblyInfo.cpp: C++ source; contains custom attributes

   • SimpleJNI.cpp: C++ source; the main file in .dll source

   • SimpleJNI.h: Header file

   • SimpleJNI.ncb: IntelliSense database

   • SimpleJNI.sln: Solution file

   • SimpleJNI.suo: Solution Options file

   • SimpleJNI.vcproj: Project file

   • ReadMe.txt: ReadMe file

   • Stdafx.cpp: C++ source; contains standard system includes

   • Stdafx.h: C++ header; contains standard system includes

3. Create your native Java class. In Example 5-1, I'll call this TempConvert.

   Example 5-1. *TempConvert.java*

```java
package com.scottpreston.javarobot.chapter5;

public class TempConvert {

    // this is a DLL in system path SimpleJNI.dll
    static {
        System.loadLibrary("SimpleJNI");
    }

    // native method
    public native float CtoF(float c);

    // native method
    public native float FtoC(float f);
```

```
// sample program
public static void main(String args[]) {
    TempConvert tc = new TempConvert();
    for (int c = 0; c < 101; c++) {
        System.out.println("c=" + c + ",f=" + tc.CtoF(c));
    }
}
}
```

4. Run javah on the compiled .class file. Javah produces C and C++ header files from your native Java class.

```
javah - jni TempConvert
```

Note From your IDE, you can either go to the compiled class path (for example, /bin/com/scottpreston/ javarobot/chapter5) or you can specify the class name from path root or a compiled JAR file.

The output of the file is shown in Example 5-2.

Example 5-2. *TempConvert.h*

```
/* DO NOT EDIT THIS FILE - it is machine generated */
#include "jni.h"
/* Header for class TempConvert */

#ifndef _Included_TempConvert
#define _Included_TempConvert
#ifdef __cplusplus
extern "C" {
#endif
/*
 * Class:     TempConvert
 * Method:    CtoF
 * Signature: (F)F
 */
JNIEXPORT jfloat JNICALL Java_com_scottpreston_javarobot_➥
 chapter5_TempConvert_CtoF
  (JNIEnv *, jobject, jfloat);
```

```
/*
 * Class:     TempConvert
 * Method:    FtoC
 * Signature: (F)F
 */
JNIEXPORT jfloat JNICALL Java_com_scottpreston_javarobot_➥
chapter5_TempConvert_FtoC
  (JNIEnv *, jobject, jfloat);

#ifdef __cplusplus
}
#endif
#endif
```

5. I had to make two modifications to this file because I compiled it from the /bin/com/scottpreston/javarobot/chapter5 directory.

   • I had to change the fully qualified class name from "Java_TempConvert" to "Java_com_scottpreston_javarobot_chapter5_TempConvert".

   • I had to replace the "<jni.h>" with "jni.h".

6. Copy jawt.h, jvmpi.h, jvmdi.h, jni_md.j, jni.h, and jawt_md.h to the project directory. These are required for jni.h and for compiling.

7. Add your native code.

■**Note** In Example 5-3, I performed the calculation using the JNIEXPORT method. Later when discussing Microsoft speech and voice recognition, calls to other classes and methods are inserted here, rather than performing 100 percent of the native action within these methods.

Example 5-3. *SimpleJNI.h*

```
// SimpleJNI.h

#include "TempConvert.h"

JNIEXPORT jfloat JNICALL➥
Java_com_scottpreston_javarobot_chapter5_TempConvert_CtoF
  (JNIEnv *, jobject, jfloat f)
{       // native code
        float out = f *1.8 + 32;
        return out;
}
```

```
JNIEXPORT jfloat JNICALL➡
Java_com_scottpreston_javarobot_chapter5_TempConvert_FtoC
  (JNIEnv *, jobject, jfloat f)
{
        // native code
return (f -= 32) /= 1.8;
}
```

8. Build the .dll and place it in system32.

9. Run the program.

By using the JNI, you can take advantage of some native voices for speech synthesis and recognition. This way, if you already have some software or have configured your machine to recognize your voice with native software, you won't have to retrain your system. I'll discuss how to use the JNI for speech synthesis in section 5.2, but first let's talk about Java Speech Synthesis.

5.1 Speech Synthesis

Java Speech API (JSAPI) and Free Text To Speech (FreeTTS) are speech synthesis programs written entirely in Java. It's important to note that FreeTTS supports only a subset of JSAPI 1.0 and has some restrictions. Please reference the FreeTTS web site (http://freetts.sourceforge.net) for more information on the software and its usage.

I'll have three implementations for speech synthesis: two Java and one native. So, to standardize behavior, I'll create an interface called JVoice and then have two implementation classes: one using JSAPI, called JavaVoice; and one using FreeTTS, called FreeTTSVoice. Figure 5-3 shows a class diagram of the setup.

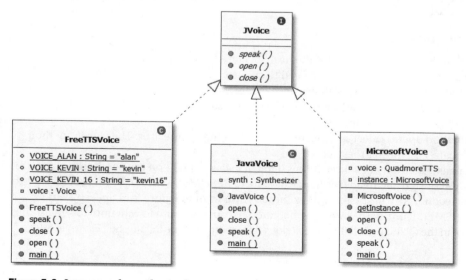

Figure 5-3. *Java speech synthesis classes*

Code Objective

Create an interface that standardizes behavior between three implementing speech synthesis classes.

Code Discussion

Our interface has only three methods. The first, open, gets the system ready for voice processing. The second, speak, takes a string input and contains the implementation for speaking. It throws an exception if there's a problem. Finally, there's close, which shuts down the voice processing. See Example 5-4.

Example 5-4. *Voice.java*

```
package com.scottpreston.javarobot.chapter5;

public interface JVoice {

    // opens or allocates voice engine
    public void open();
    // speaks
    public void speak(String words) throws Exception;
    // closes or deallocates voice engine
    public void close();

}
```

Code Objective

The code objective here is to create a speech synthesis implementation using JSAPI 1.0.

Code Discussion

The class that does all of our work for the Java Speech API is the java.speech.synthesis. Synthesizer class. To use this class, we need to create a new Synthesizer via the Central. createSynthesizer() method. This allows us to create any type of synthesizer we like with the constructor being a SynthesizerModeDesc class. After construction, the other methods follow our interface defined in Example 5-4.

The method open() calls the allocate() method on the Synthesizer. The close() method calls deallocate() on the Synthesizer.

The speak() method does three things. First, it calls resume() on the Synthesizer because it's recently allocated and needs to change its state to RESUMED so it can begin processing text to speech. Second, we call speakPlainText because we want to ignore Java Speech Markup Language (JSML). Third, we call waitEngineState() because we want to wait until the engine has placed itself in the QUEUE_EMPTY state. It does this when it's done talking. See Example 5-5.

Example 5-5. *JavaVoice.java*

```java
package com.scottpreston.javarobot.chapter5;

import java.util.Locale;

import javax.speech.Central;
import javax.speech.synthesis.Synthesizer;
import javax.speech.synthesis.SynthesizerModeDesc;

public class JavaVoice implements JVoice {

    private Synthesizer synth;

    public JavaVoice() throws Exception {
        // constructs synthesizer for US English

        synth = Central.createSynthesizer(new SynthesizerModeDesc(
                null, // engine name
                "general", // mode name
                Locale.US, // local
                null, // Boolean, running
                null)); // Voices[]
    }
    // allocates synthesizer resources, puts engine in state ALLOCATED.
    public void open() {
        try {
            synth.allocate();
        } catch (Exception e) {
            e.printStackTrace();
        }
    }
    // deallocates synthesizer resources, puts engine in state DEALLOCATED.
    public void close() {
        try {
            synth.deallocate();
        } catch (Exception e) {
            e.printStackTrace();
        }
    }
    // speaks
    public void speak(String words) throws Exception {
        // removes from paused state as set by allocate
        synth.resume();
        // speaks plain text and text is not interpreted by Java Speech Markup
        // Language JSML
        synth.speakPlainText(words, null);
```

```
        // waits until queue is empty
        synth.waitEngineState(Synthesizer.QUEUE_EMPTY);
    }

    // sample program
    public static void main(String[] args) {
        try {

            JavaVoice voice = new JavaVoice();
            voice.open();
            voice.speak("Java Robots Are Cool!");
            voice.close();

        } catch (Exception e) {
            e.printStackTrace();
        }
        System.out.println("done");
    }
}
```

Code Objective

The code objective here is to create a speech synthesis implementation using FreeTTS.

Code Discussion

First, I've created three static fields with the names alan, kevin, and kevin16. Alan sounds the best, but his domain (things he can speak) is limited to date and time sounds. Kevin is an 8-bit voice of unlimited domain (any word) and sounds very close to the JavaVoice class created in Example 5-5. Kevin16 is a 16-bit voice, is medium quality, and has unlimited domain. The remaining field is com.sun.speech.freetts.Voice called voice.

I construct voice in the class constructor via the getInstance().getVoice()method from the VoiceManager. The remaining methods, open(), speak(), and close(), are self-explanatory. See Example 5-6.

Example 5-6. *FreeTTSVoice.java*

```java
package com.scottpreston.javarobot.chapter5;

import com.sun.speech.freetts.Voice;
import com.sun.speech.freetts.VoiceManager;

public class FreeTTSVoice implements JVoice {

    // create these for use in constructor
    public static final String VOICE_ALAN = "alan";
    public static final String VOICE_KEVIN = "kevin";
    public static final String VOICE_KEVIN_16 = "kevin16";
```

```
    private Voice voice;

    // creates with name
    public FreeTTSVoice(String voiceName) {
        voice = VoiceManager.getInstance().getVoice(voiceName);
    }

    // speaks
    public void speak(String msg) {
        voice.speak(msg);
    }
    // deallocates and frees resources
    public void close() {
        voice.deallocate();
    }
    // allocates and opens resources
    public void open() {
        voice.allocate();
    }
    // sample program
    public static void main(String[] args) {
        FreeTTSVoice me = new FreeTTSVoice(FreeTTSVoice.VOICE_KEVIN_16);
        me.open();
        me.speak("Java Robots Are Cool.");
        me.close();
    }
}
```

Speech Synthesis Using JNI

Sometimes, whether I like it or not, I need to use some native code to get functionality for my robots. In the next two examples I'll create a native text-to-speech class and a native speech recognition class. The C++ project can be downloaded from www.quadmore.com.

If you recall from the introduction, I must make sure the method name for the JNIEXPORT matches the fully qualified class name. See Example 5-7.

■**Note** If you get a java.lang.UnsatisfiedLinkError, check to make sure the method names match.

Example 5-7. *QuadmoreTTS.h and QuadTTS.h*

```
JNIEXPORT jboolean JNICALL ➡
Java_com_scottpreston_javarobot_chapter5_QuadmoreTTS_SpeakDarling
```

Code Objective

The objective here is to use the JNI native class to synthesize speech.

Code Discussion

This class has a static block that calls the QuadTTS.dll. This DLL must be in the path; I put it in the c:\windows\system32 directory. The constructor is just a default QuadmoreTTS() and is excluded from the source. I have the three methods from the native code at my disposal—SpeakDarling(), setVoice(), and getVoiceToken()—but currently, I'm only using SpeakDarling(). See Example 5-8.

Example 5-8. *QuadmoreTTS.java*

```java
package com.scottpreston.javarobot.chapter5;

public class QuadmoreTTS {

    // this is a DLL in system path QuadTTS.dll
    static {
        System.loadLibrary("QuadTTS");
    }

    // native method
    public native boolean SpeakDarling(String strInput);
    // native method
    public native boolean setVoiceToken(String s);
    // native method
    public native String getVoiceToken();

    // sample program
    public static void main(String args[]) {
        QuadmoreTTS v = new QuadmoreTTS();
        boolean result = v.SpeakDarling("Java Robots Are Cool!");
        System.out.println("done!");
    }
}
```

I could use the QuadmoreTTS class in my programs, but I decided to create a wrapper class that implements the JVoice interface of my other text-to-speech classes.

There are two fields—one is the QuadmoreTTS class I created in the previous example, and the other is a static instance of the MicrosoftVoice—because I only want one program at a time accessing the voice synthesis engine.

Next, I implement the following methods from JVoice: open(), close(), and speak(). While open() and close() do nothing, speak() calls the native class SpeakDarling() method. If there's an error from this class, I've thrown an exception.

The sample program, main(), says the same phrase done earlier in the last two speech implementation classes. See Example 5-9.

Example 5-9. *MicrosoftVoice.java*

```java
package com.scottpreston.javarobot.chapter5;

public class MicrosoftVoice implements JVoice {

    // worker class for voice
    private QuadmoreTTS voice;
    // private instance to ensure only one is active
    private static MicrosoftVoice instance;

    // private constructor prevents initialization
    // called by getInstance
    private MicrosoftVoice() {
        voice = new QuadmoreTTS();
    }

    // static methods ensure one instance per class
    public static MicrosoftVoice getInstance() throws Exception {
        if (instance == null) {
            // returns self
            instance = new MicrosoftVoice();
        }
        return instance;
    }

    public void open() {
        // do nothing
    }

    public void close() {
        // do nothing
    }

    //speak, otherwise throw exception
    public void speak(String s) throws Exception {
        if (!voice.SpeakDarling(s)) {
            throw new Exception("Unable to speak");
        }
    }

    // sample usage
    public static void main(String args[]) {
        try {
            MicrosoftVoice v = MicrosoftVoice.getInstance();
            v.speak("Java Robots Are Cool!");
```

```
    } catch (Exception e) {
        e.printStackTrace();
        System.exit(1);
    }
    System.out.println("done!");
}


}
```

Now that I've created three separate implementations of the voice, it's time to see what they all sound like. Try it and see which one you like.

In TTSCompare, I'm showing a technique called factory method in getVoice(). In a nutshell, this means that I can get whatever voice I want by sending a parameter—in this case, an int enumerating one of the voices. Because all of the voices share the same interface, I can send this back from the method and use them the same way I do the sample program main(). See Example 5-10.

Example 5-10. *TTSCompare.java*

```java
package com.scottpreston.javarobot.chapter5;

public class TTSCompare {

    public static final int JAVA_VOICE = 0;
    public static final int FREETTS_VOICE = 1;
    public static final int MICROSOFT_VOICE = 2;

    public JVoice getVoice(int voiceID) throws Exception {

        JVoice voice;

        if (voiceID == FREETTS_VOICE) {
            voice = new FreeTTSVoice(FreeTTSVoice.VOICE_KEVIN_16);
        } else if (voiceID == MICROSOFT_VOICE) {
            voice = MicrosoftVoice.getInstance();
        } else {
            voice = new JavaVoice();
        }
        return voice;
    }

    // simple program to test all classes and compare quality
    public static void main(String[] args) {
        try {
```

```
            TTSCompare tts = new TTSCompare();
            // java voice
            JVoice voice1 = tts.getVoice(TTSCompare.JAVA_VOICE);
            // free tts voice
            JVoice voice2 = tts.getVoice(TTSCompare.FREETTS_VOICE);
            // microsoft voice
            JVoice voice3 = tts.getVoice(TTSCompare.MICROSOFT_VOICE);
            // open all of these
            voice1.open();
            voice2.open();
            voice3.open();
            // speak some text
            voice1.speak("Java Voice... Hello World!");
            voice2.speak("Free TTS Voice... Hello World!");
            voice3.speak("Microsoft Voice... Hello World!");
            // close them
            voice1.close();
            voice2.close();
            voice3.close();
        } catch (Exception e) {
            e.printStackTrace();
            System.exit(1);
        }


    }
}
```

If you'd like to improve the quality of the FreeTTS voice, there are other extensions available at http://freetts.sourceforge.net.

Section Summary

In this section, I programmed my PC to talk using three different implementations of the JVoice interface. Those classes are

- JavaVoice: This uses the JSAPI speech synthesis engine.

- FreeTTsVoice.java: This uses the FreeTTS speech synthesis engine.

- MicrosoftVoice.java: This uses JNI to connect the Microsoft Sound API and text-to-speech engine.

Make sure you look at that site for more details. In the next section, I'm going to talk about the second part of speech: recognition.

5.2 Speech Recognition

In this section, I'll show you two ways to create a speech recognition engine: the first using Java and the second using JNI. In these two examples, I'll show the two ways of speech recognition: one using continuous dictation, and one using command and control. Also, because I'm going to use two different implementations, I'll create an interface that both will implement.

A class diagram of the classes I'll create in this section is shown in Figure 5-4.

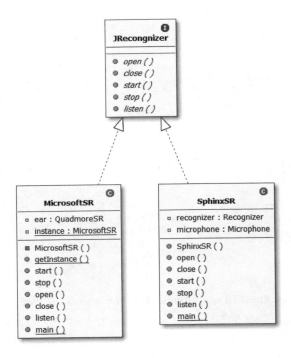

Figure 5-4. *Recognition classes*

Code Objective

The objective of this section is to create an interface that standardizes behavior between the two implementing speech recognition classes.

Code Discussion

This interface includes five methods. The open() and close() methods allocate and deallocate the same way that the JVoice interfaces implementation classes do. The start() method starts the recording device(), while the stop() method stops the recording device. Finally, the listen() method returns a String of the spoken phrase or word. See Example 5-11.

Example 5-11. *JRecognizer.java*

```
package com.scottpreston.javarobot.chapter5;

public interface JRecognizer {

    // opens device or allocates it
    public void open();
    // closes device or deallocates it
    public void close();
    // starts recognizer engine
    public void start();
    // stops recognizer engine
    public void stop();
    // starts listening
    public String listen();

}
```

First, speech recognition implementation uses the Sphinx-4 project at SourceForge. You can find more information and other detailed examples at the project home page at http://cmusphinx.sourceforge.net/sphinx4/. The Sphinx-4 is a speech recognition system written entirely in the Java programming language. It was created as a joint project between the Sphinx group at Carnegie Mellon University, Sun Microsystems, Mitsubishi Electric Research Labs (MERL), and Hewlett Packard (HP), with contributions from the University of California at Santa Cruz (USCS) and the Massachusetts Institute of Technology (MIT).

This program utilizes the "Command & Control" aspect of speech recognition. This means I must specify a grammar file. The format is called Java Speech Grammar Format.

The first part of the grammar file is the grammar header. The header format is

```
#JSGF version char-encoding local;
```

The second part is called the grammar name declaration. It's just a name; you can use either a package or a name.

```
grammar packageName.someName;
grammar someName;
```

The third part is optional and gives you the ability to import other grammars.

```
import <fullyQualifiedRuleName>;
import <fullGrammarName>;
```

The fourth part is the grammar body. This is where your rule definitions are located. You can use either pattern for the rule definition.

```
<ruleName> = rule expression;
public <ruleName> = rule expression;
```

Example 5-12 is a grammar file I'll use to open notepad. It has two rules, one for notepad and another for exiting.

Example 5-12. *notepad.gram*

```
#JSGF V1.0;

/**
 * JSGF Grammar for notepad example
 */

grammar notepad;

public <notepad> = (note pad);
public <exit> = (exit | good bye | quit);
```

Next, I need to create a class that will use this grammar file to actually launch a program.

Code Objective

The objective here is to perform basic speech recognition to open notepad, and then exit.

Code Discussion

After the grammar file, I need to create a configuration file for the recognizer. I used a provided configuration file from one of the examples, but had to make a few modifications to the grammar configuration for my class and my new grammar file. The configuration contains the other following sections:

- word recognizer
- decoder
- linguist
- dictionary
- acoustic model
- unit manager
- frontend
- monitors
- miscellaneous

In the following configuration, the dictionary is defined later in the configuration file. This contains all the words the recognizer can find.

The second line is the grammar location, which will be the class path of the project name: com.scottpreston.javarobot.chapter5.

The third line is the name of the grammar file at the location specified by the previous line.

The fourth line is required because all scores and probabilities are maintained in this class. See Example 5-13.

Example 5-13. *Grammar Configuration of notepad.config.xml*

```
<component name="jsgfGrammar" type="edu.cmu.sphinx.jsapi.JSGFGrammar">
    <property name="dictionary" value="dictionary"/>
    <property name="grammarLocation"    ➡
value="resource:/com.scottpreston.javarobot.chapter5.SphinxSR!/➡
com/scottpreston/javarobot/chapter5/"/>
    <property name="grammarName" value="notepad"/>
    <property name="logMath" value="logMath"/>
</component>
```

Now that I have both text files—notepad.gram and notepad.config.xml—I can create my speech recognition class, SphinxSR. It has two fields: recognizer and microphone. Both have parameters defined in the configuration file. I also get a copy of the grammar file. Later, I'll use the RuleGrammar to test what command I want to execute, because the rules are structured per command. Once I get the GSGFGrammar from the ConfigurationManager, I allocate() the GSFFGrammar object to create it. Then I set the private field ruleGrammar. At the end of the constructor, I loop through all the rule names and rules for informational purposes so I know what to speak.

The next methods—open() and close()—allocate() and deallocate() resources for speech recognition. The method, start(), begins recording from the microphone, while stop() halts recording from the microphone.

The listen() method calls recognize() on the recognizer. This method returns the recognition results. They can be either full or partial. As long as the result is not null, I can call a few methods on it, but the only one I care about is the one that returns the best and final result with no filler: getBestFinalResultNoFiller(). This returns a string of the spoken words. Next, to test the ruleName, I get the ruleNames from the ruleGrammar object. Then I create a RuleParse object to parse the resultText against the ruleName. If there's a match, I return the ruleName.

In main(), after constructing SphinxSR with the URL path to the configuration file, I open(), start(), and then listen() until I hear the commands/ruleNames I'm looking for. When I hear the rule "notepad", I execute notepad. When I hear the rule "exit", I exit the program. See Example 5-14.

■Note To get this to work and avoid an out-of-memory exception, you may be required to increase the memory size for your JVM by adding the arguments –Xms 128m and –Xmx 128m. To do this in Eclipse, click the Run menu, followed by Run, and then modify the VM arguments as shown in Figure 5-5.

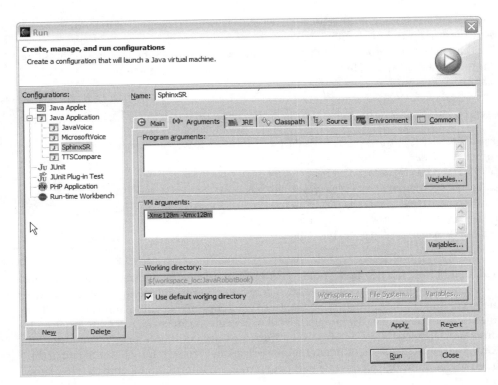

Figure 5-5. *Increasing memory in Eclipse for SphinxSR*

Example 5-14. *SphinxSR.java*

```java
package com.scottpreston.javarobot.chapter5;

import java.net.URL;

import javax.speech.recognition.RuleGrammar;
import javax.speech.recognition.RuleParse;

import edu.cmu.sphinx.frontend.util.Microphone;
import edu.cmu.sphinx.jsapi.JSGFGrammar;
import edu.cmu.sphinx.recognizer.Recognizer;
import edu.cmu.sphinx.result.Result;
import edu.cmu.sphinx.util.props.ConfigurationManager;

public class SphinxSR implements JRecognizer {

    private Recognizer recognizer;
    private Microphone microphone;
    private RuleGrammar ruleGrammar;
```

```java
    public SphinxSR(URL url) throws Exception {
        //loads configuration data from XML-based configuration file
        ConfigurationManager cm = new ConfigurationManager(url);
        // gets component by name
        recognizer = (Recognizer) cm.lookup("recognizer");
        microphone = (Microphone) cm.lookup("microphone");
        // get grammar file
        JSGFGrammar gram = (JSGFGrammar) cm.lookup("jsgfGrammar");
        // create the grammar
        gram.allocate();
        // get rules
        ruleGrammar = gram.getRuleGrammar();
        // get rule names
        String[] rules = ruleGrammar.listRuleNames();
        // display to console so you know what to speak.
        for (int i=0; i < rules.length;i++) {
            System.out.println("rule name = " + rules[i]);
            System.out.println("rule = " +ruleGrammar.getRule(rules[i]).➥
toString());;;
        }
        // separator
        System.out.println("----");
    }

    // allocates resources
    public void open() {
        try {
            recognizer.allocate();
        } catch (Exception e) {
            e.printStackTrace();
            System.exit(1);
        }
    }

    // deallocates resources
    public void close() {
        recognizer.deallocate();
    }

    // start recording
    public void start() {
        // begins capturing audio data
        if (microphone.startRecording() == false) {
            recognizer.deallocate();
            System.exit(1);
        }
    }
```

```java
    // stop capturing audio data
    public void stop() {
        microphone.stopRecording();
    }

    public String listen(){
        // gets recognition results from recognizer
        Result result = recognizer.recognize();
        String ruleName = "";
        if (result != null) {
            // gets best and final with no filler words
            String resultText = result.getBestFinalResultNoFiller();
            // display text
            System.out.println("I heard --> " + resultText);
            RuleParse rParse = null;
              String [] rules = ruleGrammar.listRuleNames();
            for (int i=0; i < rules.length;i++) {
                try {
                    // test rule name and execute
                    rParse = ruleGrammar.parse(resultText,rules[i]);
                    // set rulename
                    ruleName = rParse.getRuleName().getRuleName();
                } catch (Exception e) {
                    // do nothing
                }


            }
        }
        // return rulename
        return ruleName;
    }

    // test class
    public static void main(String[] args) throws Exception {
        // this is the configuration file
        URL url = SphinxSR.class.getResource("notepad.config.xml");
        SphinxSR sr = new SphinxSR(url);
        System.out.println("Loading...");
        sr.open();
        sr.start();
        String rule = "";
        System.out.println("Listening...");
        while (true) {
            rule = sr.listen();
            if (rule.equals("notepad")) {
                Runtime.getRuntime().exec("cmd /c notepad.exe");
            }
```

```
            if (rule.equals("exit")) {
                break;
            }
        }
        sr.stop();
        sr.close();
        System.out.println("done!");
    }

}
```

Next, I want to use JNI and implement a continuous dictation example. This will not use a grammar file, but will require you to train the recognizer as to how you dictate words.

Code Objective

The objective here is to perform basic speech recognition to open notepad, and then exit via JNI using continuous dictation.

Code Discussion

Just like the modification in Example 5-3, I'll only modify the methods to match our new package signature. See Example 5-15.

Example 5-15. *QuadmoreSR.h and QuadSR.h*

```
JNIEXPORT jstring JNICALL➡
Java_com_scottpreston_javarobot_chapter5_QuadmoreSR_TakeDictation
```

This class has a static block that calls QuadSR.dll. This DLL must be in the path, so I've put it in the c:\windows\system32 directory. After the static block, I define a single native method from the C++ project called TakeDictation. This method returns a string that I output to System.out. See Example 5-16.

Example 5-16. *QuadmoreSR.java*

```
package com.scottpreston.javarobot.chapter5;

public class QuadmoreSR {

    // this is a DLL in system path QuadSR.dll
    static {
        System.loadLibrary("QuadSR");
    }
    // from native class
    public native String TakeDictation();
```

```
// sample program
public static void main(String args[]) {
    int i;
    i = 0;
    String strRecognizedText;
    System.out.println("Beginning speech recognition...");
    // create speech recognition class
    QuadmoreSR sr = new QuadmoreSR();
    // wait until four words are heard
    while (i < 4) {
        strRecognizedText = sr.TakeDictation();
        System.out.println("\n");
        System.out.println(strRecognizedText);
        i++;
    }
    System.out.println("Done.");
}

}
```

Just like Example 5-9, I could use the QuadmoreSR class in my programs, but I decided to create a wrapper class that implements the SpeechRecognizer interface. There is no need to implement the methods start(), stop(), open(), and close(), but they are required for the interface so I will just create stubs. See Example 5-17.

Example 5-17. *MicrosoftSR.java*

```
package com.scottpreston.javarobot.chapter5;

public class MicrosoftSR implements JRecognizer {

    // class used for recognizer
    private QuadmoreSR ear;

    // holds single instance of recognizer
    private static MicrosoftSR instance;

    // private constructor prevents initialization
    // called by getInstance()
    private MicrosoftSR() {

        ear = new QuadmoreSR();
    }
```

```java
    // gets single instance of speech recognizer.
    public static MicrosoftSR getInstance() throws Exception {
        if (instance == null) {
            instance = new MicrosoftSR();
        }
        return instance;
    }

    public void start() {
    } // do nothing

    public void stop() {
    } // do nothing

    public void open() {
    } // do nothing

    public void close() {
    } // do nothing

    // starts listening and returning strings of spoken text
    public String listen() {
        return ear.TakeDictation();
    }
    // sample usage
    public static void main(String[] args) {
        try {
            // gets instance
            MicrosoftSR sr = MicrosoftSR.getInstance();
            String words = "";
            System.out.println("Listening...");
            // loops until hears exit
            while (words.equalsIgnoreCase("exit") == false) {
                words = sr.listen();
                System.out.println("I heard --> " + words);
                // if it hears note, then it opens notepad
                if (words.equalsIgnoreCase("note")) {
                    Runtime.getRuntime().exec("cmd /c notepad.exe");
                }
            }
        } catch (Exception e) {
            e.printStackTrace();
            System.exit(1);
        }
        System.out.println("done");
    }
}
```

Example 5-18 is useful when you want to hear what the Microsoft speech recognition engine "hears." You can use whatever voice you want. Here I'm using the MicrosoftVoice to repeat what it hears.

Example 5-18. *EchoTalk.java*

```java
package com.scottpreston.javarobot.chapter5;

public class EchoTalk {

    private MicrosoftVoice voice;
    private MicrosoftSR ear;

    public EchoTalk() throws Exception {
        // generic constructor gets instance of two worker classes
        voice = MicrosoftVoice.getInstance();
        ear = MicrosoftSR.getInstance();
        // give user instructions
        voice.speak("I will repeat what you say. Say exit, to end program.");
    }

    public void start() throws Exception {
        String words = "";
        // tell user to begin talking.
        voice.speak("listening");
        // this will loop until it hears 'exit'
        while (words.equalsIgnoreCase("exit") == false) {
            // gets words heard.
            words = ear.listen();
            //prints this to system out (good for debugging)
            System.out.println("I heard --> " + words);
            // say the words
            voice.speak(words);
        }
        // last words spoken.
        voice.speak("goodbye");
    }

    public static void main(String[] args) {

        try {
            EchoTalk echo = new EchoTalk();
            echo.start();
```

```
        } catch (Exception e) {
            //print error and exit.
            e.printStackTrace();
            System.exit(1);
        }


    }
}
```

Section Summary

In this section, I showed two examples of using speech recognition, both of which implemented the JRecognizer interface. The first used Sphinx-4 for Java to demonstrate command and control. The second used JNI and the Microsoft speech recognition engine to give an example of continuous dictation.

Before introducing the first example, I gave a brief overview of the Java Speech Grammar Format (JSGF). This is the format of what words the recognizer needs to understand.

The classes discussed were

- SphinxSR: This is the Java recognizer using command and control.

- MicrosoftSR: This is the continuous recognizer using JNI and Microsoft speech recognition engine. (You must train this engine prior to use.)

5.3   Chapter Summary

In this chapter, I talked about how to get your robot to talk and recognize what you're saying. I also showed you how to use speech technology written in other languages, and I gave a simple introduction to the Java Native Interface (JNI).

The JNI example, TempConvert, does a simple temperature conversion using a C++ project and class to perform the calculation. You should be able to follow the step-by-step example to create your own JNI classes.

In section 5.1, I introduced the JVoice interface to standardize implementation of the three text-to-speech classes. The first, JavaVoice, uses the Java Speech API (JSAPI) to produce speech from text. The second, FreeTTSVoice, uses the FreeTTS speech synthesis libraries to produce speech from text. The third, MicrosoftVoice, uses JNI to connect the speech synthesizer engine built in to my system after installing the Microsoft Speech API (MSAPI). Also in section 5.1, I showed a sample class that tests the voice quality of all three speech synthesis engines.

In section 5.2, I introduced the JRecognizer interface, used for standardizing implementations of the following two speech recognition classes. The first recognizer, SphinxSR, uses a grammar file, a configuration file, and the synthesizer from the Sphinx-4 project. The second recognizer uses JNI to connect to the Microsoft speech recognition engine. Also in section 5.2, I wrote a sample class that echoes what's heard in continuous dictation.

Personally, I like MicrosoftVoice for sound quality and SphinxSR for recognition. I'll use these in Chapter 9.

Now that our PC can speak and listen, it's time to get it to see, which is the topic of the next chapter.

CHAPTER 6

■■■

Vision

Vision: the art of seeing things invisible.

— Jonathan Swift

6.0 Introduction

To get my robot to see, I'll start with a webcam that has a resolution of 320×240 pixels. We'll also need the Java Media Framework and the Java Advanced Imaging APIs. The Java Media Framework is available for download from

```
http://java.sun.com/products/java-media/jmf/2.1.1/download.html
```

The Java Advanced Imaging API can be downloaded from

```
http://java.sun.com/products/java-media/jai/index.jsp
```

To make sure all your classes compile, go to your JRE or IDE and add the following JARs:

- jmf.jar: Java Media Framework

- jai_core.jar: Java Advanced Imaging Core

- jai_codec.jar: Java Advanced Imaging Codec

Up until now we've only used command-line programs, so the first thing we need to do is create a GUI (graphical user interface) in which to render the images we'll process. From there, we'll introduce a simple Swing class because up until now all we've used are command-line programs. Then we'll extend this class and use it to display an image. From there, we'll discuss how to capture images from the webcam and display and process those images.

Some of the processing performed in this chapter will include

- Thresholding: Picking color values in ranges

- Resizing: Resizing an image

- Color operations: Working with filtering and color ratios

- Smoothing: Smoothing/blurring an image

- Sharpening: Sharpening/focusing an image

- Edge finding: finding edges

- Hough transform: Line finding

We'll also use combinations of these filters to optimize and help us identify a beverage from the refrigerator. For that, we'll process three different-colored soda cans. They're also coincidentally colored red (Coke), green (7-Up), and blue (Pepsi). Or RGB for short.

What Is RGB?

RGB stands for *red, green, and blue*. The colors utilize an additive model. In this model, the three colors are added together to form other colors (see Figure 6-1).

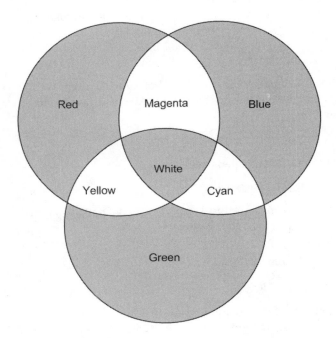

Figure 6-1. *The RGB spectrum*

For example, moving from the top left clockwise we have the following values:

Red = 255, 0, 0

Magenta = 255, 0, 255

Blue = 0, 0, 255

Cyan = 0, 255, 255

Green = 0, 255, 0

Yellow = 255, 255, 0

White = 255, 255, 255

Black = 0, 0, 0

This is the color model we'll use for this chapter.
Other models include

- CMYK: This employs subtractive color and is used in printing because it describes the light that needs to be reflected so you can see a specific color.

- YIQ: This is used in NTSC video signaling or broadcast television in North America. The YIQ stores luminance and two chrominance values.

- YUV: This color model is close to PAL video signaling or broadcast television in much of the rest of the world. It contains one luminance and two chrominance components.

- YPbPr: This is used in video compression such as MPEG and JPEG. You also might notice these labels on the back of your component video of your DVD player or television.

It's important to note that these different color models are interchangeable. For example, there are equations that will match Y, U, and V values from R, G, and B values, and vice versa. Also, of the two webcams I have, the first Logitech Webcam encodes in RGB, but my Pyro 1394 uses YUV. This won't make a difference since all the video streams get converted to BufferedImages of the ColorModel equal to RGB.

Now let's create a few helper classes and a simple Swing component before we move on to the next section, which involves capturing an image from our webcam.

Code Objective

The objective of the code in this section is to create a simple Swing component with the current operating system look and feel.

Code Discussion

In Example 6-1, I'll use the java.swing.UIManager class to set the look and feel of the window. You can choose a number of look and feels (LAFs). The one we'll use in all our examples will be the native look and feel.

Example 6-1. *WindowUtilities.java*

```
package com.scottpreston.javarobot.chapter6;

import javax.swing.UIManager;

public class WindowUtilities {
```

```
    // used in all SWING examples
    public static void setNativeLookAndFeel() {
        try {
            UIManager.setLookAndFeel(UIManager.getSystemLookAndFeelClassName());
        } catch(Exception e) {
            System.out.println("Error setting native LAF: " + e);
        }
    }

    public static void setJavaLookAndFeel() {
        try {
            UIManager.setLookAndFeel(UIManager.getCrossPlatformLookAndFeelClassName());
        } catch(Exception e) {
            System.out.println("Error setting Java LAF: " + e);
        }
    }

    public static void setMotifLookAndFeel() {
        try {
            UIManager.setLookAndFeel("com.sun.java.swing.plaf.motif.MotifLookAndFeel");
        } catch(Exception e) {
            System.out.println("Error setting Motif LAF: " + e);
        }
    }
}
```

Next, I'll create another utility class that will help the program exit in the event of closing the window. Although trivial, it does save some time. See Example 6-2.

Example 6-2. *ExitListener.java*

```
package com.scottpreston.javarobot.chapter6;

import java.awt.event.WindowAdapter;
import java.awt.event.WindowEvent;


public class ExitListener extends WindowAdapter {
    public void windowClosing(WindowEvent event) {
        System.exit(0);
    }
}
```

Now I'm ready to create a simple Swing component. In Example 6-2, the simple Swing component will extend the JFrame object.

In the constructor, I set the title of the JFrame, then chose the look and feel, and then added the Exit Listener. Next, I'll set the size to a default 320×240 pixels, change the background of the content pane to white, and set the class to visible. See Example 6-3 and Figure 6-2.

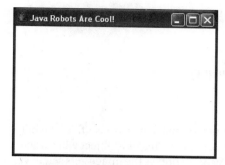

Figure 6-2. *SimpleSwing*

Example 6-3. *SimpleSwing.java*

```java
package com.scottpreston.javarobot.chapter6;

import java.awt.Color;
import java.awt.Container;

import javax.swing.JFrame;

public class SimpleSwing extends JFrame {

    // constructor
    public SimpleSwing()  {
        // calls JFrame with title
        super("Java Robots Are Cool!");
        // set look & feel
        WindowUtilities.setNativeLookAndFeel();
        // closes
        addWindowListener(new ExitListener());
        // sets size
        setSize(320, 240);
        // sets pane of content
        Container content = getContentPane();
        // sets color to white
        content.setBackground(Color.white);
        // shows frame
        setVisible(true);
    }

    public static void main(String[] args) throws Exception{
        SimpleSwing test = new SimpleSwing();

    }
}
```

We're now ready to extend this object to create an image viewer.

Code Objective

The objective here is to extend SimpleSwing to create an image viewer.

Code Discussion

Before I put the image inside the white area above, I want to create a new object that will help me with refreshing an image from a webcam later in the chapter. This new object will extend JPanel and will just contain the image that is set into it. Also, as soon as the image gets set, it will force a repaint of itself.

The fields in the class are an Image. There are two constructors: one with a default size of 320×240 and another allowing for the parameters of width (w) and height (h). See Example 6-4.

Example 6-4. *ImagePanel.java*

```java
package com.scottpreston.javarobot.chapter6;

import java.awt.Dimension;
import java.awt.Graphics;
import java.awt.Image;

import javax.swing.JPanel;

public class ImagePanel extends JPanel {

    public Image image = null;

    public ImagePanel(){
        init(320,240);
    }
    public ImagePanel(int w,int h) {
        init(w,h);
    }

    private void init(int w,int h) {
        setSize(w, h);
        setMinimumSize(new Dimension(w, h));
        setMaximumSize(new Dimension(w, h));
    }
    public void setImage(Image img) {
        image = img;
        repaint();
    }
```

```
public void paint(Graphics g) {
    if (image != null) {
        // in case image resizes background is black
        g.setColor(Color.BLACK);
        g.fillRect(0,0,this.getWidth(),getHeight());
        g.drawImage(image, 0, 0, this);
    }
  }
}
```

Now that I have a canvas to work with, it's time to create my ImageViewer class. This class has a single field, currentImage of type BufferedImage. There are two constructors, one taking a BufferedImage as a parameter, and the other taking a filename. In the second constructor to get a JPEG file, I open a FileInputStream, then pass this object to the JPEGImageDecoder, then call the decodeAsBufferedImage() method setting the currentImage. Once its construction is finished, I call init().

In the init() method, I get the size of the image, and then construct an ImagePanel with those dimensions. Next, I set the size of the window with enough room for the borders and title bar. Once sized, I add the ImagePanel to the content pane of the frame, make it visible, and then set the image into the ImagePanel. See Example 6-5 and Figure 6-3.

Figure 6-3. *The ImageViewer*

Example 6-5. *ImageViewer.java*

```java
package com.scottpreston.javarobot.chapter6;

import java.awt.BorderLayout;
import java.awt.image.BufferedImage;
import java.io.FileInputStream;

import javax.swing.JFrame;

import com.sun.image.codec.jpeg.JPEGCodec;
import com.sun.image.codec.jpeg.JPEGImageDecoder;

public class ImageViewer extends SimpleSwing {

    // to hold image
    private BufferedImage currentImage;
    // canvas for image in case we want to repaint after a process

    // constructor for buffered image
    public ImageViewer(BufferedImage bimg) {
        setTitle("ImageViewer");
        currentImage = bimg;
        init();
    }
    // constructor for filename
    public ImageViewer(String fileName) throws Exception{
        setTitle("ImageViewer - " + fileName);
        // get file
        FileInputStream fis = new FileInputStream(fileName);
        // convert jpec to buffered image
        JPEGImageDecoder decoder = JPEGCodec.createJPEGDecoder(fis);
        currentImage = decoder.decodeAsBufferedImage();
        init();
    }

    public void init() {

        int w = currentImage.getWidth();
        int h = currentImage.getHeight();
        ImagePanel imagePanel =  new ImagePanel(w,h);

        // set size of the window
        setSize(w + 8, h+35);
        // add imagePanel
        getContentPane().add(imagePanel,BorderLayout.CENTER);
        // make visible
        setVisible(true);
```

```
        // in case this is overloaded later
        imagePanel.setImage(currentImage);

    }


    public static void main(String[] args) {
        try {
          ImageViewer imageViewer = new ImageViewer("sample_images/stonehenge.jpg");
        } catch (Exception e) {
            e.printStackTrace();
            System.exit(1);
        }
    }
}
```

These are the basics. Now it's time to view images captured from a webcam. In the next section, I'll show you how to configure the Java Media Framework, use that to get the image from your webcam inside the ImageViewer, and then create a class for viewing the webcam image in real time.

So far, the classes created were

- WindowUtilities: Makes it easier to create a native look and feel for your Swing components

- ExitListener: Provides a listener to exit the program when the window exits

- SimpleSwing: Creates a simple-to-use Swing component

- ImagePanel: Provides a canvas to display and repaint images

- ImageViewer: Renders and displays images

In the next chapter, we'll use the classes created here, as well as the Java Media Framework, to display images and video from a webcam.

6.1 Image Capture

Once you install the Java Media Framework, test the installation by running JMStudio. JMStudio detects your capture devices (both audio and video). Go to File ➤ Preferences (see Figure 6-4). This brings up the JMF Registry Editor (see Figure 6-5). Select the Capture Devices tab and then click Detect Capture Devices. After a moment, the right pane will display the capture devices details.

▓**Note** The Locator identifier is on the second line of text. This locator will be what we use in the rest of the chapter to identify your webcam.

Figure 6-4. *JMStudio*

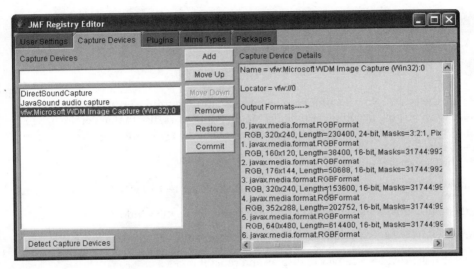

Figure 6-5. *The JMF Registry Editor*

Code Objective

The code objective in this section is to verify that the JMF was installed by finding the webcam via the MediaLocator.

Code Discussion

This will be a simple test class. The String variable URL will be the locator defined by the JMF Registry Editor. To find the camera, we need to create a MediaLocator object via the URL. Then we'll create a Processor object using the MediaLocator object. If there are no exceptions, everything works and we're ready to start doing some image capture with the webcam. If not, an exception will print to System.out. See Example 6-6.

■**Note** If you have more than one webcam, the Java Media Framework using Video For Windows can only utilize one camera per JVM. If you have this camera opened or want to use a different webcam, you'll see a Video Source window where you can select a new camera (see Figure 6-6).

Figure 6-6. *The Video Source window*

Example 6-6. *FindCamera.java*

```
package com.scottpreston.javarobot.chapter6;

import javax.media.Manager;
import javax.media.MediaLocator;
import javax.media.Processor;

public class FindCamera {

    public static void main(String[] args) {

        String url = "vfw://0";
        try {
            MediaLocator ml = new MediaLocator(url);
            Processor p = Manager.createProcessor(ml);
            System.out.println("Found camera at: " + url);
        } catch (Exception e) {
            System.out.println("Can not find camera at:" + url + ", ➥
or problem with JMF install.");
        } finally {
            System.exit(0);
        }

    }

}
```

The heart of vision processing is the capture of a single frame of a video stream into an image that can be processed. In the next example, we'll do just that: capture a single frame and then display it in the ImageViewer class created in the previous section.

Code Objective

The objective here is to capture a single frame from the web camera and display it as an image in ImageViewer.

Code Discussion

The GetFrame class has a single field, player—this is the javax.media.Player interface. See Example 6-7. The constructor takes a String that will be used to create a "realized" player via the Media Locator class sampled in the FindCamera class. To be "realized" means that the player is in the "realized" state, meaning it knows what resources it needs and has the necessary information regarding the type of media it is to present. Once the player is created, I have to start it. I then pause two and a half seconds for the camera to finish initializing.

The next method is getAwtImage(). I'll use the FrameGrabbingControl from the Java Media Framework to convert the frame to a buffer. Next, I convert the buffer to a java.awt.Image. I'll also create a similar method to get a BufferedImage that just calls the getAwtImage().

The final method of the class is close(). This closes and deallocates the player.

In the sample program in main(), I create the GetFrame object via the URL "vfw://0". This URL again can be obtained by running the JMF Registry Editor. Next, I call the getBufferedImage method and put this image in a BufferedImage. The BufferedImage is then used to construct the ImageViewer. Figure 6-7 shows the sample output of this class.

Example 6-7. *GetFrame.java*

```java
package com.scottpreston.javarobot.chapter6;

import java.awt.Image;
import java.awt.image.BufferedImage;

import javax.media.Buffer;
import javax.media.Manager;
import javax.media.MediaLocator;
import javax.media.Player;
import javax.media.control.FrameGrabbingControl;
import javax.media.format.VideoFormat;
import javax.media.util.BufferToImage;

public class GetFrame {

    private Player player;

    public GetFrame(String url) throws Exception{
```

```java
        player = Manager.createRealizedPlayer( new MediaLocator(url));
        player.start();
        // Wait a few seconds for camera to initialize (otherwise img==null)
        Thread.sleep(2500);
    }

    public Image getAwtImage() throws Exception {
        FrameGrabbingControl frameGrabber = (FrameGrabbingControl) player
                .getControl("javax.media.control.FrameGrabbingControl");
        Buffer buf = frameGrabber.grabFrame();
        Image img = (new BufferToImage((VideoFormat) buf.getFormat())
                .createImage(buf));

        if (img == null) {
            //throw new Exception("Image Null");
            System.exit(1);
        }

        return img;
    }

    public BufferedImage getBufferedImage() throws Exception {
        return (BufferedImage) getAwtImage();
    }


    public void close() throws Exception {
        player.close();
        player.deallocate();
    }

    public static void main(String[] args) {
        try {
            GetFrame getFrame = new GetFrame("vfw://0");
            BufferedImage img = getFrame.getBufferedImage();
            getFrame.close();
            ImageViewer viewer = new ImageViewer(img);

        } catch (Exception e) {
            e.printStackTrace();
            System.exit(0);
        }
    }
}
```

Figure 6-7. *GetFrame with RGB samples (Coke, 7-Up, and Pepsi)*

Displaying one frame isn't of much use. In order to do some processing, it would be nice to get more than one image, and it would be even better to get a few images per second.

Code Objective

The objective here is to display more than one frame and see live video in a JFrame.

Code Discussion

In this class, I'll use our GetFrame class, but I'll need to get those frames at an interval using a timer.

The class extends SimpleSwing, where the fields are the timer, getFrame, imagePanel, and a constant for the default URL for your webcam called DEFAULT_CAMERA. The constructors populate the DEFAULT_CAMERA or one sent in the constructor, and then call the init() method.

The init() method does the same as the ImageViewer, except it schedules the getPic() task to run. The method getPic() sets the image from the getFrame.getBufferedImage() method into the imagePanel.

The next two methods are start() and stop(). I added these for greater control regarding when the camera is processing and when it's not.

Later, I'll extend this class to include some image processing. To do this, I'll add two assessors—getFrame() and getFps()—and one setter setFps(). See Example 6-8.

Example 6-8. *WebCamViewer.java*

```
package com.scottpreston.javarobot.chapter6;

import java.awt.BorderLayout;
import java.util.Timer;
import java.util.TimerTask;

import com.scottpreston.javarobot.chapter2.Utils;
```

```java
public class WebCamViewer extends SimpleSwing {

    private Timer timer = new Timer();
    private GetFrame getFrame;
    private ImagePanel imagePanel;
    private int fps = 15;
    public static final String DEFAULT_CAMERA = "vfw://0";

    public WebCamViewer() throws Exception {
        init(DEFAULT_CAMERA);
    }

    public WebCamViewer(String camera) throws Exception{
        init(camera);
    }

    private void init(String camera) throws Exception{
        setTitle("WebCamViewer");
        // creates frame grabber
        getFrame = new GetFrame(camera);
        int w = 320;
        int h = 240;
        imagePanel =  new ImagePanel(w,h);
        // set size of the window
        setSize(w + 8, h+35);
        // add imagePanel
        getContentPane().add(imagePanel,BorderLayout.CENTER);
        // make visible
        setVisible(true);
    }

    // start the camera frame capture
    public void start() {

        timer.schedule(new TimerTask() {
            public void run() {
                getPic();
            }
        }, 200, (int)(1000 / fps));
    }

    // stop the camera frame capture
    public void stop() throws Exception{
        timer.cancel();
    }
```

```java
// get frame from GetFrame
public void getPic() {
    try {
        // set to image panel and repaint called from ImagePanel
        imagePanel.setImage(getFrame.getBufferedImage());
    } catch (Exception e) {
        e.printStackTrace();
        System.exit(1);
    }
}
// get the frame grabber
public GetFrame getGetFrame() {
    return getFrame;
}
// get frames per second
public int getFps() {
    return fps;
}
//sets frames per second
public void setFps(int fps) {
    this.fps = fps;
}


public static void main(String[] args) {
    try {

        WebCamViewer webcam = new WebCamViewer();
        webcam.start();
        Utils.pause(2000);
        webcam.stop();
    } catch (Exception e) {
        e.printStackTrace();
        System.exit(0);
    }
}
}
```

Section Summary

In this section, I used the Java Media Framework to get an image from a webcam and display it inside a viewer. Classes created in this section were

- FindCamera: Tests the JMF installation

- GetFrame: Gets a frame from the webcam

- WebCamViewer: Gets successive frames from the webcam at a defined interval

Now that we have images that can be processed, it's time to start processing them.

6.2 Basic Image Processing

There are many types of image processing. I would like to classify the processing into three types: pixel processing, area processing, and convolution and combination processing.

Pixel processing is the process of moving through an image pixel by pixel, getting a color value, and doing something with it. Many times, you'll need to remember values and place them in storage arrays. For example, take Figure 6-8. There are nine pixels. If I move from left to right and top to bottom, PixelProcessing would look at each of the color components and do something with them. So, if I wanted to turn them to grey, the pixel at (1,0) would have an RGB value of (255 + 0 + 0) / 3 = 85, and the resultant color would be (85,85,85).

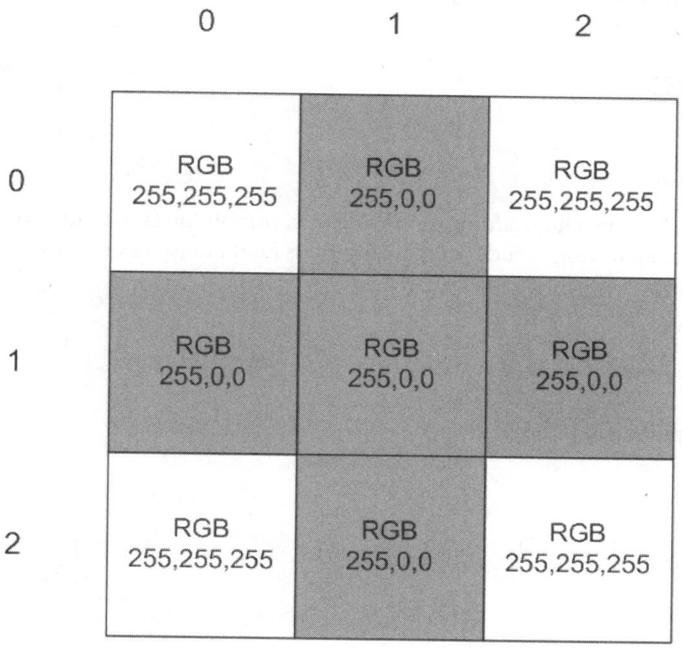

	0	1	2
0	RGB 255,255,255	RGB 255,0,0	RGB 255,255,255
1	RGB 255,0,0	RGB 255,0,0	RGB 255,0,0
2	RGB 255,255,255	RGB 255,0,0	RGB 255,255,255

Figure 6-8. *A pixel-by-pixel image*

The second type is *convolution*. This is the process of moving through an image pixel by pixel, and then doing something with it in relation to its surrounding pixels. This is done via an operator called a *kernel*. A kernel is a matrix of numbers that specify how to change the value of a single pixel as a function of its surrounding pixels. You can think of a kernel as a template that fits over each pixel and then changes it based on the values inside it. A sample matrix for smoothing an image would be

```
{1/9, 1/9, 1/9,
1/9, 1/9, 1/9,
1/9, 1/9, 1/9}
```

The calculation process moves like this. Let's start at the fifth (or center) pixel. Multiply the pixel at its top left by 1/9, then move to the pixel to the right of that, which is above the center pixel, and multiply that by 1/9. Continue this until all surrounding pixels are calculated. Afterward, add the results. You get something like

```
255 * (9/9), 255 * 4/9, 255 * 4/9 = 255, 113,113
```

which is slightly pink.

The third type is *combination processing*. This is the process of performing multiple pixel and/or convolution operations on an image at once to complete the process. For example, sometimes you might want to perform operation A before operation B, but lighting conditions might make you want to perform another operation C. Now, depending on the number of filters you have creating methods for all these combinations—and combinations of combinations—it can get downright confusing.

What I have done to simplify this is to create a FilterParameter object that will contain the following information:

- A BufferedImage to process

- The name of the filter

- An ArrayList of parameters

By creating a generic object, I can facilitate adding, removing, and combining any number of filters for a specific operation without having to code separate methods for them (see Example 6-9).

Example 6-9. *FilterParamters.java*

```java
package com.scottpreston.javarobot.chapter6;

import java.awt.image.BufferedImage;
import java.util.ArrayList;


public class FilterParameters {

    // name to identify
    private String name;
    // image to work with
    private BufferedImage image;
    // parameters
    private ArrayList parameters = new ArrayList();

    // constructor
    public FilterParameters(String n) {
        name = n;
    }

    public BufferedImage getImage() {
        return image;
    }
```

```
    public void setImage(BufferedImage image) {
        this.image = image;
    }

    public ArrayList getParameters() {
        return parameters;
    }

    public void addParameters(Object parameter) {
        parameters.add(parameter);
    }

    public String getName() {
        return name;
    }
}
```

Next, for basic image processing, I'll perform the following operations:

- Change an image to greyscale (pixel)

- Threshold an image (pixel)

- Resize an image (area)

- Detect motion (pixel)

But to render these, I want to create a class that displays two images. The first is the original image from the webcam, and the second is the image after it's processed. While you need to do this for your robot, it's nice for debugging.

Code Objective

The code objective in this section is to create a class that can view the images before and after they are processed.

Code Discussion

First, I'll reuse the WebCamViewer created in the last section by extending it. The fields in this class are two ImagePanels: one for the original image and one for the processed image. The final field is an ArrayList that I'll use to keep the list of FilterParameters.

The constructor calls super() for the camera and then calls init2(), which initializes the current class to a later size and adds the two panels side by side.

The getPic() method from the parent class is overloaded so I can, one, set the current image into the srcPanel, and two, call the doProcessing() method for the dstPanel. By overriding the parent method, I can reuse the call to getPic() from the timer created in the parent class.

The doProcessing() method creates a class ImageProcessor, and then based on the number of filters in the list, it iterates and processes all the filters before returning the image to the getPic() method, where it can be set in the dstPanel or right pane.

The main example converts the image on the left from color to greyscale, which is shown in Example 6-10.

Example 6-10. *DoubleWebCamViewer.java*

```java
package com.scottpreston.javarobot.chapter6;

import java.awt.image.BufferedImage;
import java.util.ArrayList;

import javax.swing.Box;
import javax.swing.BoxLayout;

public class DoubleWebCamViewer extends WebCamViewer {

    // source / original image
    private ImagePanel srcPanel = new ImagePanel();
    // destination image
    private ImagePanel dstPanel = new ImagePanel();
    // filters (list of FilterParameters)
    private ArrayList filters = new ArrayList();

    // constructor with no camera
    public DoubleWebCamViewer() throws Exception {
        super(DEFAULT_CAMERA);
        // separate init method
        init2();
    }

    // constructor with camera name
    public DoubleWebCamViewer(String camera) throws Exception {
        super(camera);
        // separate init method
        init2();
    }

    // common initialization block
    public void init2() throws Exception {
        setTitle("Double Webcam Viewer");
        // set frame properties
        this.setSize(648, 270);
        Box box = new Box(BoxLayout.X_AXIS);
        box.add(srcPanel);
        box.add(dstPanel);
        // clear contents added in parent
        this.getContentPane().removeAll();
```

```java
        // add new panels
        this.getContentPane().add(box);
        // show
        this.show();
    }

    // get picture where two panels are set and processing is called
    public void getPic() {
        try {

            BufferedImage bimg = getGetFrame().getBufferedImage();
            // image to left panel
            srcPanel.setImage(bimg);
            // image to right panel
            dstPanel.setImage(doProcessing(bimg));
        } catch (Exception e) {
            e.printStackTrace();
            System.exit(1);
        }
    }

    // add filters
    public void addFilter(FilterParameters filter) {
        filters.add(filter);
    }

    // processes all filters
    public BufferedImage doProcessing(BufferedImage bimg) {
        ImageProcessor imageProcessor = new ImageProcessor();
        for (int f = 0; f < filters.size(); f++) {
            FilterParameters parms = (FilterParameters) filters.get(f);
            parms.setImage(bimg);
            bimg = imageProcessor.process(parms);
        }

        return bimg;
    }

    // sample program with two filters
    public static void main(String[] args) {
        try {
            DoubleWebCamViewer webcam = new DoubleWebCamViewer();
            webcam.addFilter(new FilterParameters(ImageProcessor.FILTER_RGB_TO_GREY));
            webcam.start();
```

```
        } catch (Exception e) {
            e.printStackTrace();
            System.exit(0);
        }
    }

}
```

Code Objective

The code objective here is to convert an image from an RGB image to a greyscale image.

Code Discussion

The class containing all the image processing methods is called ImageProcessor. I've created a factory method in this class called process(), which takes a FilterParameter called parms, and then depending on its value, it calls the individual processing method. This is very similar to the Java Advanced Imaging ParameterBlock and JAI.create() methods. See Example 6-11.

Example 6-11. *ImageProcessor.java*

```java
package com.scottpreston.javarobot.chapter6;

import java.awt.Color;
import java.awt.Graphics2D;
import java.awt.Image;
import java.awt.RenderingHints;
import java.awt.Toolkit;
import java.awt.geom.AffineTransform;
import java.awt.image.BufferedImage;
import java.awt.image.renderable.ParameterBlock;

import javax.media.jai.Histogram;
import javax.media.jai.JAI;
import javax.media.jai.KernelJAI;
import javax.media.jai.PlanarImage;

public class ImageProcessor {

    private BufferedImage lastImage;

    public static final String FILTER_RGB_TO_GREY = "1";
    public static final String FILTER_MOTION = "2";
    public static final String FILTER_COLOR = "3";
    public static final String FILTER_THRESHHOLD = "4";
    public static final String FILTER_THRESHHOLD_COLOR = "5";
    public static final String FILTER_COLOR_RATIO = "6";
    public static final String FILTER_EDGE = "7";
```

```java
public static final String FILTER_SMOOTH = "8";
public static final String FILTER_SHARP = "9";
public static final String FILTER_RESIZE = "10";
public static final String FILTER_HOUGH_LINES = "11";

// generic method for processing
public BufferedImage process(FilterParameters parms) {
    BufferedImage dstImg = null;
    if (parms.getName().equalsIgnoreCase(FILTER_RGB_TO_GREY)) {
        dstImg = rgbToGrey(parms.getImage());
    }
    if (parms.getName().equalsIgnoreCase(FILTER_MOTION)) {
        dstImg = backgroundSubtract(parms.getImage());
    }
    if (parms.getName().equalsIgnoreCase(FILTER_THRESHHOLD)) {
        int min = ((Integer) parms.getParameters().get(0)).intValue();
        int max = ((Integer) parms.getParameters().get(1)).intValue();
        Boolean transparent = Boolean.FALSE;
        if (parms.getParameters().get(2) != null) {
            transparent = (Boolean) parms.getParameters().get(2);
        }
        dstImg = threshold(parms.getImage(), min, max,➥
transparent.booleanValue());
    }
    if (parms.getName().equalsIgnoreCase(FILTER_THRESHHOLD_COLOR)) {
        int min = ((Integer) parms.getParameters().get(0)).intValue();
        int max = ((Integer) parms.getParameters().get(1)).intValue();
        Color c = (Color) parms.getParameters().get(2);
        dstImg = thresholdColor(parms.getImage(), min, max, c);
    }
    if (parms.getName().equalsIgnoreCase(FILTER_COLOR)) {
        Color c = (Color) parms.getParameters().get(0);
        dstImg = filterColor(parms.getImage(), c);
    }
    if (parms.getName().equalsIgnoreCase(FILTER_COLOR_RATIO)) {
        ColorGram cg = (ColorGram) parms.getParameters().get(0);
        dstImg = colorRatio(parms.getImage(), cg);
    }
    if (parms.getName().equalsIgnoreCase(FILTER_EDGE)) {
        dstImg = sobelGradMag(parms.getImage());
    }
    if (parms.getName().equalsIgnoreCase(FILTER_SMOOTH)) {
        dstImg = smooth(parms.getImage());
    }
    if (parms.getName().equalsIgnoreCase(FILTER_SHARP)) {
        dstImg = sharpen(parms.getImage());
    }
```

```
    if (parms.getName().equalsIgnoreCase(FILTER_RESIZE)) {
        int w = ((Integer) parms.getParameters().get(0)).intValue();
        int h = ((Integer) parms.getParameters().get(1)).intValue();
        dstImg = resize(parms.getImage(), w, h);
    }
    if (parms.getName().equalsIgnoreCase(FILTER_HOUGH_LINES)) {
        dstImg = getHoughLines(parms.getImage());
    }

    return dstImg;
}
```

. . . .

```
}
```

In the rgbToGrey() method, I iterate through each pixel of the image and get its color. I then average the Red, Green, and Blue components of the color to get a grey via the first getGrey method. Then, by setting all three color components to this average, you get a 256-color greyscale image of the original. You can see the output of Example 6-12 in Figure 6-9.

Example 6-12. *rgbToGrey(), getGrey()*

```
// to greyscale image
public BufferedImage rgbToGrey(BufferedImage srcImg) {

    int h = srcImg.getHeight();
    int w = srcImg.getWidth();

    BufferedImage dstImg = new BufferedImage(w, h, BufferedImage.TYPE_INT_RGB);

    for (int y = 0; y < h; ++y) {
        for (int x = 0; x < w; ++x) {
            int srcPixel = srcImg.getRGB(x, y);
            Color c = new Color(srcPixel);
            Color g = getGrey(c);
            dstImg.setRGB(x, y, g.getRGB());
        }
    }
    return dstImg;
}

// return greyscale equivalent of pixel as color
public Color getGrey(Color color) {
    int r = color.getRed();
    int g = color.getGreen();
    int b = color.getBlue();
    int gray = (int) ((r + g + b) / 3.0);
```

```
        return new Color(gray, gray, gray);
    }

    //return greyscale equivalent of pixel as int
    public int getGrey(int colorInt) {
        return getGrey(new Color(colorInt)).getRed();
    }
```

Figure 6-9. *A color image converted to GreyScale*

One of the things you might notice from the last example is that iterating through 320×240 pixels might be really fast for converting to grey, but not if you're using a few different filters and hope to maintain your desired frame rate. Currently, it takes about 63 milliseconds from the start of this method to the end. Since the frame rate is 15 frames per second, the maximum processing time per frame is 67 milliseconds. We're getting close. If I add a 10-millisecond pause in the middle, I'd notice the frame-rate decrease. We can get around this by resizing the image. By resizing the image from 320×240 to 160×120, the time to process the image is reduced by four to about 15 milliseconds.

Code Objective

The objective in this example is to resize an image.

Code Discussion

This uses the java.awt.Graphics2D class. First, we create a destination image. Second, we give the class rendering hints on how to render the new image. Third, we draw the new, scaled version of the image using the AffineTransformation class. Finally, we return the new image. You can see the results of Example 6-13 in Figure 6-10.

Note You'll see in later sections that if we iterate through all the pixels of an image, resizing them by one-half, it will improve the performance of our algorithm by a minimum of 400 percent.

Example 6-13. *resize()*

```
public BufferedImage resize(BufferedImage srcImg, int targetW, int targetH) {

    // create new bufferedImage
    BufferedImage dstImg = new BufferedImage(targetW, targetH,
            BufferedImage.TYPE_INT_RGB);

    // create new canvas
    Graphics2D g = dstImg.createGraphics();
    g.setBackground(Color.BLACK);
    g.setRenderingHint(RenderingHints.KEY_INTERPOLATION,
            RenderingHints.VALUE_INTERPOLATION_BICUBIC);
    double sx = (double) targetW / srcImg.getWidth();
    double sy = (double) targetH / srcImg.getHeight();
    // draw src image on new object
    g.drawRenderedImage(srcImg, AffineTransform.getScaleInstance(sx, sy));
    g.dispose();
    // return new image
    return dstImg;

}
```

Figure 6-10. *The image resized to 80×60*

Another basic technique used in image processing is a process called *thresholding*. Thresholding is a valuable processing technique used in all types of image processing algorithms. In its basic form, it can be used to remove pixels from their background. When combined with other processing techniques, it's used to identify specific features like edges or lines.

Code Objective

The objective here is to demonstrate thresholding of an image. I'll remove the top half of the colors and convert them to black, leaving the bottom half as white.

Code Discussion

This is the simplest kind of comparison. If the image's greyscale pixel value is within a certain range, then color it white. If it's not in that range, color it black. You can see the output of Example 6-14 in Figure 6-11.

The parameters for this method are of course the source image, the minimum value for the threshold, the maximum value, and then a Boolean to return either the actual color or a binary representation.

Example 6-14. *threshold()*

```
// gets threshold
    public BufferedImage threshold(BufferedImage srcImg, int min, int max,
    boolean transparent) {

        // get h & w
        int h = srcImg.getHeight();
        int w = srcImg.getWidth();
        // new image for processing
        BufferedImage dstImg = new BufferedImage(w, h, BufferedImage.TYPE_INT_RGB);

        for (int y = 0; y < h; ++y) {
            for (int x = 0; x < w; ++x) {
                // get color
                int srcPixel = srcImg.getRGB(x, y);
                // get grey of color
                int colorValue = getGrey(srcPixel);
                // compare to threshold & convert to binary
                if (colorValue >= min && colorValue <= max) {
                    if (transparent) {
                        dstImg.setRGB(x, y, srcPixel);
                    } else{
                        dstImg.setRGB(x, y, Color.WHITE.getRGB());
                    }
                } else {
                    dstImg.setRGB(x, y, Color.BLACK.getRGB());
                }

            }
        }
        return dstImg;
    }
```

Figure 6-11. *Threshold image: 0 min, 127 max*

Next, I want to detect the motion in a webcam. The easiest way to do this is to subtract frames from another. The resulting difference would be a frame of motion. Depending on the number of frames per second, this will determine the size of the image.

Code Objective

The objective here is to detect motion.

Code Discussion

In this case, all we did was store the previous image globally, and then when the next image comes in, we subtract the grey pixel difference. For this to work, I created a class-level field called lastImage. This static image will be set at the end of the method for the next iteration. Also, this will take some time to process, so I've reduced the frames per second to 5. See Example 6-15 and the results in Figure 6-12.

Example 6-15. *backgroundSubtract()*

```
// get motion by subtracting background between current old image
public BufferedImage backgroundSubtract(BufferedImage srcImg) {
    // make sure to set the frames per second to about 5!
    int h = srcImg.getHeight();
    int w = srcImg.getWidth();

    // create dst image
    BufferedImage dstImg = new BufferedImage(w, h, BufferedImage.TYPE_INT_RGB);

    if (lastImage != null) {
        for (int y = 0; y < h; ++y) {
            for (int x = 0; x < w; ++x) {
                // get grey of image
                int srcPixel = getGrey(srcImg.getRGB(x, y));
                // get color of last image
                int diffPixel = getGrey(lastImage.getRGB(x, y));
```

```
        // calculate difference
        int diff = Math.abs(srcPixel - diffPixel);
        // make difference color
        Color diffColor = new Color(diff, diff, diff);
        // set into image
        dstImg.setRGB(x, y, diffColor.getRGB());
      }
    }
  }
  // set last frame
  lastImage = srcImg;
  return dstImg;
}
```

Figure 6-12. *Motion detect*

Section Summary

In this section, we performed some processing and provided a mechanism to add multiple processing operations together. The classes created in this section were

- FilterParameters: Creates a parameter object that can be passed to the ImageProcessor

- DoubleWebCamViewer: Creates a dual-view webcam that shows the original image on one side and the processed image on the other

- ImageProcessor: The class containing all image processing code. We looked at the following methods:

  - ImageProcessor.rgbToGrey(): Converts an image to greyscale

  - ImageProcessor.resize(): Resizes an image

  - ImageProcessor.threshold(): Gets a greyscale color range from a minimum and maximum value

  - ImageProcessor.backgroundSubtract(): Detects motion

Next, it's time to look at some techniques for processing color images.

6.3 Color Processing

In the last section, we processed pixels but did not use their individual color components for anything. To illustrate how we can use the colors of an image, we'll threshold the colors of an image versus the image's greyscale. In the next few examples, I'll threshold three colors—red, green, and blue—for the three beverage cans.

Code Objective

The objective here is to perform a threshold operation on the three different color components.

Code Discussion

This method is similar to thresholding except for the added parameter Color. This color is then used to get the specific color component for the threshold. You can see from the three images that you can almost make out which cans are red, green, and blue. See Example 6-16 and Figures 6-13, 6-14, and 6-15.

Example 6-16. *thresholdColor()*

```java
public BufferedImage thresholdColor(BufferedImage srcImg, int min, int max,
        Color c) {
    // get h & w
    int h = srcImg.getHeight();
    int w = srcImg.getWidth();
    //destination image
    BufferedImage dstImg = new BufferedImage(w, h, BufferedImage.TYPE_INT_RGB);
    // get pixels
    for (int y = 0; y < h; ++y) {
        for (int x = 0; x < w; ++x) {
            // get color
            int srcPixel = srcImg.getRGB(x, y);
            int colorValue = 0;
            // get color values for color sent
            if (c == null) {
                colorValue = getGrey(srcPixel);
            } else if (c == Color.RED) {
                colorValue = new Color(srcPixel).getRed();
            } else if (c == Color.GREEN) {
                colorValue = new Color(srcPixel).getGreen();
            } else if (c == Color.BLUE) {
                colorValue = new Color(srcPixel).getBlue();
            }
```

```
            // filter for color in range
            if (colorValue >= min && colorValue <= max) {
                dstImg.setRGB(x, y, Color.WHITE.getRGB());
            } else {
                dstImg.setRGB(x, y, Color.BLACK.getRGB());
            }

        }
    }
    // return image
    return dstImg;
}
```

Figure 6-13. *The red threshold*

Figure 6-14. *The green threshold*

Figure 6-15. *The blue threshold*

Still another way to use color is to filter it. So, rather than getting certain color components, I'll just show certain colors as greyscale images.

Code Objective

In this section, the objective is to use a color filter to show only the red pixels of an image in greyscale, where higher reds appear white, and lower reds appear black.

Code Discussion

Here, instead of thresholding, we're just converting the red components of an image into greyscale. See Example 6-17 and Figure 6-16.

Example 6-17. *filterColor()*

```
public BufferedImage filterColor(BufferedImage srcImg, Color c) {
        int h = srcImg.getHeight();
        int w = srcImg.getWidth();

        BufferedImage dstImg = new BufferedImage(w, h, BufferedImage.TYPE_INT_RGB);

        for (int y = 0; y < h; ++y) {
            for (int x = 0; x < w; ++x) {
                int srcPixel = srcImg.getRGB(x, y);
                int colorValue = 0;
                // gets colors
                if (c == null) {
                    colorValue = getGrey(srcPixel);
                } else if (c == Color.RED) {
                    colorValue = new Color(srcPixel).getRed();
```

```
        } else if (c == Color.GREEN) {
            colorValue = new Color(srcPixel).getGreen();
        } else if (c == Color.BLUE) {
            colorValue = new Color(srcPixel).getBlue();
        }
        // set that color as grey version
        dstImg.setRGB(x, y, new Color(colorValue, colorValue, colorValue)
                .getRGB());
        }
    }
    // return image
    return dstImg;
}
```

Figure 6-16. *The red filter*

One way to study the color of an image is by computing image statistics. If I wanted to find the average red, average green, or average blue of an image, there are two ways to do it: I can go through pixel by pixel and count the colors, or I can use Java Advanced Imaging.

Code Objective

The objective in this example is to calculate the average red, green, and blue values of an image pixel by pixel.

Code Discussion

I've found this method to be slightly faster than using Java Advanced Imaging. The following method sums all the color values of the image together and then divides the quantities by the total pixels in the image. See Example 6-18.

Example 6-18. *getMean()*

```java
public int[] getMean(BufferedImage srcImg) {

        int h = srcImg.getHeight();
        int w = srcImg.getWidth();

        BufferedImage dstImg = new BufferedImage(w, h, BufferedImage.TYPE_INT_RGB);

        double red = 0;
        double green = 0;
        double blue = 0;

        for (int y = 0; y < h; ++y) {
            for (int x = 0; x < w; ++x) {
                int srcPixel = srcImg.getRGB(x, y);
                // tally total colors for 3 components
                red = red + new Color(srcPixel).getRed();
                green = green + new Color(srcPixel).getGreen();
                blue = blue + new Color(srcPixel).getBlue();
            }
        }
        // get averages
        int redAvg = (int) (red / (h * w));
        int greenAvg = (int) (green / (h * w));
        int blueAvg = (int) (blue / (h * w));
        System.out.println("color mean=" + redAvg + "," + greenAvg + "," + blueAvg);
        return new int[] { redAvg, greenAvg, blueAvg };
    }
```

Code Objective

The objective here is to calculate the average red, green, and blue values of the image, using the javax.media.jai.Histogram class.

Code Discussion

The first thing we do is set the number of bins and the minimum and maximum of the histograms. Then we construct the histogram with those parameters. After that, we create a parameter block for the operation. This is very similar to what I did with the FilterParameter class.

Next because Java Advanced Images uses PlanarImages instead of BufferedImages, we have to create an output image to perform the operation. Once the operation completes, we simply extract the histogram property from the output image and get the mean values for the red, green, and blue of the image before writing the output to System.out. See Example 6-19.

Example 6-19. *getHistogram();*

```java
public int[] getHistogram(BufferedImage bufImg) {
        // Set up the parameters for the Histogram object.
        int[] bins = { 256, 256, 256 }; // The number of bins.
        double[] low = { 0.0D, 0.0D, 0.0D }; // The low value.
        double[] high = { 256.0D, 256.0D, 256.0D }; // The high value.

        // Construct the Histogram object.
        Histogram hist = new Histogram(bins, low, high);

        // Create the parameter block.
        ParameterBlock pb = new ParameterBlock();
        pb.addSource(bufImg); // Specify the source image
        pb.add(null); // No ROI
        pb.add(1); // Sampling
        pb.add(1); // periods

        // Perform the histogram operation.
        PlanarImage output = (PlanarImage) JAI.create("histogram", pb, null);

        // Retrieve the histogram data.
        hist = (Histogram) output.getProperty("histogram");

        // Print 3-band histogram.
        int[] mean = new int[] {(int)hist.getMean()[0],
                (int)hist.getMean()[1],(int)hist.getMean()[2]};
        System.out.println("histogram2=" + mean[0] + "," + mean[1] + ","
                + mean[2]);
        return mean;
    }
```

Getting the mean values helps us compute the desired color of an image. From Example 6-17 with colorFilter(), knowing that you first want the red, and second the green, and third the blue can help you optimize the filter to give you an exact color.

What I've found through experimentation is that it's not so much the colors that make a difference, but their relationship to each other that's important. So instead, I'll create a class called a ColorGram that represents not only the colors, but also the ratio of those colors to one another.

Code Objective

The objective here is to create a class that represents colors and their ratios to one another.

Code Discussion

The ColorGram class itself is nothing more than a data structure. I have constructed it such that the combination of any target ColorGram is the function of all the colors in this form: x * red + y * green + z * blue + c, where red, green, and blue are the colors of a pixel, and x, y, z, and c are the values of the ColorGram.

The function isMatch() just checks the current pixel color to see if it's in the range of the ColorGram's minimum and maximum values. When it is, it returns true.

The very last method of the class is clone(). Here I'm creating an exact copy of the ColorGram. Later in this section, I'll continuously modify and optimize a ColorGram object, but right now I just want to optimize the value of the ColorGram, so by cloning it I can get an exact copy without making changes to its reference. See Example 6-20.

Example 6-20. *ColorGram.java*

```java
package com.scottpreston.javarobot.chapter6;

import java.awt.Color;

public class ColorGram implements Cloneable{

    private double[] colorGram;

    public ColorGram() {
    // blank
        colorGram = new double[] {
                0, 0, 0, 0, // min
                0, 0, 0, 255, // max red color
                0, 0, 0, 0, // min green color
                0, 0, 0, 255, // max green color
                0, 0, 0, 0, // min blue color
                0, 0, 0, 255 };
    }


    public ColorGram(double[] cg) {
        colorGram = cg;
    }

    public int getRedMin(Color c) {
        return getColor(c, 0);
    }

    public int getRedMax(Color c) {
        return getColor(c, 4);
    }
```

```java
    public int getGreenMin(Color c) {
        return getColor(c, 8);
    }

    public int getGreenMax(Color c) {
        return getColor(c, 12);
    }

    public int getBlueMin(Color c) {
        return getColor(c, 16);
    }

    public int getBlueMax(Color c) {
        return getColor(c, 20);
    }

    public double getIndex(int index) {
        return colorGram[index];
    }
    public void setMins(int[] mins) {
        colorGram[3] = mins[0]; // red
        colorGram[3+8] = mins[1]; // green
        colorGram[3+16] = mins[2]; // blue
    }

    public void setMaxs(int[] maxs) {
        colorGram[7] = maxs[0]; // red
        colorGram[7+8] = maxs[1]; // green
        colorGram[7+16] = maxs[2]; // blue
    }

    // column == r,g,b if primary color
    // row = r,g,b of secondary color
    // constant value
    public void setRatio(int column, int row, double value) {
        // rows will be 2,4,6
        colorGram[(column + ((row-1)*4))-1] = 1;
        colorGram[(row*4) -1] = value;
    }


    private int getColor(Color c, int index) {
        int out = (int) (c.getRed() * colorGram[index]
                + c.getGreen() * colorGram[index + 1]
                + c.getBlue() * colorGram[index + 2]
                + colorGram[index + 3]);
```

```
            if (out > 255)
                out = 255;
            if (out < 0)
                out = 0;

            return out;
        }

        public String toString() {
            StringBuffer out = new StringBuffer("ColorGram =   {\n");
            for (int x = 0; x < colorGram.length; x++) {
                out.append(colorGram[x]);
                if ((x % 4) == 3) {
                    if (x == colorGram.length) {
                        out.append("\n");
                    } else {
                        out.append(",\n");
                    }
                } else {
                    out.append(",");
                }
            }
            out.append("}");
            return out.toString();
        }

        public boolean isMatch(Color c) {

            boolean hit = false;
            int count = 0;
            // eliminate black since it's 0
            if (c.getRed() > getRedMin(c) && c.getRed() <= getRedMax(c)) {
                count++;
            }
            if (c.getGreen() > getGreenMin(c) && c.getGreen() <= getGreenMax(c)) {
                count++;
            }
            if (c.getBlue() > getBlueMin(c) && c.getBlue() <= getBlueMax(c)) {
                count++;
            }
            if (count > 2) {
                hit = true;
            }
            return hit;
        }
```

```
public double[] getColorGram() {
    return colorGram;
}
public void setColorGram(double[] colorGram) {
    this.colorGram = colorGram;
}

public Object clone() {
    double[] newCg = new double[24];
    for (int d=0;d<24;d++) {
        newCg[d] = colorGram[d];
    }
    return new ColorGram(newCg);
}
}
```

In Example 6-21, this is the filter applied in the ImageProcessing class. Again, it's very similar to the thresholding class, except I call isMatch() by passing in the ColorGram.

Example 6-21. *ImageProcessing.colorRatio() and colorRatioCount()*

```
public BufferedImage colorRatio(BufferedImage srcImg, ColorGram cg) {

    int h = srcImg.getHeight();
    int w = srcImg.getWidth();

    BufferedImage dstImg = new BufferedImage(w, h, BufferedImage.TYPE_INT_RGB);

    for (int y = 0; y < h; ++y) {
        for (int x = 0; x < w; ++x) {
            int srcPixel = srcImg.getRGB(x, y);
            Color c = new Color(srcPixel);
            // calls hard work done here.
            if (cg.isMatch(c)) {
                // for real color
                dstImg.setRGB(x, y, c.getRGB());
                // for binary color
                //dstImg.setRGB(x, y, Color.BLACK.getRGB());
            } else {
                dstImg.setRGB(x, y, Color.BLACK.getRGB());
            }

        }
    }
    return dstImg;
}
```

```
public int colorRatioCount(BufferedImage srcImg, ColorGram cg) {

    int h = srcImg.getHeight();
    int w = srcImg.getWidth();
    int count = 0;
    BufferedImage dstImg = new BufferedImage(w, h, BufferedImage.TYPE_INT_RGB);

    for (int y = 0; y < h; ++y) {
        for (int x = 0; x < w; ++x) {
            int srcPixel = srcImg.getRGB(x, y);
            Color c = new Color(srcPixel);
            if (cg.isMatch(c)) {
                count++;
            }
        }
    }
    return count;
}
```

These sample ColorGrams represent the cans of soda. In the first ColorGram, you see that red is optimized with two thresholds: 104 and 158. Second, the green thresholds are set so that they're 22 points lower than the red pixel. Third, the blue threshold is 31 points lower than the red pixel.

For the 7-Up, the optimized color is green, followed by the tuning of red and blue with respect to the green pixel. And finally for Pepsi, the optimized color is blue, followed by the tuning of the red and green pixels with respect to blue. See Example 6-22 and Figures 6-17 through 6-19.

Example 6-22. *Sample ColorGrams (Coke, 7-Up, and Pepsi)*

```
public static ColorGram COKE = new ColorGram (new double[] {
            0.0,0.0,0.0,104.0,
            0.0,0.0,0.0,158.0,
            0.0,0.0,0.0,0.0,
            1.0,0.0,0.0,-22.0,
            0.0,0.0,0.0,0.0,
            1.0,0.0,0.0,-31.0
            });

public static ColorGram SEVEN_UP = new ColorGram (new double[] {
            0.0,0.0,0.0,0.0,
            0.0,1.0,0.0,-38.0,
            0.0,0.0,0.0,90.0,
            0.0,0.0,0.0,147.0,
            0.0,0.0,0.0,0.0,
            0.0,1.0,0.0,-6.0
            });
```

```
public static ColorGram PEPSI = new ColorGram (new double[] {
            0.0,0.0,0.0,0.0,
            0.0,0.0,1.0,-26.0,
            0.0,0.0,0.0,0.0,
            0.0,0.0,1.0,-19.0,
            0.0,0.0,0.0,87.0,
            0.0,0.0,0.0,162.0
            });
```

Figure 6-17. *The Coke ColorGram*

Figure 6-18. *The 7-Up ColorGram*

Figure 6-19. *The Pepsi ColorGram*

You might be wondering how I came up with these numbers. Well, at first I experimented until I got a match. Then I wrote a program to help create the ColorGram from a cropped image.

To get the three images for the three cans, I used an image editor and cropped just the target image. Then I wrote a program that would optimize the cropped image until it gave me the desired color ratio most prominent in the sample image.

Code Objective

The objective here is to create a ColorGram calibration program.

Code Discussion

In this class, I have 11 fields: currentImage, which is the current image loaded from the filename passed to the constructor; ImagePanel, to display and repaint the image as it changes; maxCount, which will be used to count pixels in a particular color range; the array meanValues and redAvg, greenAvg, and blueAvg to hold the averages of the primary colors and order them from most color to least color; a threshold value to determine what percentage of the image it should be optimized to; and finally, bestColorGram, which is the optimized, processed ColorGram and ImageProcessor used to perform the ColorRatio and ColorRatioCount on the sampled images.

I overloaded the constructor to take an optional Boolean value. This tells the class whether or not to show the GUI component. The constructor with no parameter defaults to true. Then it sends the filename and the toShow parameter to init().

During init(), the class gets the file as it did in ImageViewer, but I also process the image getting the top-bottom 150 greyscale colors from the image. This removes the background of the object I'm looking for without any modification to the image via the image editor. Next, I get the mean values of the remaining colors. After that, I construct the image panel with the image dimensions. Then I set the other frame properties and add an Exit Listener before I show it.

The next method called is optimize(). This looks at the colors and sorts them. If any are equal, then I increment the values of the second color by one so I can create an order for the colors: RED, GREEN, and BLUE.

Next, I take my primary color and move the minimum value up until I still have 95 percent of the colors I want. Then I move down from the maximum until I have 95 percent of that image; this should be 90 percent of the original.

Finally, I move the ratios from the second and third colors down to 50 percent of the pixels. I don't want that many of these colors, so the percentage is lower.

The methods optmizeMin(), optmizeMax(), and optmizeRatio() call doProcessing() with a ColorGram as modified by their descriptors.

The doProcessing() method calls colorRatioCount(), shown after Example 6-23, where the total colors in the ColorGram are counted and returned as an int. The first reading will always be the highest, so this is set as the maxCount. Then during each successive call, the threshold is measured as a percentage of the maxCount, and the total colors are compared. If the number is greater than the percentage, I save the ColorGram as my bestColorGram. This is where I used the clone() method because I keep sending in a new cg (ColorGram), and if I would have set it to the instance created in the optimize methods, it would change as well.

In main(), I feed a sample image of the Coke can, and then the program creates the ColorGram. See Figure 6-20.

Example 6-23. *ColorGramCalibration.java*

```java
package com.scottpreston.javarobot.chapter6;

import java.awt.BorderLayout;
import java.awt.Color;
import java.awt.image.BufferedImage;
import java.io.FileInputStream;
import java.util.Arrays;

import javax.swing.JFrame;

import com.sun.image.codec.jpeg.JPEGCodec;
import com.sun.image.codec.jpeg.JPEGImageDecoder;

public class ColorGramCalibration extends JFrame {

    // image to calibrate
    private BufferedImage currentImage;
    // panel to hold image
    private ImagePanel imagePanel;
    // count of colors
    private int maxCount = 0;
    // values of histogram mean values
    private int[] meanValues;
    // current best ColorGram
    private ColorGram bestColorGram = new ColorGram();
    // mean values for color components
    private int redAvg = 0;
    private int greenAvg = 0;
    private int blueAvg = 0;
    // initial threshold
    private double threshhold = .95;
    // to display or not
    private boolean toShow = true;
    private ImageProcessor imageProcessor = new ImageProcessor();

    public ColorGramCalibration(String fileName) throws Exception {
        init(fileName, true);
    }

    public ColorGramCalibration(String fileName, boolean gui) throws Exception {
        init(fileName, gui);
    }
```

```java
    private void init(String fileName, boolean toShow) throws Exception{
        setTitle("ColorGram Calibration");
        FileInputStream fis = new FileInputStream(fileName);
        JPEGImageDecoder decoder = JPEGCodec.createJPEGDecoder(fis);
        currentImage = decoder.decodeAsBufferedImage();
        // get important part of image, not background, which is white
        currentImage = imageProcessor.threshold(currentImage, 0, 150, true);
        // gets mean values
        meanValues = imageProcessor.getMean(currentImage);
        // used later
        redAvg = meanValues[0];
        greenAvg = meanValues[1];
        blueAvg = meanValues[2];

        // init panel
        imagePanel = new ImagePanel(currentImage.getWidth(), ➥
currentImage.getHeight());

        // set frame properties
        WindowUtilities.setNativeLookAndFeel();
        addWindowListener(new ExitListener());
        setBackground(Color.BLACK); // gets image
        setSize(currentImage.getWidth() + 8, currentImage.getHeight() + 30);
        getContentPane().add(imagePanel, BorderLayout.CENTER);
        if (toShow) {
            setVisible(true);
            show();
        }
    }
    // processing called from optimize methods
    private void doProcessing(ColorGram cg) {
        // get maximum color ratio count for image and colorgram passed
        int max = imageProcessor.colorRatioCount(currentImage, cg);
        // if zero initialize count
        if (maxCount == 0) {
            maxCount = max;
        }
        // get threshold for colors to be counted
        double maxThresh = maxCount * threshhold;
        // if current color count greater than threshhold, set as best colorgram
        if (max > maxThresh) {
            currentImage = imageProcessor.colorRatio(currentImage, cg);
            // since cg is changing and by reference
            bestColorGram = (ColorGram) cg.clone();
        }
```

```java
        // set image
        imagePanel.setImage(currentImage);


}


    // move primary color minimum value up
    public void optimizeMin(Color color) {
        int min = 0;
        for (min = 0; min < 256; min++) {
            ColorGram tempColorGram = new ColorGram();
            int[] rgb = null;
            // checks to see what color is primary
            if (color.equals(Color.RED)) {
                rgb = new int[] { min, 0, 0 };
            }
            if (color.equals(Color.GREEN)) {
                rgb = new int[] { 0, min, 0 };
            }
            if (color.equals(Color.BLUE)) {
                rgb = new int[] { 0, 0, min };
            }
            // adjust colorgram
            tempColorGram.setMins(rgb);
            // process colorgram in image
            doProcessing(tempColorGram);
        }
    }

    // move maximum of primary color down to threshold
    public void optimizeMax(Color color) {

        // reset max count
        maxCount = 0;
        // make sure I start with copy of current best colorgram (getting min
        // value)
        ColorGram tempColorGram = (ColorGram) getBestColorGram().clone();
        int max = 255;
        for (max = 255; max > 0; max--) {
            int[] rgb = null;
            if (color.equals(Color.RED)) {
                rgb = new int[] { max, 255, 255 };
            }
            if (color.equals(Color.GREEN)) {
                rgb = new int[] { 255, max, 255 };
            }
```

```
            if (color.equals(Color.BLUE)) {
                rgb = new int[] { 255, 255, max };
            }
            tempColorGram.setMaxs(rgb);
            doProcessing(tempColorGram);
        }
    }

    // get ratio of two colors
    public void optmizeRatio(Color primaryColor, Color secondaryColor) {
        // get copy of current best colorgram
        ColorGram tempColorGram = (ColorGram) getBestColorGram().clone();
        // value of ratio
        int value = 0;
        // what color (r,g,b)
        int column = 0;
        // what min/max value of component r,g,b
        int row = 0;
        // move values from 0 to 255
        for (value = 0; value < 255; value++) {
            if (primaryColor.equals(Color.RED)) {
                column = 1;
            }
            if (primaryColor.equals(Color.GREEN)) {
                column = 2;
            }
            if (primaryColor.equals(Color.BLUE)) {
                column = 3;
            }
            if (secondaryColor.equals(Color.RED)) {
                row = 2;
            }
            if (secondaryColor.equals(Color.GREEN)) {
                row = 4;
            }
            if (secondaryColor.equals(Color.BLUE)) {
                row = 6;
            }
            tempColorGram.setRatio(column, row, -value);
            doProcessing(tempColorGram);
        }
    }
```

```
// optimization
public void optimize() {
    // sort values getting order of most color, 2nd and 3rd
    Arrays.sort(meanValues);
    Color[] colors = new Color[3];
    // correct in case they are equal.
    if (meanValues[0] == meanValues[1]) {
        meanValues[1]++;
    }
    if (meanValues[0] == meanValues[2]) {
        meanValues[2]++;
    }
    if (meanValues[1] == meanValues[2]) {
        meanValues[2]++;
    }
    for (int i = 0; i < 3; i++) {
        if (meanValues[i] == redAvg) {
            colors[2 - i] = Color.RED;
        }
        if (meanValues[i] == greenAvg) {
            colors[2 - i] = Color.GREEN;
        }
        if (meanValues[i] == blueAvg) {
            colors[2 - i] = Color.BLUE;
        }
    }
    // go in this order
    // i want most of primary color
    threshhold = .95;
    optimizeMin(colors[0]);
    System.out.println("done min");
    optimizeMax(colors[0]);
    System.out.println("done max");
    // i don't want much of 2nd and 3rd colors
    threshhold = .5;
    optmizeRatio(colors[0], colors[1]);
    System.out.println("done ratio 1");
    optmizeRatio(colors[0], colors[2]);
    System.out.println("done ratio 2");
}

public ColorGram getBestColorGram() {
    return bestColorGram;
}
```

```
// sample program
public static void main(String[] args) {
    try {
        // load image
        ColorGramCalibration cg2 = new ColorGramCalibration(
                "sample_images//coke.jpg", true);
        // optimize it
        cg2.optimize();
        // print colorgram for cut-paste if needed
        System.out.println(cg2.getBestColorGram().toString());
    } catch (Exception e) {
        e.printStackTrace();
        System.exit(1);
    }
}
```

Figure 6-20. *All ColorGrams after optimization (Coke, 7-Up, and Pepsi)*

Section Summary

In this section, I showed you a few ways to use color to identify objects. For my goal of getting a beverage from the refrigerator, this was all I needed. The six methods and two classes created in this section were

- ImageProcessor.thresholdColor(): A method to get the color thresholds of certain minimum and maximum values for a particular color band: RED, GREEN, or BLUE

- ImageProcessor.filterColor(): A method to filter colors of a particular band

- ImageProcessor.getMean(): A method to compute some image statistics and get the average colors of each band

- ImageProcessor.getHistogram(): A method that offers an alternative method of getting the same statistics using Java Advanced Imaging and the histogram operation

- ImageProcessor.colorRatio(): A method that processes an image by colors' ratios between one another

- ImageProcessor.colorRatioCount(): A method that counts the colors in a ratio

- ColorGram: A data structure that represents the color ratios as a linear equation

- ColorGramCalibration: A program that creates a ColorGram from a thumbnail of the desired image

Next, I'll describe image processing using Java's Advanced Imaging API.

6.4   Advanced Image Processing

To find the edge of an image requires *area-level processing*. Area-level processing is the process of looking at a specific pixel in relation to the pixels around it. This is done by applying a kernel to an image. Some operations we will show are low-pass filters or smoothing, high-pass filters or sharpening, and line-finding filters known as Sobel Gradient masks.

Code Objective

The following objectives are handled in this example:

- Smooth an image by passing it through a low-pass filter.

- Sharpen an image by passing it through a high-pass filter.

- Get the edges of an image by passing it through a Sobel Gradient filter.

Code Discussion

Smoothing involves a kernel containing values of 1/9 in a 3×3 matrix. When applying this kernel to the image, you get the results shown in Figure 6-21.

Sharpening involves a kernel of 0, –1, 0, –1, 5, –1, –1, 0 in a 3×3 matrix. When applying this kernel to the image, you get the results shown in Figure 6-22.

The Sobel Gradient filter involves taking the gradient of neighboring pixels to find edges. When applying this kernel to an image, you get the results shown in Figure 6-23. (See Examples 6-24 through 6-27.)

Example 6-24. *bufferedToPlanar() and planarToBuffered()*

```java
private PlanarImage bufferedToPlanar(BufferedImage bImg) {
    Image awtImg = Toolkit.getDefaultToolkit().createImage(bImg.getSource());
    return JAI.create("awtimage", awtImg);

}

private BufferedImage planarToBuffered(PlanarImage pImg) {
    return pImg.getAsBufferedImage();
}
```

Example 6-25. *smooth()*

```
public BufferedImage smooth(BufferedImage srcImg) {

    PlanarImage input = bufferedToPlanar(srcImg);
    float ninth = 1.0f / 9.0f;
    float[] k = { ninth, ninth, ninth, ninth, ninth, ninth, ninth, ninth, ➡
ninth };
    KernelJAI kern = new KernelJAI(3, 3, k);
    ParameterBlock pb = new ParameterBlock();
    pb.addSource(input);
    pb.add(kern);
    PlanarImage output = JAI.create("Convolve", pb).createInstance();
    return planarToBuffered(output);
}
```

Figure 6-21. *Low-pass/smoothing filter*

Example 6-26. *sharp()*

```
public BufferedImage sharpen(BufferedImage srcImg) {

    PlanarImage input = bufferedToPlanar(srcImg);
    float[] k = { 0.0f, -1.0f, 0.0f, -1.0f, 5.0f, -1.0f, 0.0f, -1f, 0.0f };
    KernelJAI kern = new KernelJAI(3, 3, k);
    ParameterBlock pb = new ParameterBlock();
    pb.addSource(input);
    pb.add(kern);
    PlanarImage output = JAI.create("Convolve", pb).createInstance();
    return planarToBuffered(output);
}
```

Figure 6-22. *The high-pass/sharpening filter*

Example 6-27. *sobelGradient(): edges*

```
public BufferedImage sobelGradMag(BufferedImage srcImg) {

    PlanarImage input = bufferedToPlanar(srcImg);
    KernelJAI vert = KernelJAI.GRADIENT_MASK_SOBEL_VERTICAL;
    KernelJAI horz = KernelJAI.GRADIENT_MASK_SOBEL_HORIZONTAL;
    ParameterBlock pb = new ParameterBlock();
    pb.addSource(input);
    pb.add(vert);
    pb.add(horz);
    PlanarImage output = JAI.create("gradientmagnitude", pb).createInstance();
    return planarToBuffered(output);
}
```

Figure 6-23. *The Sobel Gradient filter*

The last filter to find edges is very useful in image analysis because you can start to see the lines formed by the objects. Those lines when applied with another algorithm—called the *Hough transform*—can be used to recognize and differentiate between objects.

Code Objective

The code objective here is to use the Hough transform to find the lines in an image.

Code Discussion

Our algorithm will follow the next sequence of steps:

1. Smooth the image. We do this to give us better transitions for the edges and less noise.

2. Find the edges of the image. We do this to give us the most potential lines.

3. Threshold the edges. We do this to separate softer edges into hard black-and-white edges.

4. Create an accumulator array of angles and distances (polar coordinates) for lines. This is a way of counting all possible lines. We use polar coordinates because the standard line equation, y = mx + b, has problems with vertical lines (that is, an infinite slope).

5. Move through the image pixel by pixel, looking for edge points.

6. When there is a hit, cycle through all possible lines at that point and increment the accumulator vote total by 1 for each angle and distance, while solving for the equation p = x * cos(theta) + y * sin(theta).

7. Convert the polar coordinates with the most votes back to Cartesian coordinates as representations of lines. (See Example 6-28 and Figure 6-24.)

Example 6-28. *getHoughLines.java*

```
public BufferedImage getHoughLines(BufferedImage srcImg) {

        double hough_thresh = .25;
        // since all points are being traversed, most lines will be found by
        // only moving through 90 degrees
        // also i only care about grid lines
        int angle_range = 90;
        // angular resolution
        int aRes = 1;

        int h = srcImg.getHeight();
        int w = srcImg.getWidth();

        // maximum radius of image is diagonal
        int pMax = (int) Math.sqrt((w * w) + (h * h));

        int[][] acc = new int[pMax][angle_range]; // create accumulator
        // pre-process image
        srcImg = smooth(srcImg);
        srcImg = sobelGradMag(srcImg);
        srcImg = threshold(srcImg, 127, 255);
```

```java
int maxPoints = 0;
double totalPoints = 0;
// move through image row by row from top to bottom

for (int y = 0; y < h; ++y) {
    for (int x = 0; x < w; ++x) {
        int srcPixel = srcImg.getRGB(x, y);
        Color c = new Color(srcPixel);
        // build accumulator image
        // this will get the grey value of the image
        // even though i get red here, they are all same value.
        int colorValue = getGrey(c).getRed();
        // if color is white, then we want to move through all
        // lines at this point
        if (colorValue == 255) {
            // moving through each line from zero to max angle
            // at resolution defined.
            for (int theta = 0; theta < angle_range; theta = theta + aRes) {
                // get the angle 0-90
                double radians = (theta / 180.0) * Math.PI ;
                // get potential line
                // p = radius
                // radians = angle
                // x = x-coordinate
                // y = y-coordinate
                int p = (int) (Math.cos(radians) * x + Math
                        .sin(radians)
                        * y);
                // get absolute radius
                p = Math.abs(p);
                // add the accumulator at this angle and radius
                acc[p][theta] = acc[p][theta] + 1;
                // want to add the total points accumulated
                totalPoints = totalPoints + acc[p][theta];
                // get the maximum number of points accumulated
                // for a particular bin
                if (acc[p][theta] > maxPoints) {
                    maxPoints = acc[p][theta];
                }
            }
        }
    }
}
// now work with the parameters space of the accumulator to find the x,y
// coordinates of the lines
// a = normalized to width
// b = normalized height
```

```
    for (int b = 0; b < pMax; b++) { // all pixels
        for (int a = 0; a < angle_range; a = a + aRes) { // all angles
            // created x coordinate from angles and distances
            double xx = (a / (double)angle_range) * (double) w;
            // created y coordinate from angles and distances
            double yy = (b / (double) pMax) * (double) h;
            // look at threshold of lines relative to max value of the
            if (acc[b][a] > (hough_thresh * maxPoints)) {
                // now find tangent lines
                drawHoughLines(srcImg, b, a);
            }
        }
    }

    return srcImg;

}

private void drawHoughLines(BufferedImage img, int p, int theta) {

    // h & w of image
    int h = img.getHeight();
    int w = img.getWidth();

    double radians = (theta / 360.0) * Math.PI * 2;
    // get line coordinates
    int x = (int) (p * Math.cos(radians));
    int y = (int) (p * Math.sin(radians));

    double x1 = (double) x;
    double y1 = (double) y;
    double x2 = x;
    double y2 = y;
    //double tx = Math.cos(radians);
    //double ty = Math.sin(radians);

    // add all points on line in one direction
    while (y1 > 0 && x1 < w && y1 < h && x1 > 0) {
        x1 = (x1 + Math.sin(radians));
        y1 = (y1 - Math.cos(radians));
    }

    // add all points on line in the other direction
    while (y2 > 0 && x2 < w && y2 < h && x2 > 0) {
        x2 = (x2 - Math.sin(radians));
        y2 = (y2 + Math.cos(radians));
    }
```

```
    // draw line from end of direction one, to end of direction 2
    Graphics2D g = img.createGraphics();
    g.setColor(Color.GREEN);
    g.drawLine((int)x1,(int) y1, (int) x2, (int) y2);

}
```

Figure 6-24. *The Hough transform of the three cans*

Section Summary

In this section, I used a combination of filters from pixel processing and some from Java's Advanced Imaging API to process images. The methods created were

- ImageProcessor.smooth(): Uses JAI to smooth an image using a low-pass filter

- ImageProcessor.sharpen(): Uses JAI to sharpen an image using a high-pass filter

- ImageProcessor.sobelGradMag(): Uses JAI to find the edges of an image

- ImageProcessor.getHoughLines(): Uses the Hough transform to find the lines in an image

- ImageProcessor.drawHoughLines(): Iterates through the Hough array to create lines on the processed image

6.5 Chapter Summary

In this chapter, I wanted to show you how to process images from a web camera. By the final chapter, you should be able to do some complex analysis and give your robot a lot of information about its world using a few algorithms and data structures.

In the introduction, I created two utility classes—WindowUtilities and ExitListener—to assist with Swing class creation. I created an ImagePanel to provide a canvas for working with processed images and generated a sample ImageViewer that renders JPEGs.

In section 6.1, I showed you how to install and test the Java Media Framework with FindCamera, and then created a class to get a single frame from the camera called GetFrame. Finally, in this chapter I created a WebCamViewer to show images in real time from your webcam.

In section 6.2, I introduced a new webcam viewer called DoubleWebCamViewer that allows for real-time viewing of image processing. I also introduced a class called FilterParameters that allows for generic combinations of filters to be added to the DoubleWebCamViewer class. Finally, I introduced the ImageProcessor class for performing some basic image analysis.

In section 6.3, I showed you how to process images by color and introduced more methods in the ImageProcessor class to process with color and get color statistics from the webcam image. I then introduced a data structure called ColorGram that represents the ratios of colors to one another in the form of a linear equation, which when used with its corresponding ColorGramCalibration class can take a thumbnail image and optimize its ColorGram as something to look for during processing.

Finally, in section 6.4, I used some methods of image processing from Java Advanced Imaging to smooth, sharpen, and find edges, and perform the Hough transform for finding lines.

I'm now almost ready to have my robot get me a can of soda. I just need to teach it to move, which is the topic of the next chapter.

CHAPTER 7

■ ■ ■

Navigation

Though we travel the world over to find the beautiful, we must carry it with us or we find it not.

— Ralph Waldo Emerson

7.0 Introduction

Navigation is one of the holy grails of robotics. Of all the challenges in robotics, navigation has the most applications. If you want a robot that can clean a rug, mop a floor, mow a lawn, or deliver medicine, all you need is a robot that can navigate.

You will find soon after you begin navigation with your robot that many unforeseen, unplanned things will happen. They happen because your sensors didn't interpret the environment with the precision you would have liked. I call this poor data or poor interpretation "noise." In this chapter, we will start by having the robot navigate within an environment that has little to zero noise and then increase the environment's complexity and noise as we go.

Before I begin though, I'd like to introduce a little terminology. The terms come from a branch of mathematics called Graph Theory.

- A *vertex* is a synonym for point or node and represents a single element of a set.

- An *edge* is a connection between vertices.

- A *graph* is the set of vertices V, and the edges of V.

- A *simple graph* is an unweighted, undirected graph.

- A *directed graph* indicates travel between two vertices in a specific direction only.

- A *weighted graph* is a graph with weights on the edges.

Figure 7-1 shows the different types of graphs.

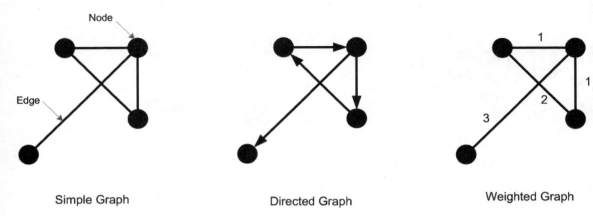

Simple Graph   Directed Graph   Weighted Graph

Figure 7-1. *A simple graph, a directed graph, and a weighted graph*

To illustrate how you can use graphs with navigation, let's take your commute to the grocery store. You start at vertex A, and end at vertex B. For fun, let's add a trip to the gas station, which will be vertex C, and a trip to the automatic teller machine (ATM) for some cash, at vertex D. If you add miles or the time it takes to get to and from each of these vertices, the graph now becomes a weighted graph (as shown in Figure 7-1).

The graph in Figure 7-2 also has other qualities; you cannot get from the ATM or the gas station to home without going to the grocery. So your robot program only needs to know how to go from A to B. Then from B it just has to know how to get to C, or D.

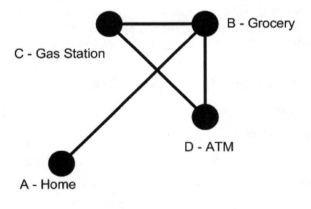

Trip Graph

Figure 7-2. *The trip graph*

To represent vertices and edges, I am going to create two classes: one Vertex with a name field, and an Edge with a name field and two vertices. Later, I will extend these classes so that the problems of navigation can be broken down into analyzing a path through a graph. See Examples 7-1 and 7-2.

Example 7-1. *Vertex.java*

```
package com.scottpreston.javarobot.chapter7;

public class Vertex {

    public String name;

    public Vertex() {}

    public Vertex(String n) {
        name = n;
    }
}
```

Example 7-2. *Edge.java*

```
package com.scottpreston.javarobot.chapter7;

public class Edge {

    public String name;
    public Vertex v1;
    public Vertex v2;
    public int w;

    public Edge() {}

    // constructs with two vertices and a weight
    public Edge(Vertex v1, Vertex v2, int w) {
        this.v1 = v1;
        this.v2 = v2;
        this.w = w;
    }
    public String toString() {
        return "{v1=" + v1.name +",v2=" + v2.name + ",w=" + w +"}";
    }
}
```

In this chapter, I will create 19 classes and one basic Stamp program. There will be five navigational classes:

- Navigation: Performs basic navigation (best in ideal regions)

- Localization: Provides a start point for a robot and gives it the ability to navigate to other coordinates

- ObstacleNavigation: Provides for obstacle avoidance during navigation

- IndoorNavigation: Shows you how to create maps indoors and how to navigate

- OutdoorNavigation: Shows you how to use GPS to navigate your robot

Figure 7-3 shows a class diagram of all these together.

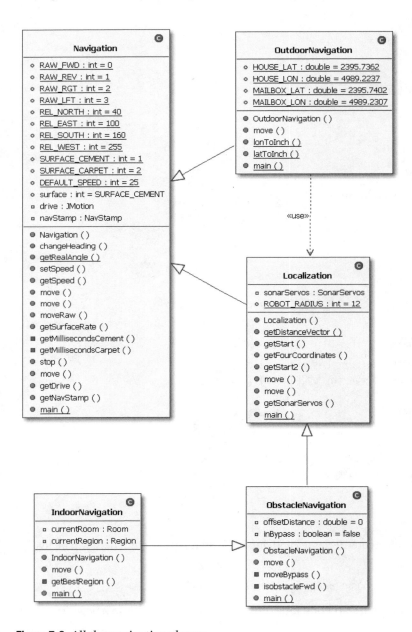

Figure 7-3. *All the navigation classes*

Before I begin navigation with these classes, I need to tell you about the robot used, Feynman5 (see Figure 7-4), because you'll need to make adjustments to some of the classes in this chapter depending on the configuration of your robot.

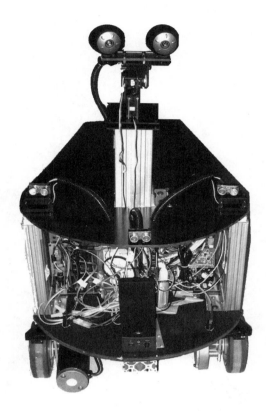

Figure 7-4. *The Feynman5 robot*

First, some background on the name. I started building robots a long time ago, and my first PC robot was named Feynman. I called it that because I named all the PCs in my house after famous physicists. I had computers named Einstein, Hawking, Newton, and Feynman. The one that was eventually converted into a robot was Feynman. The robot pictured in Figure 7-4 is the fifth generation of the original, hence the name Feynman5.

Feynman5 was built during the writing of this book in the spring of 2005. His chassis is 80-20 aluminum extrusion and black PVC, which I got at McMaster.Com. For brains, he has a VIA EPOA M1000, Mini-ITX with 256MB of RAM, and a 3.5" 20GB hard disk. The microcontroller is a BASIC Stamp 2 on a Parallax Board of Education.

For power, I use two 33-amp hour batteries—one for the motors and one for the computer and peripherals.

For motion, I use a Scott Edwards MiniSSC-II, two Victor 833 Speed Controls from IFI Robotics, and two NPC-41250 wheelchair motors. I connected the MiniSSC in parallel with my BASIC Stamp 2 to the PC's serial port.

For sensing, I use a Devantech CMPS03 digital compass, two GP2D02 Sharp Infrared sensors, three SRF04 sonar devices, and two Pyro 1394 webcams. To move the webcams, I used the Pan & Tilt Kit from Lynxmotion. To connect the sensors, I used a Preston Research Sonar Distribution Module and a CMPS03 carrier board.

Table 7-1 shows what all 16 I/O pins of the Stamp are connected to.

Table 7-1. *The BASIC Stamp Pin Out*

Stamp Pin	Function
0	Reserved for Bluetooth
1	Reserved for Bluetooth
2	Sharp IR #1 out
3	Sharp IR #1 in
4	Sharp IR #2 out
5	Sharp IR #2 in
6	Spare
7	Spare
8	Sonar 1 – Init
9	Sonar 1 – Echo
10	Sonar 2 – Init
11	Sonar 2 – Echo
12	Sonar 3 – Init
13	Sonar 3 – Echo
14	CMPS03 compass
15	GPS serial in

Now that you know what my robot looks like, let's see what makes it navigate, starting with the microcontroller. Figure 7-5 shows a class diagram of the data structures and the NavStamp class using those structures.

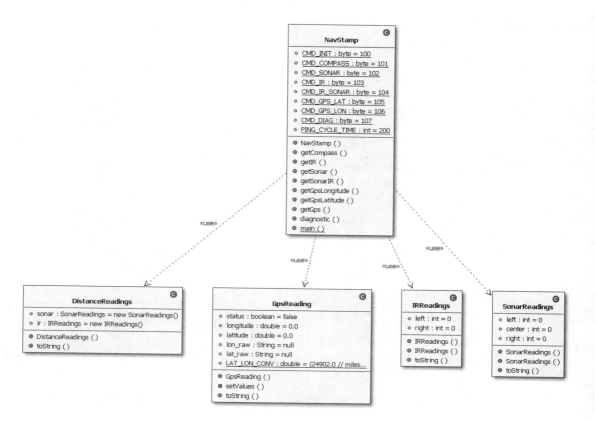

Figure 7-5. *A class diagram of NavStamp and Data structures*

Before I get data from the microcontroller, I decided to create some data structures to hold this information. Those structures include the following:

- SonarReadings: To hold sonar data

- IRReadings: To hold infrared data.

- DistanceReadings: To hold combination data

- GPSReadings: To hold GPS longitude and latitude data

All the readings discussed next will be a ~ (tilde)-delimited string. While having a byte array is just as useful for these numbers, the returns come from either a web serial port or a standard serial port. If it was just coming from a serial port, I could use a byte[], but byte streams over the Web are less convenient.

All readings also have public fields. I avoid the typical Java setter/getter convention because I want to access these data structures like I access java.awt.Point.

In SonarReadings (see Example 7-3), the constructor takes a string of value Sonar1~Sonar2~Sonar3.

Example 7-3. *SonarReadings.java*

```java
package com.scottpreston.javarobot.chapter7;

import java.io.Serializable;

public class SonarReadings implements Serializable {

    public int left = 0;
    public int center = 0;
    public int right = 0;

    public SonarReadings() {
        // default
    }

    public SonarReadings(String readings) {
        // sample input "11~22~33"
        String[] values = readings.split("~");
        left = new Integer(values[0]).intValue();
        center = new Integer(values[1]).intValue();
        right = new Integer(values[2]).intValue();
    }

    public String toString() {
        return "left=" + left + ",center=" + center + ",right=" + right;
    }
}
```

The second data structure is for the two sharp infrared detectors above and in front of the wheels. The constructor takes a string of value Ir1~Ir2. See Example 7-4.

Example 7-4. *IRReadings.java*

```java
package com.scottpreston.javarobot.chapter7;

import java.io.Serializable;

public class IRReadings implements Serializable {

    public int left = 0;
    public int right = 0;

    public IRReadings() {
        // default
    }
```

```java
    public IRReadings(String readings) {
        String[] values = readings.split("~");
        left = new Integer(values[0]).intValue();
        right = new Integer(values[1]).intValue();
    }

    public String toString() {
        return "left=" + left + ",right=" + right;
    }
}
```

The final reading is from all sonar and infrared detectors at the same time. The constructor takes a string of value Ir1~Ir2~ Sonar1~Sonar2~Sonar3. See Example 7-5.

Example 7-5. *DistanceReadings.java*

```java
package com.scottpreston.javarobot.chapter7;

import java.io.Serializable;

public class DistanceReadings implements Serializable {

    public SonarReadings sonar = new SonarReadings();
    public IRReadings ir = new IRReadings();

    public DistanceReadings(String readings) throws Exception {

        String[] values = readings.split("~");
        ir.left = new Integer(values[0]).intValue();
        ir.right = new Integer(values[1]).intValue();
        sonar.left = new Integer(values[2]).intValue();
        sonar.center = new Integer(values[3]).intValue();
        sonar.right = new Integer(values[4]).intValue();
    }

    public String toString() {
        return ir.toString() + "," + sonar.toString();
    }

}
```

I will leave the discussion of GPSReadings.java until section 7.5, "Outdoor Navigation."

For the NavStamp class in Example 7-6, this should look very familiar to the classes I created in Chapter 2. The command bytes at the top match the bytes expected in the BASIC Stamp program. The other static primitive PING_CYCLE_TIME will be used by navigation classes that need to know how long to wait until the microcontroller is finished getting sensor data.

The constructor uses the JSerialPort interface I created in Chapter 2. The other methods correspond to getting specific data from the microcontroller, for example:

- getCompass(): Gets an int back as a heading. This will tell the robot what direction it is facing relative to magnetic north.

- getIr(): Gets the infrared sensors at the base of the robot.

- getSonar(): Gets the sonar at the top of the robot.

- getSonarIR(): Gets both the sonar and infrared information from the robot.

- getGpsLongitude(), getGpsLatitude(), and getGps(): These will be discussed later in section 7.5.

Example 7-6. *NavStamp.java*

```java
package com.scottpreston.javarobot.chapter7;

import com.scottpreston.javarobot.chapter2.Controller;
import com.scottpreston.javarobot.chapter2.JSerialPort;
import com.scottpreston.javarobot.chapter2.Utils;
import com.scottpreston.javarobot.chapter2.WebSerialClient;

public class NavStamp extends Controller {

    // command bytes to microcontroller
    public static byte CMD_INIT = 100;
    public static byte CMD_COMPASS = 101;
    public static byte CMD_SONAR = 102;
    public static byte CMD_IR = 103;
    public static byte CMD_IR_SONAR = 104;
    public static byte CMD_GPS_LAT = 105;
    public static byte CMD_GPS_LON = 106;
    public static byte CMD_DIAG = 107;
    public static int PING_CYCLE_TIME = 200;

    public NavStamp(JSerialPort port) throws Exception {
        super(port);
    }

    // get compass reading
    public int getCompass() throws Exception {
        String heading = execute(new byte[] { CMD_INIT, CMD_COMPASS }, 175);
        String[] h2 = heading.split("~");
        String heading2 = "";
        for (int h = 0; h < h2.length; h++) {
            heading2 = heading2 + (char) new Integer(h2[h]).intValue();
        }
        return new Integer(heading2).intValue();
    }
```

```java
// get ir
public IRReadings getIR() throws Exception {
    String readings = execute(new byte[] { CMD_INIT, CMD_IR }, 75);
    return new IRReadings(readings);
}

// get sonar
public SonarReadings getSonar() throws Exception {
    String readings = execute(new byte[] { CMD_INIT, CMD_SONAR }, 75);
    return new SonarReadings(readings);
}

// get both ir and sonar
public DistanceReadings getSonarIR() throws Exception {
    String readings = execute(new byte[] { CMD_INIT, CMD_IR_SONAR }, 200);
    return new DistanceReadings(readings);
}

// get gps longitude
public String getGpsLongitude() throws Exception {
    byte[] readings = execute2(new byte[] { CMD_INIT, CMD_GPS_LON }, 5000);
    return Utils.toAscii(readings);
}

// get gps latitude
public String getGpsLatitude() throws Exception {
    byte[] readings = execute2(new byte[] { CMD_INIT, CMD_GPS_LAT }, 5000);
    return Utils.toAscii(readings);
}

// get both longitude and latitude
public GpsReading getGps() throws Exception {
    String lon = getGpsLongitude();
    String lat = getGpsLatitude();
    return new GpsReading(lon, lat);
}

// get diagnostic signal
public boolean diagnostic() throws Exception {
    String s = execute(new byte[] { CMD_INIT, CMD_DIAG }, 80);
    if (s.equals("1~2~3")) {
        return true;
    }
    return false;
}
```

```java
// test all methods
public static void main(String[] args) {
    try {
        WebSerialClient com = new WebSerialClient("10.10.10.99", "8080", "1");
        NavStamp s = new NavStamp(com);
        System.out.println("diag=" + s.diagnostic());
        Utils.pause(500);
        System.out.println("compass=" + s.getCompass());
        Utils.pause(500);
        System.out.println("ir=" + s.getIR().toString());
        Utils.pause(500);
        System.out.println("diag=" + s.getSonar().toString());
        Utils.pause(500);
        System.out.println("all dist=" + s.getSonarIR());
        s.close();
        System.out.println("done");
    } catch (Exception e) {
        e.printStackTrace();
        System.exit(1);

    }
}

}
```

Next is the program for the BASIC Stamp. In the main label, it waits for a start byte of 100, following which it waits for the next commands.

■Note Because the SSC is hooked to the same serial connection as the BASIC Stamp, the SSC might send a byte of 100 to the SSC for a position. However, because the Stamp is looking for two bytes in the 100s, it will ignore the second byte to the SSC, if there is one, since it will be a 255 sync byte (see SSCProtocol.java in Example 3-3).

The first section of this program initializes variables for all constants, working variables, and return variables. You can see that the constants defined below correspond to the BASIC Stamp 2 pin out in Table 7-1.

The second section consists of the main program area, where it looks and waits for an input request byte[] from the NavStamp class and then branches to the subroutine depending on the command.

The third section consists of subroutines specifically designed to get infrared, sonar, and compass readings, and then return the output to the NavStamp class in the form of a serial byte[]. See Example 7-7.

Example 7-7. *nav1.bs2*

```
' {$STAMP BS2}
' {$PBASIC 2.5}
' {$PORT COM1}
' cmd variable
cmd           VAR    Byte
N9600         CON    16468
' GPDO2 IR
dout1         CON    2      'output to the DIRRS.   (green)
din1          CON    3      'input from the DIRRS.  (yellow)
dout2         CON    4      'output to the DIRRS.   (green)
din2          CON    5      'input from the DIRRS.  (yellow)
dout3         CON    6      'output to the DIRRS.   (green)
din3          CON    7      'input from the DIRRS.  (yellow)
dist1         VAR    Byte   'ir dist 1
dist2         VAR    Byte   'ir dist 2
dist3         VAR    Byte   'ir dist 3
' CMPS03 COMPASS
cin           CON    14     'serial data out     GREEN (a)
heading       VAR    Word   'heading

' srf04 sonar
convfac       CON    74     '74 inches, 29 cm
ECHO1         CON    9      'input from the SRF04.   (red)
INIT1         CON    8      'output to the SRF04.    (gry)
ECHO2         CON    11     'input from the SRF04.   (yel)
INIT2         CON    10     'output to the SRF04.    (grn)
ECHO3         CON    13     'input from the SRF04.   (blu)
INIT3         CON    12     'output to the SRF04.    (pur)

wDist1        VAR    Word   'sonar1
wDist2        VAR    Word   'sonar2
wDist3        VAR    Word   'sonar3
status        VAR    Byte
gpsData1      VAR    Byte(5)
gpsData2      VAR    Byte(4)

N4800   CON 16572 'GPS baudrate (4800)


main:
  cmd = 0
  SERIN 16,16468,main,[WAIT(100), cmd]
  IF cmd = 101 THEN get_compass      ' gets compass reading    (READ-ms) ➡
- return after a time
  IF cmd = 102 THEN ping_sonar       ' pings the sonar     (READ-ms) ➡
- return after a time
```

```
    IF cmd = 103 THEN ping_ir          ' pings the sonar      (READ-ms) ➡
- return after a time
    IF cmd = 104 THEN ping_all          ' pings the sonar      (READ-ms) ➡
- return after a time
    IF cmd = 105 THEN get_lat          ' gets gps latitude
    IF cmd = 106 THEN get_lon          ' gets gps longitude
    IF cmd = 107 THEN get_diag          ' gets diagnostic
    PAUSE 5
    GOTO main

get_compass:
    PULSIN cin, 1, heading                        ' Get reading
    heading = (heading-500)/50                    ' BS2(e) ➡
- Calculate Bearing in degrees
    SEROUT 16,N9600,[DEC heading]                 ' out to PC
    GOTO main
ping_sonar:
    GOSUB sonar1
    GOSUB sonar2
    GOSUB sonar3
    ' output is s1~s2~s3
    SEROUT 16,N9600,[wDist1,wDist2,wDist3]
    GOTO main
ping_ir:
    GOSUB ir1
    GOSUB ir2
    ' output is ir1~ir2
    SEROUT 16,N9600,[dist1,dist2]
    GOTO main
ping_all:
    GOSUB ir1
    GOSUB ir2
    GOSUB sonar1
    GOSUB sonar2
    GOSUB sonar3
    ' output is ir1~ir2~s1~s2~s3
    SEROUT 16,N9600,[dist1,dist2,wDist1,wDist2,wDist3]
    GOTO main
ir1:
    LOW dout1
ir1b:
    IF IN3=0 THEN ir1b
    SHIFTIN din1,dout1,2,[dist1\8]
    HIGH dout1
    RETURN
ir2:
    LOW dout2
```

```
ir2b:
    IF IN5=0 THEN ir2b
    SHIFTIN din2,dout2,2,[dist2\8]
    HIGH dout2
    RETURN
sonar1:
  PULSOUT INIT1,5                        ' 10us init pulse
  OUTPUT INIT1                           ' (delay)
  RCTIME ECHO1,1,wDist1                  ' measure echo time
  wDist1=wDist1/convfac                  ' convert to inches
  RETURN
sonar2:
  PULSOUT INIT2,5                        ' 10us init pulse
  OUTPUT INIT2 ' (delay)
  RCTIME ECHO2,1,wDist2                  ' measure echo time
  wDist2=wDist2/convfac                  ' convert to inches
  RETURN
sonar3:
  PULSOUT INIT3,5                        ' 10us init pulse
  OUTPUT INIT3                           ' (delay)
  RCTIME ECHO3,1,wDist3                  ' measure echo time
  wDist3=wDist3/convfac                  ' convert to inches
  RETURN
get_lat:
  *SERIN GPS,N4800,2000,get_lat,[WAIT("GPRMC,"),SKIP 7,status,SKIP 1,➥
STR gpsData1\4,SKIP 1,STR gpsData2\4]
  *SEROUT 16,N9600,[status,",0",gpsData1(0),gpsData1(1),":",gpsData1(2), ➥
gpsData1(3),".",gpsData2(0),gpsData2(1),gpsData2(2),gpsData2(3)]
  *GOTO main
get_lon:
  *SERIN GPS,N4800,2000,get_lon,[WAIT("GPRMC,"),SKIP 7,status,SKIP 13,➥
STR gpsData1\5,SKIP 1,STR gpsData2\4]
  *SEROUT 16,N9600,[status,",",gpsData1(0),gpsData1(1),gpsData1(2),➥
":",gpsData1(3),➥
gpsData1(4),".",gpsData2(0),gpsData2(1),gpsData2(2),gpsData2(3)]
  *GOTO main
get_diag:
  SEROUT 16,N9600,["1","2","3"]
  goto main
```

Section Summary

Now I am ready to get the robot to navigate. Though the previous section was just an introduction, I covered various foundational topics, such as

- Basic Graph Theory: Describing ideal navigation scenarios

- Robot Configuration: Describing the components and structure of the robot being used to demonstrate navigation

- Data Structures: Describing holding of the information coming from the microcontroller

- Sensor Data Retrieval: Describing the exact mechanisms for requesting data from the microcontroller for my robot configuration

The next section will demonstrate the most basic navigational process: dead reckoning.

7.1 Navigation Basics

The most basic type of navigational process is dead reckoning. Dead reckoning is the process of deducing the position of a vehicle or robot based on course and distance. To perform this type of navigation you need a way of measuring both heading and distance.

To demonstrate this, I am going to navigate in a space defined by coordinates of 100 inches × 100 inches. I will call this space a Perfect World (see Figure 7-6) and from it you can see that if your robot is starting from point a, and needs to move to point b, it's a trigonometric calculation based on the distance you traveled in the y direction and the distance you traveled in the x direction, or angle theta through a distance c.

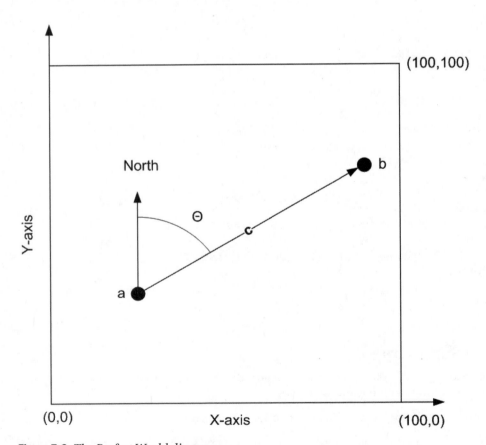

Figure 7-6. *The Perfect World diagram*

In order for a robot to do this, it must accomplish the following:

- Move in a straight line.

- Face a specific direction.

- Move a specified distance.

Setup

Our robot will require the following to perform basic dead reckoning:

- SpeedDiffDrive.java (Chapter 4)

- A Compass Reading (Chapter 5)

To refresh the differential drive class and how it relates to movement, please see the diagram in Figure 7-7.

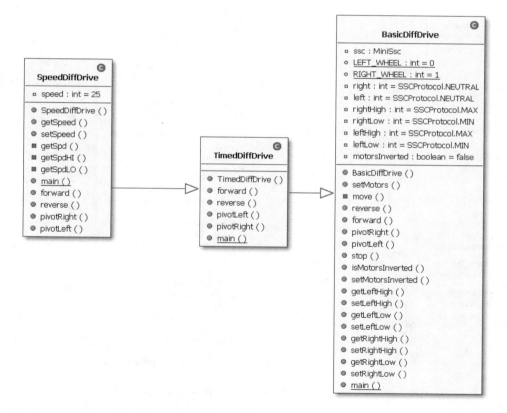

Figure 7-7. *The SpeedDiffDrive class diagram from Chapter 2*

Next, I decided not to calibrate our robot to move in a straight line since the speed control and servo controllers send precise analog voltages to the motors. As long as your motors have identical rotation characteristics, you should be fine with setting them at the same speed. However, make sure you take some measurements of how fast your robot moves for a given speed in a given unit of time. Since I am not using encoders, I had to calibrate Feynman5 on two surfaces—cement and carpet—for specific speeds.

Code Objective

The code objective here is to create a navigation class that gives the robot the ability to dead reckon.

Code Discussion

Figure 7-8 shows the three classes that will handle basic navigation.

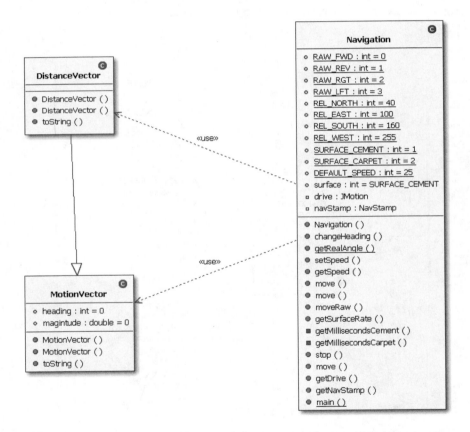

Figure 7-8. *The three classes that handle basic navigation: Navigation, MotionVector, and DistanceVector*

Of the two classes required to get our robot to perform dead reckoning, the first one we are going to discuss is MotionVector. MotionVector represents the heading and time of any movement the robot will want to make. Its child class, DistanceVector, is used to help the programmer differentiate between moving with units of distance or units of time.

The two public fields are heading and magnitude. The heading I chose to be an int for degrees and the magnitude can be any double value. See Example 7-8.

Example 7-8. *MotionVector*

```java
package com.scottpreston.javarobot.chapter7;

public class MotionVector extends Edge{

    public int heading = 0;
    public double magnitude = 0;

    public MotionVector(int h, double seconds) {
        heading = h;
        magnitude = seconds;
        weight= (int)seconds;
    }

    public MotionVector(String h, String seconds) throws Exception {
        heading = new Integer(h).intValue();
        magnitude = new Double(seconds).doubleValue();
        weight= (int)magnitude;
    }

    public String toString() {
        return "Heading: " + heading + " Seconds: " + magnitude;
    }
}
```

The next class, DistanceVector, is basically the same as the MotionVector except that in this navigation class I convert inches to seconds via a conversion based on a calibration of the robot's speed and surface. See Example 7-9.

Example 7-9. *DistanceVector*

```java
package com.scottpreston.javarobot.chapter7;

public class DistanceVector extends MotionVector {

    public DistanceVector(int h, double inches) {
        super(h, inches);
    }
```

```
    public DistanceVector(String h, String inches) throws Exception {
        super(h, inches);
    }

    public String toString() {
        return "Heading: " + heading + " Inches: " + magnitude;
    }
}
```

The next thing I want to do is create the navigation class. The three instance fields in this class are for the drive, the microcontroller, and the current surface type, since the surface could change during a robot's journey.

The first of the static constants are four enumerations to specify that when given a command the robot should move in a specific direction for a specific time. The second set consists of relative coordinate readings taken from the compass while the robot was facing a specific direction. In this new coordinate system, north is to the front of the house, east is to the right side, south is to the rear, and west is to the left side. The final static constant is the default speed, which I set to 25.

Note I modified the SpeedDiffDrive class from Chapter 3 to take timing from 1 to 10 to 1 to 100 for greater precision.

The constructors for this class are the same: JSerialPort. With this JSerialPort, I create an instance of the SpeedDiffDrive, NavStamp, and SonarServos. Right now, all I need is the NavStamp and the SpeedDiffDrive. I also set the default speed to the constant value DEFAULT_SPEED; this can be any value from 1 to 100.

The next method is changeHeading() with an input parameter of an int that will represent the robot's goal heading. The goal heading will be from 0 to 360, where 0 is north, 90 is east, 180 is south, and 270 is west. However, these numbers are ideal and do not match the relative headings taken via experimentation. To get the robot's goal heading to match the real-world headings, I created a method called getRealAngle() to do the conversion.

Now, because of the robot's speed I had to slow my robot down considerably during the turn process. Otherwise, it will move too fast and take longer to find the correct heading because of overshoot. An overshoot happens when the robot is trying to go from, say, 90 to 100 degrees and it moves too far—perhaps 130 degrees. Overshoot happens because of the time of the turn and the speed of the turn.

To prevent overshoot, I created a Boolean called toggle. When the method is in the toggle state, it tells the method that it already overshot once and that it's time to reduce the speed of the turn size by 250 milliseconds.

I have found through experimentation that the robot works best with an accuracy of plus or minus 2 degrees, a speed of 12, and a turn size of 1 second.

For the actual change heading part of the algorithm, I wanted to ensure that the robot took readings and refined its position until it was within the accuracy defined ~4 degrees. For this, I had it loop continuously via a while(true) conditional.

While inside the loop, the robot checks its current heading relative to the direction it wants to face. I call this reading relHeading (short for relative heading), and to keep the degrees always between 0 and 360, I added 360 to those relative headings less than zero. Once the robot knows its relative heading, it can begin turning. If the relative heading is between 0 and 180, then I tell it to pivot left. If the relative heading is between 180 and 360, then I tell it to pivot right. Depending on how far away the robot is from its target position, I decrease the turn time. Then once the accuracy is reached, I make sure the drive is stopped. I break out of the loop and I reset the speed to 2.

The next methods in the class are two move() methods. One takes a DistanceVector and the other takes a MotionVector. For the method taking the DistanceVector as a parameter, inches get converted to seconds using the getSurfaceRate() method. It is important to take measurements for this if you are not using an encoder. If you are using an encoder, then your drive class will already have a mechanism for stopping you at a specified distance, so here you would call that method from your drive class rather than do a conversion.

Finally, in the main() test method, the robot moves in a 3-foot square box in the directions east, north, west, and south. In the end, it should be right back where it started, provided that your calibrations are correct. (See Example 7-10.)

Example 7-10. *Navigation.java*

```java
package com.scottpreston.javarobot.chapter7;

import com.scottpreston.javarobot.chapter2.JSerialPort;
import com.scottpreston.javarobot.chapter2.Utils;
import com.scottpreston.javarobot.chapter2.WebSerialClient;
import com.scottpreston.javarobot.chapter3.JMotion;
import com.scottpreston.javarobot.chapter3.SpeedDiffDrive;

public class Navigation {

    // movement constants for raw movement
    public static final int RAW_FWD = 0;
    public static final int RAW_REV = 1;
    public static final int RAW_RGT = 2;
    public static final int RAW_LFT = 3;
    // relative readings for 4 coordinate axes
    public static final int REL_NORTH = 40;
    public static final int REL_EAST = 100;
    public static final int REL_SOUTH = 160;
    public static final int REL_WEST = 255;
    // surface constants
    public static final int SURFACE_CEMENT = 1;
    public static final int SURFACE_CARPET = 2;
    // default speed
    public static final int DEFAULT_SPEED = 25;
```

```
// instance variables
public int surface = SURFACE_CEMENT;
private JMotion drive;
private NavStamp navStamp;

public Navigation(JSerialPort serialPort) throws Exception {
    // drive with default speed
    drive = new SpeedDiffDrive(serialPort);
    drive.setSpeed(DEFAULT_SPEED);
    // stamp for sensors
    navStamp = new NavStamp(serialPort);
}

// change heading
public void changeHeading(int newHeading) throws Exception {
    // this will calculate a real angle from a relative measure of
    // the coord axis.
    newHeading = getRealAngle(newHeading);
    int accuracy = 2; // degrees
    // autoadjust speed depending on the surface
    if (surface == SURFACE_CEMENT) {
        // slow so don't overshoot 15 degrees at 1sec intervals
        drive.setSpeed(12);
    } else {
        // moves slower on carpet
        drive.setSpeed(20);
    }
    // used to record lats turn
    int lastTurn = 0;
    boolean toggle = false;
    int turnSize = 1000;
    while (true) {
        // get compass
        int currentHeading = navStamp.getCompass();
        // get relative heading from compass to where you want to go
        int relHeading = currentHeading - newHeading;

        // adjust for negative
        if (relHeading < 0) {
            relHeading = 360 + relHeading;
        }
        // if within bounds, stop
        if (relHeading <= accuracy || relHeading >= 360 - accuracy) {
            drive.stop();
            break;
        }
```

```java
        // in case it overshoots direction twice
        if (toggle) {
            // reset
            toggle = false;
            // reduce turn time by 250ms
            turnSize = turnSize - 250;
        }
        // turn for a second left
        if (relHeading < 180 && relHeading > 15) {
            if (lastTurn == 'R') {
                toggle = true;
            }
            drive.pivotLeft(turnSize);
            // record what turn
            lastTurn = 'L';
            // turn for a second right
        } else if (relHeading >= 180 && relHeading < 345) {
            // records toggle
            if (lastTurn == 'L') {
                toggle = true;
            }
            drive.pivotRight(turnSize);
            lastTurn = 'R';
        } else if (relHeading >= 345) {
            drive.pivotRight(250);
        } else if (relHeading <= 15) {
            drive.pivotLeft(250);
        }
    }
    // set back to default speed
    drive.setSpeed(DEFAULT_SPEED);
}

// adjust for angle measured to absolute angle
public static int getRealAngle(int theta) {

    int phi = 0;
    double ratio = 0.0;
    // if in 1st quadrant
    if (theta > 0 && theta < 90) {
        // 1. get % of the total range
        // 2. get range
        // 3. multiply range by percentage, add it to current north reading.
        phi = (int) ((theta / 90.0) * (REL_EAST - REL_NORTH)) + REL_NORTH;
    }
```

```java
        if (theta > 90 && theta < 180) {
            theta = theta - 90;
            phi = (int) ((theta / 90.0) * (REL_SOUTH - REL_EAST)) + REL_EAST;
        }
        if (theta > 180 && theta < 270) {
            theta = theta - 180;
            phi = (int) ((theta / 90.0) * (REL_WEST - REL_SOUTH)) + REL_SOUTH;
        }
        if (theta > 270 && theta < 360) {
            theta = theta - 270;
            phi = (int) ((theta / 90.0) * ((360 + REL_NORTH) - REL_WEST)) ➡
+ REL_WEST;
        }
        // in case actual directions
        if (theta == 0) {
            phi = REL_NORTH;
        }
        if (theta == 90) {
            phi = REL_EAST;
        }
        if (theta == 180) {
            phi = REL_SOUTH;
        }
        if (theta == 270) {
            phi = REL_WEST;
        }
        if (phi > 360) {
            phi = phi - 360;
        }
        return phi;

    }

    // setter for drive speed
    public void setSpeed(int s) throws Exception {
        drive.setSpeed(s);
    }

    // getter for drive speed
    public int getSpeed() {
        return drive.getSpeed();
    }

    //  distance vector is in inches
    public void move(DistanceVector dVect) throws Exception {
        // convert since in inches
        dVect.magnitude = getSurfaceRate(dVect.magnitude);
```

```
        // converted to MotionVector
        move(dVect);
    }


    // motion vector is in inches
    public void move(MotionVector vect) throws Exception {
        // change heading
        Utils.log("MV=" + vect.toString());
        changeHeading(vect.heading);
        // move fwd or reverse
        if (vect.magnitude > 0) {
            drive.forward((int) (vect.magnitude * 1000));
        } else if (vect.magnitude < 0) {
            drive.reverse((int) (-vect.magnitude * 1000));
        }
    }


    public void moveRaw(int dir, int ms) throws Exception {
        if (dir == RAW_FWD) {
            drive.forward(ms);
        }
        if (dir == RAW_REV) {
            drive.reverse(ms);
        }
        if (dir == RAW_RGT) {
            drive.pivotRight(ms);
        }
        if (dir == RAW_LFT) {
            drive.pivotLeft(ms);
        }
    }


    // surface rate when adjusting inches to seconds
    public int getSurfaceRate(double inches) {
        if (surface == SURFACE_CARPET) {
            return getMillisecondsCarpet(inches);
        }
        if (surface == SURFACE_CEMENT) {
            return getMillisecondsCement(inches);
        }
        return 0;
    }


    //  surface rate when adjusting inches to seconds
    private int getMillisecondsCement(double inches) {
```

```java
        double convFactor = 0.0; // this will be second/inches
        switch (drive.getSpeed()) {
        case 10:
            convFactor = 1 / 4.0;
            break;
        case 20:
            convFactor = 1 / 7.0;
            break;
        case DEFAULT_SPEED:
            convFactor = 1 / 14.0;
            break;
        case 30:
            convFactor = 1 / 20.0;
            break;
        }
        // will return seconds
        return (int) (inches * convFactor);

    }

    //  surface rate when adjusting inches to seconds
    private int getMillisecondsCarpet(double inches) {

        double convFactor = 0.0; // this will be second/inches
        switch (drive.getSpeed()) {
        case 10:
            convFactor = 1 / 16.0;
        case 20:
            convFactor = 1 / 36.0;
        case 30:
            convFactor = 1 / 48.0;
        }
        return (int) (inches * convFactor);

    }

    // call to stop since in case of emergency
    public void stop() throws Exception {
        drive.stop();
    }

    // move for multiple vectors
    public void move(MotionVector[] path) throws Exception {
        for (int i = 0; i < path.length; i++) {
            move(path[i]);
        }
    }
```

```java
public JMotion getDrive() {
    return drive;
}

public NavStamp getNavStamp() {
    return navStamp;
}

public static void main(String[] args) {

    try {
        WebSerialClient sPort = new WebSerialClient("10.10.10.99", "8080", "1");
        Navigation nav = new Navigation(sPort);
        // move east 36 inches
        nav.move(new DistanceVector(90, 36));
        // move north 36 inches
        nav.move(new DistanceVector(0, 36));
        // move west 36 inches
        nav.move(new DistanceVector(270, 36));
        // move south 36 inches
        nav.move(new DistanceVector(180, 36));

    } catch (Exception e) {
        e.printStackTrace();
        System.exit(1);
    }
}
}
```

Section Summary

With the code in this section, you should be able to perform dead reckoning using Java with a differential drive and a compass. The three classes I created in this section were

- MotionVector: Heading in degrees and magnitude in seconds

- DistanceVector: Heading in degrees and magnitude in inches

- Navigation: Navigational class that implements dead reckoning for both DistanceVectors and MotionVectors

What you will notice as you begin to experiment with this type of navigation are the types of errors you will get. I experienced the following types of errors:

- Errors in conversion factors relating to surface rates and headings.

- Position accuracy decreased as the number of movements increased.

- The robot did not avoid obstacles.

- The compass readings were not consistent at different locations in the test environment.

- Wheel slippage, inclines, and obstacles caused large inaccuracies in navigation.

In the next section, I will discuss how I can reduce some of the errors relating to positional inaccuracy by giving the robot the ability to know where it is absolutely in an environment. This process is called localization.

7.2 Localization

Localization is the process of giving the robot the ability to position itself in its environment. In the last chapter, the robot was able to move in a vector, but this vector had no start point, and its end point had large amounts of error because of environmental factors like wheel slippage, errors in conversion, and so on. In this section, I'll show you how to reduce this error by using sonar to calculate a start and an end position.

To begin, I am going to set the environment of the robot to be in a Perfect World as defined in the last section. This is a 100-inch × 100-inch grid with no obstacles. (See Figure 7-9.)

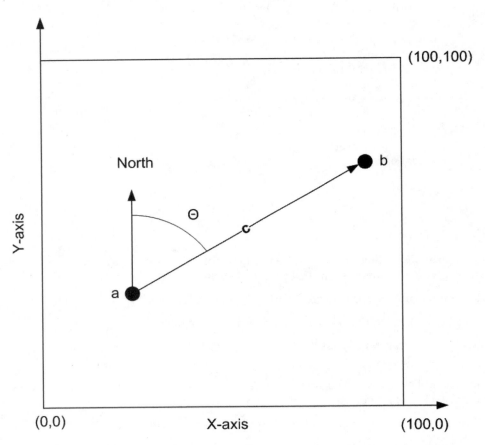

Figure 7-9. *Perfect World*

Again, to move successfully in this area, the robot will need the following information:

- A start point (a)

- An end point (b)

- A way to orient ourselves (find a heading) Θ (theta)

- A way to know how far we need to go (c)

From the previous section, the robot moved in the path of vector c with a heading and a time (or distance), but without a starting point or knowing whether or not it was at its end point. It moved relative to nothing, which is not that useful in navigation. So, how can the robot find its start point? There are two ways: I could tell the robot where it starts, or the robot could figure it out by itself.

To tell the robot where it should start, I added a single static method to the Localization class. This method takes any two points and returns a DistanceVector. Though the calculations speak for themselves, I needed to convert the angles from the Cartesian plane to the plane of compass readings. For Cartesian, the readings (clockwise from the top) are 90, 0, 270, and 180, with compass readings of 0, 90, 180, and 270. I performed this conversion by comparing the points with respect to one another and the arc tangent of the two points slope. See Example 7-11.

Example 7-11. *Localization.getDistanceVector()*

```
// calculate vector from 2 points.
    public static DistanceVector getDistanceVector(Point a, Point b) ➥
throws Exception {

        int d;
        int dx = a.x - b.x;
        int dy = a.y - b.y;
        System.out.println(a.toString());
        System.out.println(b.toString());
        // get distance
        double mag = Math.sqrt(dx * dx + dy * dy);
        // get angle
        if ((dx) == 0) {
            d = 90;
        } else {
            double slope = (double) (dy) / (double) (dx);
            d = (int) Math.toDegrees(Math.atan(slope));
        }
        // adjust angle to coordinate system of N,E,S,W
        if (a.y <= b.y) { // if 1st point(Y) higher
            if (a.x > b.x) { // if 1st point(X) is more to right
                d = 360 - (90 + d);
            } else {
                d = 90 - d;
            }
```

```
        } else {
            if (a.x < b.x) {
                d = 90 - d;
            } else {
                d = 180 + (90 - d);
            }
        }
        return new DistanceVector(d, mag);
    }
```

Next, I want to create a data structure with a name I could store and recall at a later time. I can't do this with a Point, but I can reuse a Point by just extending it and giving my new class a variable called name. I called this class NavPoint and added the string name to its constructor. See Example 7-12.

Example 7-12. *NavPoint.java*

```
package com.scottpreston.javarobot.chapter7;

import java.awt.Point;

public class NavPoint extends Point {

    public static final String START_POINT = "start";
    public static final String EXIT_POINT = "exit";
    public static final String CENTER_POINT = "center";

    public String name = null;


    public NavPoint(String name) {
        super();
        this.name = name;
    }

    public NavPoint(String name, int x, int y) {
        super(x, y);
        this.name = name;
    }

    public NavPoint(String name, Point p) {
        super(p);
        this.name = name;
    }
}
```

Next, it's time for the robot to figure out its start position on its own.

Code Objective

The code objective here is to give the robot the ability to find its start position, and then to navigate with dead reckoning.

Code Discussion

Given my robot has two moving sonar, one fixed sonar, and a known environment (a Perfect World), it will just have to perform two tasks. First, it will face north so it can align itself with the walls of its environment. Second, it will need to take readings of the south and west walls to determine my location. To perform this task, I'll need to create a class for my movable sonar called SonarServos.

The class has three instance fields, two to hold the positions of the servos and one for the MiniSsc. The other static fields in the class are specific for Feynman5 and were obtained through experimentation.

The constructor of the class takes a JSerialPort and is used to construct the MiniSsc class responsible for moving the sonar.

The move() method takes two arguments: left and right. These raw positions move the sonar. You can use this method when calibrating your robot for its AFT and FORE positions.

The moveLeft() and moveRight() methods take angles in degrees. Once again, I need to convert the angles to match the N, E, S, W coordinate system. So 0 is in front of the robot, 90 is to its right, and so on.

The left sonar only has valid angles from 180 to 360, while the right sonar only has valid angles from 0 to 180. The methods take into account the FORE and AFT positions of the sonar so that the robot moves the left or right sonar to the best approximation of the angle from the byte resolution servo position.

In main(), the sonar moves to the front, to the back, and to the side of the robot. This will validate that you have set the constants correctly. Then program the moves through angles from 0 to 360. Here you can observe the robot moving one sonar at a time since the sonar are each only capable of moving through 180 degrees. See Example 7-13.

Example 7-13. *SonarServos.java*

```java
package com.scottpreston.javarobot.chapter7;

import com.scottpreston.javarobot.chapter2.JSerialPort;
import com.scottpreston.javarobot.chapter2.Utils;
import com.scottpreston.javarobot.chapter2.WebSerialClient;
import com.scottpreston.javarobot.chapter3.MiniSsc;

public class SonarServos {

    public static final int LEFT_SONAR = 2;
    public static final int RIGHT_SONAR = 3;
    public static final int LEFT_AFT = 60;
    public static final int LEFT_NEUTRAL = 150;
    public static final int RIGHT_NEUTRAL = 110;
    public static final int LEFT_FORE = 245;
```

```java
public static final int RIGHT_AFT = 200;
public static final int RIGHT_FORE = 20;

private int leftPos = 127;
private int rightPos = 127;

private MiniSsc ssc;

public SonarServos(JSerialPort serialPort) throws Exception {
    ssc = new MiniSsc(serialPort);
}

public void move(int left, int right) throws Exception {
    Utils.pause(250); // wait for servo settle
    ssc.move(LEFT_SONAR, left, RIGHT_SONAR, right);
    Utils.pause(250); // wait for servo settle
}

// this will be from 180 to 360 of the robot.
public void moveLeft(int angle) throws Exception {
    if (angle > 360) {
        angle = angle - 360;
    }
    if (angle < 0) {
        angle = angle + 360;
    }
    double thirdQuad = (LEFT_FORE - LEFT_NEUTRAL); // > 127
    double fourthQuad = (LEFT_NEUTRAL - LEFT_AFT); // < 127
    int pos = LEFT_NEUTRAL;
    if (angle < 270 && angle > 180) {
        angle = 270 - angle;
        pos = (int) ((angle / 90.0) * thirdQuad) + LEFT_NEUTRAL;
    } else if (angle > 270) {
        angle = 360 - angle;
        pos = LEFT_NEUTRAL - (int) ((angle / 90.0) * fourthQuad);
    } else if (angle < 180) {
        pos = LEFT_AFT;
    }
    ssc.move(LEFT_SONAR, pos);
}

// this will be from 0 to 180 of the robot.
public void moveRight(int angle) throws Exception {
    if (angle > 360) {
        angle = angle - 360;
    }
```

```java
    if (angle < 0) {
        angle = angle + 360;
    }
    double firstQuad = (RIGHT_NEUTRAL - RIGHT_FORE); // < 127
    double secondQuad = (RIGHT_AFT - RIGHT_NEUTRAL); // > 127
    int pos = RIGHT_NEUTRAL;
    if (angle < 90) {
        pos = RIGHT_NEUTRAL - (int) ((angle / 90.0) * firstQuad);
    } else if (angle > 90 && angle > 180) {
        angle = 180 - angle;
        pos = (int) ((angle / 90.0) * secondQuad) + RIGHT_NEUTRAL;
    } else if (angle > 180) {
        pos = RIGHT_AFT;
    }
    ssc.move(RIGHT_SONAR, pos);
}

public void lookSide() throws Exception {
    move(LEFT_NEUTRAL, RIGHT_NEUTRAL);
}

public void lookFore() throws Exception {
    move(LEFT_FORE, RIGHT_FORE);
}

public void lookAft() throws Exception {
    move(LEFT_AFT, RIGHT_AFT);
}

public static void main(String[] args) throws Exception {
    try {
        WebSerialClient com = new WebSerialClient("10.10.10.99", "8080", "1");
        SonarServos ss = new SonarServos(com);
        ss.lookFore();
        Utils.pause(1000);
        ss.lookAft();
        Utils.pause(1000);
        ss.lookSide();
        // get 360 readings from sonar
        for (int a = 0; a < 360; a = a + 10) {
            ss.moveLeft(a);
            ss.moveRight(a);
            Utils.pause(1000);
        }
        com.close();
```

```
        } catch (Exception e) {
            e.printStackTrace();
            System.exit(1);
        }
    }
}
```

Now that the robot can move its sonar, it needs to look at four coordinate axes (N, E, S, and W), and because the robot is in a perfect world and knows where the walls are located, it just needs to take readings for west and south to give the robot its start position.

The Localization class extends Navigation. There is one field for the SonarServos class and one for the robot radius during measurements of the robot's position. This is needed because the sonar servos are 12 inches from the center of the robot and the position of the robot will always be relative to its center.

The next method, getStart(), changes the heading of the robot to north, and then moves the sonar servos to the side so the robot can get the sonar reading to its left (west). Next, the sonar servos moves AFT (south), and then takes the average of the two readings since both are facing the same direction.

The next method describes how to calculate the start position if the robot is facing some direction other than north. In this case, the program will need to know how to look at its heading, and then move the sonar servos to their best approximation of the coordinate axis N, E, S, and W.

To determine its heading, the method first calls its parents accessor to the NavStamp class and then calls getCompass(). Next, the positions of the four axes need to be calculated based on the heading of the robot. Here, the four coordinate axes are calculated by subtracting the heading from the four coordinate axes angular values (0, 90, 180, and 270). For example, if the robot is facing east, then its east position is in front of it or at 0 degrees. If the robot is facing southeast, it's –90 degrees, or to it's left at 270, and so on. Don't worry about the negative numbers on the degrees, because the SonarServos will adjust this reading to the degree corresponding from 0 to 360 degrees.

Note The trigonometric functions can use either –90 or 270 to produce the correct number; however, it's easier to explain when talking about the range 0 to 360.

Next, depending on the heading of the robot, it will need to move its sonar to the corresponding closest position. So, from 0 to 90 degrees, its best positions are to the south and west. But while facing from 90 to 180 degrees, the west position is out of range of the left sonar, and while I could make two readings for south and west with the right sonar, it's not as efficient. So instead I will take a north reading with the left sonar, and measure the west with the right. I continue alternating what sonar takes what readings by recording the "bestReadings" for a given heading for 180 to 270 degrees, and from 270 to 360 degrees.

Finally, at the end of the method, depending on the measurements taken, I either subtract the north or the east reading from 100, since the room is a 100 × 100 grid. Then at the end I adjust the readings based on the radius of the robot.

For this adjustment, let's say the robot is facing 30 degrees: westPos = 270 – 30 or 240 degrees, and the southPos = 180 – 30 or 150 degrees. The left sonar moves counterclockwise a little, while the right sonar moves clockwise a little. The best readings are one west of 48 and one south of 36. Because the radius of the robot is 12 inches, the x measurement is cos(30) * radius or about 10 inches, while the y measurement is sin(30) or 6 inches. The final coordinates are 48 + 10, 36 + 6, or 58,42.

In another example, if the robot turns to, say, 225 degrees or southwest, the readings will be for the north and the east. For this angle, cos(225) and sin(225) = –8, so the readings will be subtracted by 8, which makes sense because the robot's center is away from the readings. See Example 7-14.

Example 7-14. *Localization.java*

```java
package com.scottpreston.javarobot.chapter7;

import java.awt.Point;

import com.scottpreston.javarobot.chapter2.JSerialPort;
import com.scottpreston.javarobot.chapter2.Utils;
import com.scottpreston.javarobot.chapter2.WebSerialClient;

public class Localization extends Navigation {

    private SonarServos sonarServos;

    public static final int ROBOT_RADIUS = 12;

    public Localization(JSerialPort serialPort) throws Exception {
        super(serialPort);
        sonarServos = new SonarServos(serialPort);
    }

    // calculate vector from 2 points.
    public static DistanceVector getDistanceVector(Point a, Point b) ➥
throws Exception {

        int d;
        int dx = a.x - b.x;
        int dy = a.y - b.y;
        // get distance
        double mag =  Math.sqrt(dx * dx + dy * dy);
        // get angle
        if ((dx) == 0) {
            d = 90;
        } else {
            double slope = (double) (dy) / (double) (dx);
            d = (int) Math.toDegrees(Math.atan(slope));
        }
```

```java
        // adjust angle to coordinate system of N,E,S,W
        if (a.y <= b.y) { // if 1st point(Y) higher
            if (a.x > b.x) { // if 1st point(X) is more to right
                d = 360 - (90 + d);
            } else {
                d = 90 - d;
            }
        } else {
            if (a.x < b.x) {
                d = 90 - d;
            } else {
                d = 180 + (90 - d);
            }
        }
        return new DistanceVector(d, mag);
    }

    // this uses sonarServos, add your own sensors here if needed
    public NavPoint getStart() throws Exception {

        int[] nesw = getFourCoordinates();
        return new NavPoint(NavPoint.START_POINT, nesw[3], nesw[2]);
    }

    public int[] getFourCoordinates() throws Exception {
        // first face north.
        changeHeading(0);
        sonarServos.lookSide();
        Utils.pause(500);
        SonarReadings sonarReadings = getNavStamp().getSonar();
        int north = sonarReadings.center;
        int east = sonarReadings.right - ROBOT_RADIUS;
        int west = sonarReadings.left + ROBOT_RADIUS;
        sonarServos.lookAft();
        Utils.pause(500);
        sonarReadings = getNavStamp().getSonar();
        // average of two readings
        int south = (int) ((sonarReadings.left + sonarReadings.right) / 2.0);
        return new int[] {north,east,south,west};
    }

    // this uses sonarServos, add your own sensors here if needed
    public NavPoint getStart2() throws Exception {

        int heading = getNavStamp().getCompass();
        int north = 0, south = 0, east = 0, west = 0;
        int eastPos = 90 - heading;
```

```java
    int southPos = 180 - heading;
    int westPos = 270 - heading;
    int northPos = 360 - heading;
    SonarReadings sonarReadings = null;

    int bestReadings[] = null; // order x,y
    if (heading >= 0 && heading < 91) { //1st quad
        sonarServos.moveLeft(westPos);
        sonarServos.moveRight(southPos);
        Utils.pause(500);
        sonarReadings = getNavStamp().getSonar();
        west = sonarReadings.left;
        south = sonarReadings.right;
        bestReadings = new int[] { REL_WEST, REL_SOUTH };
    } else if (heading > 90 && heading < 181) {
        sonarServos.moveLeft(northPos);
        sonarServos.moveRight(westPos);
        Utils.pause(500);
        sonarReadings = getNavStamp().getSonar();
        north = sonarReadings.left;
        west = sonarReadings.right;
        bestReadings = new int[] { REL_WEST, REL_NORTH };
    } else if (heading > 180 && heading < 271) {
        sonarServos.moveLeft(eastPos);
        sonarServos.moveRight(northPos);
        Utils.pause(500);
        sonarReadings = getNavStamp().getSonar();
        east = sonarReadings.left;
        north = sonarReadings.right;
        bestReadings = new int[] { REL_EAST, REL_NORTH };
    } else if (heading > 270 && heading < 360) {
        sonarServos.moveLeft(southPos);
        sonarServos.moveRight(eastPos);
        Utils.pause(500);
        sonarReadings = getNavStamp().getSonar();
        south = sonarReadings.left;
        east = sonarReadings.right;
        bestReadings = new int[] { REL_EAST, REL_SOUTH };
    }

NavPoint navPoint = new NavPoint(NavPoint.START_POINT, 0, 0);
int xOffset = 0;
int yOffset = 0;
if (bestReadings[0] == REL_EAST) {
    xOffset = (int)(ROBOT_RADIUS * Math.cos(Math.toRadians(eastPos)));
    navPoint.x = 100 - east;
```

```java
        } else {
            xOffset = (int)(ROBOT_RADIUS * Math.cos(Math.toRadians(westPos)));
            navPoint.x = west;
        }
        if (bestReadings[1] == REL_NORTH) {
            yOffset = (int)(ROBOT_RADIUS * Math.sin(Math.toRadians(northPos)));
            navPoint.y = 100 - north;
        } else {
            yOffset = (int)(ROBOT_RADIUS * Math.sin(Math.toRadians(southPos)));
            navPoint.y = south ;
        }
        navPoint.x = navPoint.x + xOffset;
        navPoint.y = navPoint.y + yOffset;
        return navPoint;
    }

    // move from a to b
    public void move(Point a, Point b) throws Exception {
        MotionVector v = getDistanceVector(a, b);
        move(v);
    }

    public void move(Point b) throws Exception {
        move(getStart(), b);
    }

    public SonarServos getSonarServos() {
        return sonarServos;
    }

    public static void main(String[] args) {
        try {
            WebSerialClient sPort = new WebSerialClient("10.10.10.99", "8080", "1");
            Localization local = new Localization(sPort);
            local.move(new Point(36, 36));
        } catch (Exception e) {
            e.printStackTrace();
            System.exit(1);
        }
    }

}
```

Section Summary

With localization, your robot should be able to figure out its start position with relative ease, providing the environment is not that noisy. By repeating this process at the end of your algorithm, your robot can determine whether it's close enough to its goal to move again or exit.

The classes created in this section were

- NavPoint: A class that extends java.awt.Point but provides a name field

- SonarServos: A class that controls the sonar servos on top of the robot

- Localization: A class that extends Navigation that provides for the robot to estimate its start position

Next, it's time for the robot to move into a real environment with obstacles and avoid them.

7.3   Obstacle Detection

In the last two sections, we spoke of dead reckoning and localization in a finite known environment. How a robot deals with obstacles in this finite environment translates directly into how it deals with noisy environments and obstacles. To start with, I'll classify obstacles into six types: Useful Static, Useful Semi-static, Useful Dynamic, Useless Static, Useless Semi-static, and Useless Dynamic. They're shown in Table 7-2.

Table 7-2. *Obstacle Classification*

Obstacle Type	Useful	Useless
Static	Walls, furniture, landmarks, sidewalks, lawn	Floor lamps, closely spaced items, trees, creeks, potholes
Semi-static	Beverage cans, toys?	Toys on the floor, boxes, lawn sprinklers
Dynamic	Faces, hands, puppies	Walking person, toy or box on the floor, tree

The useful items are things that assist us in navigation. Static items like walls, landmarks, sidewalks are all items that don't move but can be used to give us a start point, way point, or end point. The semi-static items don't help the robot navigate because even though they don't move, they are not always at the same location. However, they could be goals for a robot (for example, cleaning the floor of items before I vacuumed or getting cans out of the refrigerator). The final ones don't help the robot navigate, but like semi-static obstacles they can be end points or goals for a robot (for example, following hand signals, or following a specific person in a crowded room).

The useless items are things that create noise for the robot. Noise can cause large or small errors in how the robot determines its routes or whether it hits anything. Static items that are useless are things that are very difficult for the robot to detect with its sensors. These are obstacles that it may hit and that could damage the robot (or the obstacle, too). Semi-static obstacles are items that we don't really care about but are not moving and have to be adjusted for during navigation. Finally, dynamic obstacles are those that usually get out of the robot's way if given enough time, so in this case the robot just needs to be patient and then resume its movement.

Currently, I have only talked about one type of obstacle: the static, useful kind. Now I'll show you how to create a class to handle the useless semi-static and useless dynamic kind of obstacles while our robot is navigating.

In Figure 7-10, the original path of the robot was from point a to point b. However, in Figure 7-10 an obstacle lies in the path between *a* and *b*. So in order for the robot to get to its goal (point b), it must calculate an alternate path around the obstacle.

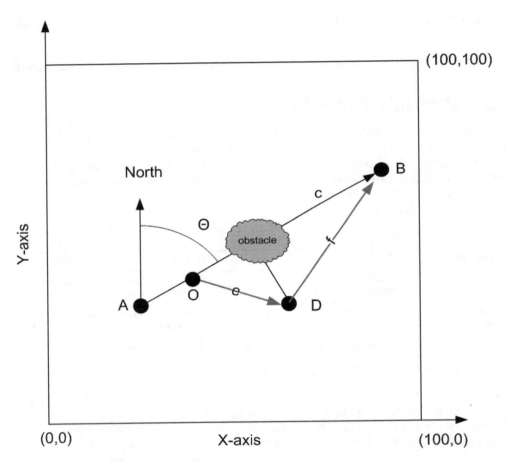

Figure 7-10. *Obstacle detection and path planning*

To calculate point D, take a point perpendicular to the right or the left of the obstacle. To choose right or left depends on what side has the most space in front of the robot. If it's to the right, the angle will be the heading 45 degrees, while the path to the left of the angle will be the heading –45 degrees.

Code Objective

The objective here is to give the robot the ability to navigate around obstacles.

Code Discussion

The ObstacleNavigation class builds on the Localization class from the last chapter. It has a single variable, offsetDistance, which will always be the diameter of the robot away from the original path. The constructor passes JSerialPort to the parent class Localization, and then any references required for the SonarServos, NavStamp, and SpeedDiffDrive classes can be used from the parents' accessor methods.

The only public method in this class is move(), which overrides the move() method in the Navigation class. The first thing I do in this method is log the MotionVector sent to the method. This was helpful to me while debugging, and it's also good to have a log for the robot's movements. Next it calls changeHeading() like its parent. Second, in the event of a negative magnitude, an exception is thrown because the sensors are configured for forward detection. If I had more sensors, I would adjust this for any direction, forward or reverse.

The next variable in the method, totalMs, holds the calculation of the total distance in milliseconds for the entire move. This is needed so that if the robot encounters an obstacle it can be calculated where the obstacle was encountered, permitting the bypass vectors to determine the position of the original coordinates. In Figure 7-10, the totalMs will represent the length of line c.

The next variable is offsetTime. This calculates the time based on the surface rate and the current offsetDistance. For the current robot, this is 34 inches divided by 14 inches per second, which translates to about 2400 milliseconds.

The first calculation that needs to be made is the number of times the sensors can take readings during the total range of motion. I'll call these variables sweeps. By knowing the number of sweeps calculated, the number of interval calls can be made to the isObstacleFwd() methods. If an obstacle does get in the way of the robot, the interval count is maintained. Using this number, the remaining time can be calculated in the current MotionVector. The variable used to calculate the remaining time is remainingMS, which is the count multiplied by the cycle time of the sensors.

The final bit of logic in this method is checking to see if an obstacle was encountered. If it was, then I pause the robot for a second before moving in reverse for 1 second. This clears the robot's path so it can turn and move along the bypass vector path without hitting the obstacle. Next, I need to increase the total remainingMS by the second it moved in reverse. Finally, before calling moveBypass(), I check to see if the remainingMS is greater than the offsetTime. This is because it's still possible that the robot is close enough to its desired position that any bypass would not get it any closer to its goal than if it just stayed put. Finally, if no obstacle is detected, the robot just moves forward for the remaining milliseconds.

The first of the two private methods is ObsicalForward(), which determines if there's an obstacle in the way of the robot. Again, you want to adjust the values in this method for your robot's configuration. Here I get all the sonar readings from the NavStaqmp, and depending on the readings, I return a true for obstacle and a false for no obstacle.

The second method, moveBypass(), creates two bypass vectors. These are vectors e and f in Figure 7-10. To calculate them, first the robot needs to determine the direction of the obstacle. To calculate the direction, I used a probability approach for each of the readings.

The first measurements are the infrared detectors. If the left side is greater than the right, I increase the left's probability of having an obstacle closer (higher means closer for the infrared sensors). If the sonar reading on the left is smaller, I increase the left's probability of an obstacle because there is more room on the right.

In the next set of calculations, I need to determine the final length of vector f. This is the second vector in the bypass path. Since I know the length of the first vector, I will have to calculate the second vector so that the robot will move to its original target point. The calculation first looks at the distance the robot has traveled parallel to its original heading. This is the COS of the angle multiplied by the offsetDistance. Now I can calculate the remaining distance in the direction of the original heading by subtracting the remaining time from this value.

Finally, the robot has a new distance it needs to travel such that the angle that is computed by the right triangle of one side is the remaining distance on the original path, and the second side is the distance traveled from the original path. I can calculate the angle by taking the arc tangent of these two ratios, and then I can calculate the distance by squaring the sides, adding them, and then taking the square root.

Now the robot will recursively call move() with two new headings. Because of this recursion, it's theoretically possible for the robot to move in a circle until it avoids the obstacle(s). This is better handled with mapping (which will be discussed in the next section), so an exception is thrown if more than one bypass is required. See Example 7-15.

Example 7-15. *ObstacleNavigation.java*

```java
package com.scottpreston.javarobot.chapter7;

import com.scottpreston.javarobot.chapter2.JSerialPort;
import com.scottpreston.javarobot.chapter2.Utils;
import com.scottpreston.javarobot.chapter2.WebSerialClient;

public class ObstacleNavigation extends Localization {


    private double offsetDistance = 0;
    private boolean inBypass = false;

    public ObstacleNavigation(JSerialPort serialPort) throws Exception {
        super(serialPort);
        offsetDistance = Math.sin(Math.toRadians(45)) * ROBOT_RADIUS * 2;

    }

    public void move(MotionVector vect) throws Exception {
        Utils.log("MV=" + vect.toString());
        if (vect.magnitude < 0) {
            throw new Exception("Only avoids obstacles in forward direction");
        }
        changeHeading(vect.heading);
```

```java
        // get total time in MS for motion (vector length)
        int totalMS = (int) Math.abs(vect.magnitude) * 1000;
        int offsetTime = (int) getSurfaceRate(offsetDistance) * 1000;
        // this will be minimum bypass distance
        // get number of sonar scans for range of motion
        int sweeps = (int) (totalMS / NavStamp.PING_CYCLE_TIME);
        // this will start motion
        getSonarServos().lookFore();
        Utils.pause(2000); // time to move sonar
        getDrive().forward();
        int count = 0;
        boolean Obstacle = false;
        while (count < sweeps) {
            // moves until it hits something or is done.
            if (isObstacleFwd()) {
                Utils.log("***fwd Obstacle***");
                getDrive().stop();
                Obstacle = true;
                break;
            }
            count++;
        }
        getDrive().stop();
        // get remaining time in vector
        int remainingMS = totalMS - (count * NavStamp.PING_CYCLE_TIME);
        if (Obstacle) {
            if (inBypass) {
                throw new Exception("Already in bypass find another route.");
            }
            Utils.pause(1000); // so not rough change of direction
            moveRaw(RAW_REV, 1000);
            remainingMS = remainingMS + 1000;
            // since both an Obstacle and it can be bypassed
            if (remainingMS > offsetTime) {
                inBypass = true;
                moveBypass(new MotionVector(vect.heading, remainingMS), offsetTime);
                inBypass = false;
            }
        } else {
            // since can't detect this distance anyway
            getDrive().forward(remainingMS);
        }
    }

    private void moveBypass(MotionVector remainingVect, int offsetTime) ➥
throws Exception {
```

```java
    // since readings in milliseconds
    remainingVect.magnitude = remainingVect.magnitude;
    DistanceReadings readings = getNavStamp().getSonarIR();
    // to move around obstacle to the left or to the right
    int newHeading = remainingVect.heading;
    double sq2 = (Math.sqrt(2) / 2.0);
    double leftProb = 0;
    double rightProb = 0;

    // ir is more important use this first
    // ir high means close, low means far
    if (readings.ir.left - 20 > readings.ir.right) {
        //  since something closer on left, then turn right
        leftProb = leftProb + 0.15;
        // if so close turning will cause hit
        if (readings.ir.left > 100)
            leftProb = leftProb + 0.1;
    } else {
        rightProb = rightProb + 0.15;
        // if so close not turning will cause hit
        if (readings.ir.right > 120)
            rightProb = rightProb + 0.1;
    }
    // checking sonar if left < right more room to right so turn right by
    // increasing prob.
    if (readings.sonar.left < readings.sonar.right) {
        leftProb = leftProb + 0.1;
        // if close
        if (readings.sonar.left < 24)
            leftProb = leftProb + 0.1;
        // if so close not turning will cause hit
        if (readings.sonar.left < 12)
            leftProb = leftProb + 0.1;
    } else {
        rightProb = rightProb + 0.1;
        if (readings.sonar.right < 24)
            rightProb = rightProb + 0.1;
        if (readings.sonar.right < 12)
            rightProb = rightProb + 0.1;
    }
    int headingOne = 0;
    int headingTwo = 0;
    // int offset distance
    double offsetAdjacent = Math.cos(Math.toRadians(45)) * offsetDistance;
    double offsetOpposite = Math.sin(Math.toRadians(45)) * offsetDistance;
```

```java
            // remaining time for original heading
            double remainingTime = remainingVect.magnitude - offsetAdjacent;
            int finalAngle = (int) Math.toDegrees(Math.atan(offsetOpposite / ➥
    remainingTime));
            double finalMagnitude = Math.sqrt(offsetAdjacent * offsetAdjacent + ➥
    remainingTime
                    * remainingTime);
            Utils.log("Obstacle prob=" + rightProb + "," + leftProb);
            if (rightProb < leftProb) {
                // turn right
                headingOne = newHeading + 45;
                headingTwo = newHeading - finalAngle;
            } else {
                headingOne = newHeading - 45;
                headingTwo = newHeading + finalAngle;
            }

            MotionVector bypassOne = new DistanceVector(headingOne, offsetTime);
            move(bypassOne);
            MotionVector bypassTwo = new MotionVector(headingTwo, finalMagnitude);
            move(bypassTwo);
        }

        private boolean isObstacleFwd() throws Exception {
            DistanceReadings dist = getNavStamp().getSonarIR();
            if (dist.ir.left > 100 || dist.ir.right > 120 || dist.sonar.left < 12
                    || dist.sonar.center < 12 || dist.sonar.right < 12) {
                return true;
            } else {
                return false;
            }
        }

        public static void main(String[] args) {
            try {
                WebSerialClient com = new WebSerialClient("10.10.10.99", "8080", "1");
                ObstacleNavigation nav = new ObstacleNavigation(com);
                // in seconds
                MotionVector[] v = new MotionVector[] { new MotionVector(90, 10) };
                nav.move(v);
            } catch (Exception e) {
                e.printStackTrace();
                System.exit(1);
            }
        }
    }
}
```

Section Summary

Detecting obstacles can be as sophisticated as your sensors are. I have demonstrated one way to find them using infrared and sonar, but you could use other methods as your budget allows. The class created in this section was ObstacleNavigation and it achieved this by constructing a path around an obstacle.

Currently, the algorithm only works well for a single obstacle, or if you have things temporarily getting in the way of your robot as it moves. If you think your robot will encounter multiple obstacles, it may save you time to construct a map with a path where the robot doesn't have to deal with more than one object at a time. For that, we'll have to use a little Graph Theory and create a software map of our environment.

7.4 Indoor Navigation

Up until now, all our navigation has been in the perfect world of a 100-inch × 100-inch grid. Rooms in a house or an office do not fit very well in this environment because there are things like tables, halls, doors, and so on. But as I began to experiment with navigation, I found it easier to join a few idealized environments together (like the 100 × 100 grid) into a graph than it was to model an entire room with all its quirks.

For example, using the graph from the introduction, I can create four vertices that each represent 100 × 100 regions. If I move from A to B, I don't need to know anything about C and D. Likewise, if I move from C to D, I don't need to know anything about A, though I could move via B if I wanted to take a longer path. (See Figure 7-11.)

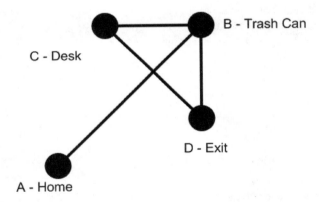

Room Graph

Figure 7-11. *A room graph*

The question is how can I model this in Java? Earlier I created two classes called Vertex and Edge. I'll now extend the Vertex class to create an object that models the perfect world on a 100 × 100 grid. I'll call this class a region.

A region has four fields. The first is inherited from Vertex and will be so named, while the second is an int size that gives the distance from the outermost point of the region to its center. The third is an ArrayList, which stores NavPoints denoting specific locations in the region to which the robot might want to navigate. The fourth field is an int[] called characteristic. This field represents the four coordinate axes as they would be measured in this region. The array {1,0,0,1} would represent readings in the north and west direction, but not long or out-of-range readings in east and south.

The region has a constructor of a name and a size. In the constructor, I also add the center waypoint since it will be needed later for navigation.

Outside of standard getter and accessor methods, I have three methods, one that will get the point in the region by name, and two other methods that do point translations. The method getScaledPoint() converts points taken in this region, say, from a sonar to a scaled point in the region within the bounds of 100 × 100. The method getScaledMagnitude() converts the final distance vector back to actual inches for any movement. See Example 7-16.

Example 7-16. *Region.java*

```java
package com.scottpreston.javarobot.chapter7;

import java.awt.Point;
import java.util.ArrayList;

public class Region extends Vertex{

    //list of way points in center
    private ArrayList wayPoints = new ArrayList();
    // start point in region absolute coordinates
    private int size = 0;
    // used to determine position within region N,E,S,W readings
    private int[] characteristic = new int[]{0,0,0,0};

    // constructor
    public Region(String name, int size) {
        super(name);
        this.size = size;
        // just add center point for later use.
        addWayPoint(NavPoint.CENTER_POINT,50,50);
    }

    // navigation points
    public void addWayPoint(NavPoint p) {
        wayPoints.add(p);
    }
    public void addWayPoint(String name,int x, int y) {
        addWayPoint(new NavPoint(name,x,y));
    }
```

```java
    //  get scaled start point
    //  output will be percentage from measured
    public Point getScaledPoint(int x,int y) {
        double totalSize = size * 2;
        int x2 = (int)(x/totalSize*100);
        int y2 = (int)(y/totalSize*100);
        return new Point(x2,y2);
    }

    // returns in actual inches
    public double getScaledMagnitude(double m) {
        double scale = size * 2 / 100.0;
        return m*scale;
    }

    //get points by name
    public NavPoint getPointByName(String name) {
        NavPoint pt = null;
        for (int x=0; x<wayPoints.size() ; x++) {
            NavPoint tmp = (NavPoint)wayPoints.get(x);
            if (tmp.name.equalsIgnoreCase(name)){
                pt = tmp;
                break;
            }
        }
        return pt;
    }

    public ArrayList getWayPoints() {
        return wayPoints;
    }

    public int getSize() {
        return size;
    }
    public void setSize(int size) {
        this.size = size;
    }
    public int[] getCharacteristic() {
        return characteristic;
    }
    public void setCharacteristic(int[] characteristic) {
        this.characteristic = characteristic;
    }
}
```

While moving inside the regions is no problem since we have been doing that, it's navigating from region to region inside the same room that we have not done. To help me with that, I'll create a new object called, simply enough, Room.

A Room will connect and orient all the regions in it relative to one another. I will do this by connecting them with edges. This is convenient since we already have edges as DistanceVectors. I will always construct the distance vectors so they are measured from each region's center point. To illustrate the creation of the region map in a real environment (my basement), see Figure 7-12.

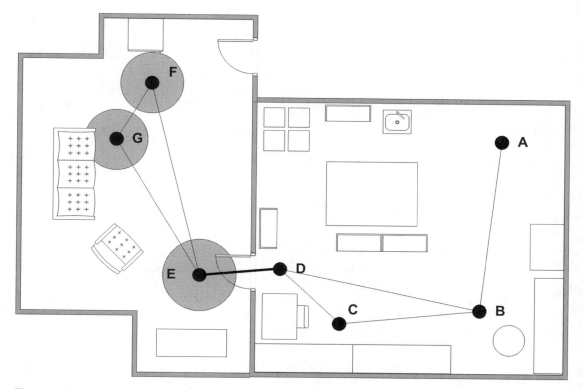

Figure 7-12. *The basement model*

The next step is to create a data structure that can represent this, called Room. The Room class, like the region class, has regions as vertices and edges, which will be DistanceVectors. I have added a sample Room in the static method called getBasement(), which defines the room in the previous figure. See Example 7-17.

Example 7-17. *Room.java*

```java
package com.scottpreston.javarobot.chapter7;

import java.util.ArrayList;

public class Room extends Vertex {

    private ArrayList regions = new ArrayList();
    private ArrayList edges = new ArrayList();

    public Room(String name) {
        super(name);
    }

    public void addRegion(Region r) {
        regions.add(r);
    }

    public void addEdge(Region r1, Region r2, DistanceVector vect) {
        vect.v1 = r1;
        vect.v2 = r2;
        edges.add(vect);
    }

    public static Room getBasement() {
        // 1st create regions
        Region a = new Region("home",36);
        a.setCharacteristic(new int[]{0,0,1,1});
        // add specific location of the trash can
        Region b = new Region("trash",36);
        b.setCharacteristic(new int[]{1,0,0,1});
        b.addWayPoint("can",80,20);
        Region c = new Region("desk",24);
        c.setCharacteristic(new int[]{1,1,0,0});
        Region d = new Region("exit",24);
        d.setCharacteristic(new int[]{0,1,0,1});
        Region e = new Region("treadmill",48);
        c.setCharacteristic(new int[]{0,1,1,0});
        Region f = new Region("fridge",36);
        c.setCharacteristic(new int[]{1,0,0,0});
        Region g = new Region("sofa",24);
        c.setCharacteristic(new int[]{0,0,0,1});
```

```
    // create room by linking regions
    Room basement = new Room("shop");
    basement.addEdge(a,b,new DistanceVector(190,260));
    basement.addEdge(b,d,new DistanceVector(290,288));
    basement.addEdge(b,c,new DistanceVector(260,216));
    basement.addEdge(c,d,new DistanceVector(315,60));
    basement.addEdge(d,e,new DistanceVector(280,72));
    basement.addEdge(e,f,new DistanceVector(345,260));
    basement.addEdge(e,g,new DistanceVector(325,200));
    basement.addEdge(g,f,new DistanceVector(210,72));
    return basement;

}

public ArrayList getRegions() {
    return regions;
}
public ArrayList getEdges() {
    return edges;
}
public void setEdges(ArrayList edges) {
    this.edges = edges;
}

}
```

The graph that I need to navigate is almost complete. The only thing that's missing is an algorithm that tells the robot the shortest path to take from one vertex to another. The algorithm I'll use for that is called Dijkstra's Algorithm (named after Edsger Dijkstra), which determines the shortest path for a directed weighted graph.

To illustrate this example, I'll take the following graph of the right side of the basement. But give the weights to the graph that correspond to the distance between them.

- AB = 260

- BD = 288

- BC = 216

- CD = 60

Next, instead of imagining a robot moving between these points, let's say we're using pipes and water instead. The water would be running in a line, with a constant speed.

Now, let's put special valves at each of the vertices—B, C, and D—such that if water gets there first from any incoming pipe, it closes the valve to all the other pipes coming into the valve. The valve then puts up a flag saying that this vertex is the shortest path.

If you can imagine the flow of water, you can find the shortest distance, in this case the vertices will be from A to B to C to D as the sum from BD = 288, which is greater than BC + CD = 276. See Figure 7-13.

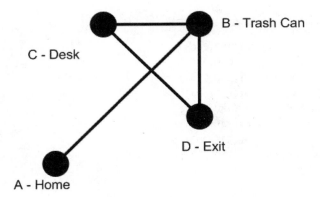

Room Graph

Figure 7-13. *The room graph*

If you want to understand the inner workings of the algorithm more deeply than the plumbing analogy, pick up the book *A Discipline of Programming* by Dijkstra himself, or check out my reference page on it at www.scottsbots.com/definitiveguide. See Example 7-18.

Example 7-18. *Dijkstra.java*

```java
package com.scottpreston.javarobot.chapter7;

import java.util.ArrayList;
import java.util.Collections;
import java.util.HashMap;
import java.util.HashSet;
import java.util.Iterator;

public class Dijkstra {

    private ArrayList vertices = new ArrayList();
    private ArrayList edges = new ArrayList();
    private HashMap oldVertex = new HashMap();
    private HashMap distances = new HashMap();
    private HashSet unsettled = new HashSet();
    private HashSet settled = new HashSet();

    public void addEdge(Edge e) {
        edges.add(e);
    }

    public void addAllEdges(ArrayList e) {
        edges = e;
    }
```

```java
    public void addVertex(Vertex v) {
        vertices.add(v);
    }

    public void addAllVertices(ArrayList v) {
        vertices = v;
    }

    public int getDist(Vertex start, Vertex end) {
        int[][] adj = getAdj();
        int size = vertices.size();
        int w = 0;
        for (int i = 0; i < size; i++) {
            Vertex vi = (Vertex) vertices.get(i);
            for (int j = 0; j < size; j++) {
                Vertex vj = (Vertex) vertices.get(j);
                if (vi.equals(start) && vj.equals(end)) {
                    w = adj[i][j];
                }
            }

        }
        return w;
    }

    public void setShortDistance(Vertex v, int dist) {
        unsettled.remove(v);
        distances.put(v, new Integer(dist));
        unsettled.add(v);
    }

    public void setPred(Vertex a, Vertex b ){
        oldVertex.put(a,b);
    }

    public Vertex getPred(Vertex a) {
        return (Vertex)oldVertex.get(a);
    }

    public int getShortDistance(Vertex v) {
        Integer d = (Integer) distances.get(v);
        if (d == null) {
            return Integer.MAX_VALUE;
        } else {
            return d.intValue();
        }
    }
}
```

```java
public Vertex extractMinimum() {
    Iterator i = unsettled.iterator();
    int min = Integer.MAX_VALUE;
    Vertex minV = null;
    while (i.hasNext()) {
        Vertex tmp = (Vertex) i.next();
        if (getShortDistance(tmp) < min) {
            min = getShortDistance(tmp);
            minV = tmp;
        }
    }
    unsettled.remove(minV);
    return minV;
}

public void relaxNeighbors(Vertex u) {
    int[][] adj = getAdj();
    int size = vertices.size();
    for (int i = 0; i < size; i++) {
        Vertex vi = (Vertex) vertices.get(i);
        if (vi.equals(u)) { // only check this i'th column
            for (int j = 0; j < size; j++) {
                Vertex v = (Vertex) vertices.get(j);
                int w2 = adj[i][j];
                // should give all adjacent vertices not settled
                if (w2 > 0 && w2 < Integer.MAX_VALUE
                        && (settled.contains(v) == false)) {
                    // does a shorter distance exist?
                    if (getShortDistance(v) > getShortDistance(u)
                            + getDist(u, v)) {
                        int d = getShortDistance(u) + getDist(u, v);
                        setShortDistance(v, d);
                        setPred(v,u);
                    }
                }
            }

        }
    }

}


public ArrayList getShortestPath( Vertex start, Vertex end) {
    unsettled.add(start);
    setShortDistance(start,0);
    while (unsettled.size() > 0) {
```

```
            Vertex u = extractMinimum(); // gets shortest Vertext
            settled.add(u);
            relaxNeighbors(u);
        }
        ArrayList l = new ArrayList();
        for (Vertex v = end; v != null; v = getPred(v)) {
            l.add(v);
        }
        Collections.reverse(l);

        System.out.println("--- PRINT ORDER ---");
        for (int d=0;d < l.size();d++) {
            Vertex v = (Vertex) l.get(d);
            System.out.println(v.name);
        }
        return l;
    }

    public Vertex getVertexByName(String n) {
        int size = vertices.size();
        for (int i = 0; i < size; i++) {
            Vertex vi = (Vertex) vertices.get(i);
            if (vi.name.equals(n)) {
                return vi;
            }
        }
        return null;

    }

    private int[][] getAdj() {

        int[][] adjMatrix = new int[vertices.size()][vertices.size()];
        // init all large
        for (int i = 0; i < vertices.size(); i++) {
            for (int j = 0; j < vertices.size(); j++) {
                adjMatrix[i][j] = Integer.MAX_VALUE;
            }
        }
        // set to actual values  to zero
        for (int i = 0; i < vertices.size(); i++) {
            Vertex vi = (Vertex) vertices.get(i);
            for (int j = 0; j < vertices.size(); j++) {
                Vertex vj = (Vertex) vertices.get(j);
                if (i == j) {
                    adjMatrix[i][j] = 0;
```

```java
            } else {
                for (int k = 0; k < edges.size(); k++) {
                    Edge e = (Edge) edges.get(k);
                    if (e.v1.equals(vi) && e.v2.equals(vj))
                        adjMatrix[i][j] = e.weight;
                    if (e.v2.equals(vi) && e.v1.equals(vj))
                        adjMatrix[i][j] = e.weight;
                }
            }
        }
    }

    return adjMatrix;
}


public static void main(String[] args) {
    Dijkstra dijkstra = new Dijkstra();
    Vertex a = new Vertex("a");
    dijkstra.addVertex(a);
    Vertex b = new Vertex("b");
    dijkstra.addVertex(b);
    Vertex c = new Vertex("c");
    dijkstra.addVertex(c);
    Vertex d = new Vertex("d");
    dijkstra.addVertex(d);
    dijkstra.addEdge(new Edge(a, d, 2));
    dijkstra.addEdge(new Edge(a, b, 2));
    dijkstra.addEdge(new Edge(a, c, 4));
    dijkstra.addEdge(new Edge(b, c, 1));
    dijkstra.getShortestPath(d,c);

    //System.out.println(d.adjToString(d.getAdj()));
}

/**
 * @return Returns the vertices.
 */
public ArrayList getVertices() {
    return vertices;
}
/**
 * @param vertices The vertices to set.
 */
public void setVertices(ArrayList vertices) {
    this.vertices = vertices;
}
```

```java
/**
 * @return Returns the edges.
 */
public ArrayList getEdges() {
    return edges;
}
/**
 * @param edges The edges to set.
 */
public void setEdges(ArrayList edges) {
    this.edges = edges;
}
}
```

Code Objective

The code objective here is to give the robot the ability to navigate indoors, and most importantly to the fridge.

Code Discussion

The IndoorNavigation class extends ObstacleNavigation because I don't want my robot hitting anything on its way to the refrigerator. It has two fields of type Room and Region where the region will be the current region and the room will be the room passed through the constructor.

The move() method in this algorithm takes a single String parameter end, which will be the name of the end NavPoint. The method itself consists of three parts: first, to get the current region and start point through localization; second, to move from its current region to its end region via the shortest path determined by the Dijkstra Algorithm; third, to move to the desired end point in the end region.

Getting the start position is done via the getBestRegion() method. This method gets four coordinate axes from the getFourCoordinates() method in Localization. These four coordinates are measured against all the regions' sizes and characteristics to produce a vote. The region with the largest vote will then be the best region, and from there the start position will be obtained from the best readings of the four axes: N, E, S, and W. See Example 7-19.

Example 7-19. *IndoorNavigation.java*

```java
package com.scottpreston.javarobot.chapter7;

import java.util.ArrayList;

import com.scottpreston.javarobot.chapter2.JSerialPort;
import com.scottpreston.javarobot.chapter2.WebSerialClient;

public class IndoorNavigation extends ObstacleNavigation {

    private Room currentRoom;
    private Region currentRegion;
```

```java
    public IndoorNavigation(JSerialPort serialPort, Room room) throws Exception {
        super(serialPort);
        currentRoom = room;
    }

    public void move(String end) throws Exception{
        ArrayList path = new ArrayList();
        getBestRegion();
        NavPoint start = currentRegion.getPointByName(NavPoint.START_POINT);
        NavPoint startCenter = currentRegion.getPointByName(NavPoint.CENTER_POINT);
        // start vector will be in virtual points 100x100
        DistanceVector startVector = getDistanceVector(start,startCenter);
        // convert from 100x100 to scaled version
        startVector.magnitude = currentRegion.getScaledMagnitude➥
(startVector.magnitude);
        path.add(startVector);
        // middle vectors
        ArrayList regions  = currentRoom.getRegions();
        Region endRegion = null;
        NavPoint endPoint = null;
        for (int r=0;r<regions.size();r++) {
            endRegion = (Region)regions.get(r);
            if (endRegion.getPointByName(end) != null){
                endPoint = endRegion.getPointByName(end);
                break;
            }
        }
        Dijkstra dijkstra = new Dijkstra();
        dijkstra.setVertices(regions);
        dijkstra.setEdges(currentRoom.getEdges());
        path.addAll(dijkstra.getShortestPath(currentRegion,endRegion));
        // end vector
        NavPoint endCenterPoint = currentRegion.getPointByName➥
(NavPoint.CENTER_POINT);
        DistanceVector endVector = getDistanceVector(endCenterPoint,endPoint);
        endVector.magnitude = endRegion.getScaledMagnitude(endVector.magnitude);
        path.add(endVector);
        DistanceVector[] path2 = (DistanceVector[]) path.toArray();
        // conversion will be made to seconds from Navigation
        move(path2);
    }
```

```java
private void getBestRegion() throws Exception{
    // get 4 coordinate measures
    int[] nesw = getFourCoordinates();
    // get regions
    ArrayList regions  = currentRoom.getRegions();
    Region bestRegion = null;
    int maxVote=0;
    // iterate through all regions
    for (int r=0;r<regions.size();r++) {
        Region tmpRegion = (Region)regions.get(r);
        int longDist = tmpRegion.getSize()*2;
        int[] rChar = tmpRegion.getCharacteristic();
        int vote = 0;
        // vote on if measurements match readings
        for (int v=0;v<4;v++) {
            if (rChar[v] == 0 && nesw[v] > longDist) {
                vote++;
            }
            if (rChar[v] == 1 && nesw[v] < longDist) {
                vote++;
            }
        }
        if (vote > maxVote) {
            bestRegion = tmpRegion;
        }
    }
    int [] bestChar = bestRegion.getCharacteristic();
    int x=0,y=0;
    if (bestChar[2] == 1) {
        y=nesw[2];
    }
    if (bestChar[0] == 1 && bestChar[2] == 0) {
        y= 100 - nesw[0];
    }
    if (bestChar[3] == 1) {
        y=nesw[3];
    }
    if (bestChar[1] == 1 && bestChar[3] == 0) {
        y= 100 - nesw[1];
    }
    bestRegion.addWayPoint(new NavPoint(NavPoint.START_POINT,➥
bestRegion.getScaledPoint(x,y)));
    currentRegion = bestRegion;
}
```

```
public static void main(String[] args) {

    Room basement = Room.getBasement();
    try {
        WebSerialClient sPort = new WebSerialClient("10.10.10.99", "8080", "1");
        IndoorNavigation nav = new IndoorNavigation(sPort,basement);
        nav.move("fridge");
    } catch (Exception e) {
        e.printStackTrace();
        System.exit(1);
    }


    }
}
```

Section Summary

In this section, I showed you that by adding some structure to where you want your robot to travel, your robot can navigate any place you need it to indoors. The classes created in this section were

- Region: The idealized coordinate system of a 100 × 100 grid

- Room: A room consisting of many regions connected by DistanceVectors

- Dijkstra: An algorithm for finding the shortest path through a weighted graph between vertices

- IndoorNavigation: A navigation program using regions and rooms for moving to any named point

Since my robot can now move indoors quite well, I thought it time I teach it to move outdoors. Though I have not perfected mowing the lawn, getting the mail, or walking the dog, I have been able to get the robot to move close to the mailbox using GPS. And that's what I am going to talk about next.

7.5 Outdoor Navigation

What is GPS? Global Positioning System (GPS) is a satellite navigation system made up of 24 satellites traveling in very precise orbits. While GPS was originally intended for use by the military, it was opened up for civilian use in the 1980s.

GPS triangulates the signals of these satellites by measuring the time difference between when the signals were transmitted and when they were received. It's the difference that allows a GPS device to fix a position at some coordinate on the earth. A GPS receiver must lock on to at least three satellites to get a 2-D position of longitude (N/S) and latitude (E/W), and lock on to four satellites to get a 3-D position that includes altitude.

GPS receivers range in accuracy of from 10 meters to 3 meters. So, if you need precise navigation, you'll still need to use the methods discussed in section 7.3. However, you can use the global positioning of a GPS receiver to get you pretty darn close.

The GPS device we'll use is a $100 unit called the Garmin eTrex (www.garmin.com/products/etrex). This unit outputs serial signals at 4800 baud in simple text format every few seconds. The format name is called NMEA (National Marine Electronics Association). In order to make use of this GPS signal, we'll need to modify our BASIC Stamp program to retrieve and parse this text into a usable format.

The sample output from the eTrex in NMEA format is displayed in Example 7-20.

The first line, beginning with $GPRMC, is the line that gives us the time and the position. The last line in bold (starting with $PGRMZ) gives us our elevation. The following BASIC Stamp program waits for the first line, and then parses it as it arrives.

Example 7-20. *NMEA Output from eTrex*

```
$GPRMC,144710,A,3955.7362,N,08309.2237,W,0.0,351.7,060705,6.5,W,A*17
$GPRMB,A,,,,,,,,,,,,A,A*0B
$GPGGA,144710,3955.7362,N,08309.2237,W,1,07,1.3,291.8,M,-33.3,M,,*72
$GPGSA,A,3,,06,,09,,15,18,21,,26,29,,3.1,1.3,2.8*36
$GPGSV,3,1,11,03,06,323,00,06,22,204,36,08,00,024,00,09,25,147,37*7F
$GPGSV,3,2,11,10,06,080,00,15,38,312,39,18,51,293,38,21,79,308,35*7C
$GPGSV,3,3,11,22,20,275,00,26,55,049,37,29,40,046,39*41
$GPGLL,3955.7362,N,08309.2237,W,144710,A,A*5E
$GPBOD,,T,,M,,*47
$PGRME,4.7,M,7.2,M,9.5,M*2B
$PGRMZ,957,f,3*10
$GPRTE,1,1,c,*37
```

The only thing we need to do is connect our eTrex to our BASIC Stamp via the data cable [01-10205-00]. I used the bare wire version because it's easier to connect to my Stamp. Another version connects directly to a DB9. See Figure 7-14.

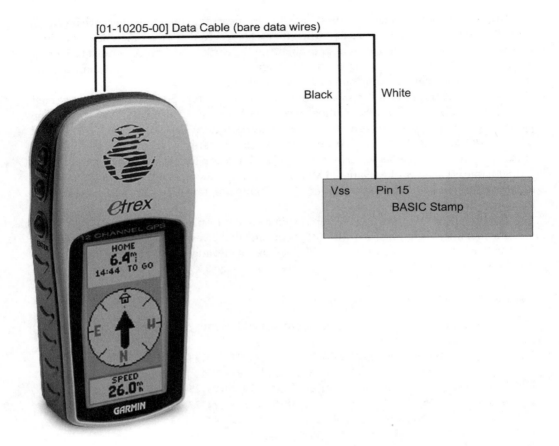

Figure 7-14. *eTrex and Stamp*

Code Objective

The objective here is to get the robot to do dead reckoning outdoors using GPS.

Code Discussion

The Parallax BASIC Stamp 2 has a limited amount of memory. If you employ the BASIC Stamp 2P, you could use a function to input the serial data to a RAM scratchpad and do all the parsing from there. Here, we're going to parse everything as a single line, skipping parts of the line and pushing data into variables where they are needed.

Also, we have to make two separate calls to get the exact longitude and latitude because the variable space in my standard BASIC Stamp 2 is limited. So, in Example 7-21, you should see the two functions get_lat and get_lon. This will effectively get all the information I need for the GPS information.

Example 7-21. *get_lat and get_lon*

```
get_lat:
    SERIN GPS,N4800,2000,get_lat,[WAIT("GPRMC,"),SKIP 7,➡
status,SKIP 1,STR gpsData1\4,SKIP 1,STR gpsData2\4]
    SEROUT 16,N9600,[status,",0",gpsData1(0),gpsData1(1),"➡
:",gpsData1(2),gpsData1(3),".",gpsData2(0),gpsData2(1),gpsData2(2),gpsData2(3)]
    GOTO main
get_lon:
    SERIN GPS,N4800,2000,get_lon,[WAIT("GPRMC,"),SKIP 7,status,SKIP ➡
13,STR gpsData1\5,SKIP 1,STR gpsData2\4]
    SEROUT 16,N9600,[status,",",gpsData1(0),gpsData1(1),gpsData1(2),"➡
:",gpsData1(3),gpsData1(4),".",gpsData2(0),gpsData2(1),gpsData2(2),gpsData2(3)]
    GOTO main
```

Now we have the BASIC Stamp code written. I have only added the parameters for the $GPRMC line of the NMEA reading. You can modify this for altitude, time, and other items as you see fit.

Those readings act as the status, which gives an indication of whether or not the reading is valid. This is from the GPS receiver and will be a W if it's not a valid reading. The other readings are the RAW output from the device in (DD:MM.NNNN) format, where the DD is degrees, the MM is minutes, and the NNNN is the fractional minute reading.

The output values for double longitude and double latitude are in minutes. To get this, I multiplied the hour reading by 60. See Example 7-22.

Example 7-22. *GpsReading.java*

```java
package com.scottpreston.javarobot.chapter7;

import java.io.Serializable;

public class GpsReading implements Serializable {

    public boolean status = false;
    public double longitude = 0.0;
    public double latitude = 0.0;
    public String lon_raw = null;
    public String lat_raw = null;

    // gives an equivalent of about 7 inches.
    public static final double LAT_LON_CONV = (24902.0 // miles around earth
            * 5280.0 // feet in a mile
            * 12 // inches per feet
            ) / (360.0 // degrees in a circle
            * 60.0 // minutes in a degree
            * 10000 // resolution of minutes
            ); // inches in a foot
```

```java
    public GpsReading(String lon, String lat) throws Exception {
        lon_raw = lon;
        lat_raw = lat;
        setValues();
    }

    private void setValues() throws Exception {
        if (lon_raw.startsWith("A") && lon_raw.startsWith("A")) {
            status = true;
        }
        String lonHr = lon_raw.substring(2, 5);
        String latHr = lat_raw.substring(2, 5);
        String lonMn = lon_raw.substring(6, 12);
        String latMn = lat_raw.substring(6, 12);

        longitude = new Double(lonHr).doubleValue() * 60
                + (new Double(lonMn).doubleValue());
        latitude = new Double(latHr).doubleValue() * 60
                + (new Double(latMn).doubleValue());

    }

    public String toString() {
        return "GpsReading = {longitude = " + lon_raw + " = " + longitude
                + ", latitude = " + lat_raw + " = " + latitude;
    }

}
```

Now that we have the data structure, all we have left to do is create the methods in the NavStamp class to get the data from our BASIC Stamp program. I have to create three methods to get the data from the Stamp: the first gets the longitude, the second gets the latitude, and the third combines the two and returns the GpsReading object. See Example 7-23.

Example 7-23. *NavStamp Command Programs*

```java
    public String getGpsLongitude() throws Exception {
        byte[] readings = execute3(new byte[] { CMD_INIT, CMD_GPS_LON }, 5000);
        return Utils.toAscii(readings);
    }
    public String getGpsLatitude() throws Exception {
        byte[] readings = execute3(new byte[] { CMD_INIT, CMD_GPS_LAT }, 5000);
        return Utils.toAscii(readings);
    }
    public GpsReading getGps() throws Exception{
        String lon = getGpsLongitude();
        String lat = getGpsLatitude();
        return new GpsReading(lon,lat);
    }
```

The last step is adding this functionality to our navigation class. I have set four static variables that represent the coordinates of my house's garage and the mailbox. These are in minutes and can be converted to inches using the conversion constant defined in GpsReading. The important thing I need to know is not the distance in inches itself, but the distance between the points.

In Example 7-24, I'll calculate a DistanceVector from my garage to the mailbox. Because the points in the Localization.getDistanceVector() method take whole numbers, I'll convert the numeral in the 10,000th place to a whole number by multiplying the coordinate by 10,000. Next, I pass in the start point and end point to the getDistanceVector() method, and then scale the magnitude to inches. My resulting vector from the garage to the mailbox is a heading of 61, with a distance of 452 inches (or a little over 37 feet).

Example 7-24. *OutdoorNavigation.java*

```java
package com.scottpreston.javarobot.chapter7;

import java.awt.Point;

import com.scottpreston.javarobot.chapter2.JSerialPort;

public class OutdoorNavigation extends Navigation {

    public static double HOUSE_LAT = 2395.7362;
    public static double HOUSE_LON = 4989.2237;

    public static double MAILBOX_LAT = 2395.7402;
    public static double MAILBOX_LON = 4989.2307;

    public OutdoorNavigation(JSerialPort serialPort) throws Exception {
        super(serialPort);
    }

    public void move(GpsReading end) throws Exception {
        GpsReading start = getNavStamp().getGps();
        Point startPoint = new Point(lonToInch(start.longitude),
                lonToInch(start.latitude));
      Point endPoint = new Point(lonToInch(end.longitude), lonToInch(end.latitude));
        DistanceVector v = Localization.getDistanceVector(startPoint,
                endPoint);
        // convert to inches
        v.magnitude = v.magnitude * GpsReading.LAT_LON_CONV;
        move(v);
    }
}
```

```java
    public static int lonToInch(double d) {
        double conv = Math.cos(Math.toRadians(HOUSE_LAT/60));
        d = conv * d;
        return (int) (d * 10000);
    }

    public static int latToInch(double d) {
        return (int) (d * 10000);
    }

    public static void main(String[] args) {
        try {
            System.out.println("inches per point of resolution =" + GpsReading.➥
LAT_LON_CONV);
            System.out.println("house lon to inches=" + lonToInch(HOUSE_LON));
            System.out.println("house lat to inches=" + latToInch(HOUSE_LAT));
            System.out.println("mail lon to inches=" + lonToInch(MAILBOX_LON));
            System.out.println("mail lat to inches=" + latToInch(MAILBOX_LAT));
            Point startPoint = new Point(lonToInch(HOUSE_LON),➥
 lonToInch(HOUSE_LAT));
        Point endPoint = new Point(lonToInch(MAILBOX_LON), lonToInch(MAILBOX_LAT));
            DistanceVector v = Localization.getDistanceVector(startPoint,
                    endPoint);
            v.magnitude = v.magnitude * GpsReading.LAT_LON_CONV;
            System.out.println(v.toString());
        } catch (Exception e) {
        }
    }
}
```

Section Summary

In this section, I showed you how to get a NMEA reading from your BASIC Stamp and then send it to your Java program. Then you converted that reading to a coordinate system you could perform calculations with (for example, get a DistanceVector) so you could pass it to a navigation class to move.

The classes created in this section were

- GPSReading: A data structure to hold the data from the BASIC Stamp

- OutdoorNavigation: A navigational class that converts between longitude and latitude to get my robot from the house to the mailbox and back again

Stay tuned for updates at www.scottsbots.com, since this should be the perfect outdoor navigation to walk the dog.

7.6 Chapter Summary

In this chapter, I showed some classes that allow your robot to navigate, via dead reckoning, around obstacles, indoors and out.

In the introduction, I covered some of the following foundational topics:

- Basic Graph Theory: Describing ideal navigation scenarios

- Robot Configuration: Describing the components and structure of the robot being used to demonstrate navigation

- Data Structures: Describing holding the information coming from the microcontroller

- Sensor Data Retrieval: Describing the exact mechanisms for requesting data from the microcontroller for our robot configuration

In section 7.1, I demonstrated the most basic navigational process, dead reckoning. The three classes I created in this section were

- MotionVector: A heading in degrees with a magnitude in seconds

- DistanceVector: A heading in degrees, with a magnitude in inches

- Navigation: A navigational class that implements dead reckoning for both DistanceVectors and MotionVectors

In section 7.2, I discussed how to reduce some of the errors relating to positional inaccuracy by giving the robot the ability to know where it is absolutely in an environment. That process is called localization.

With localization, your robot should be able to figure out its start position with relative ease, provided the environment is not too noisy. By repeating this process, at the end of your algorithm your robot can determine whether it's close enough to its goal to move again or exit. The classes created in this section were

- NavPoint: A class that extends java.awt.Point but provides a name field

- SonarServos: A class that controls the sonar servos on top of the robot

- Localization: A class that extends Navigation, thus allowing the robot to estimate its start position

In section 7.3, I demonstrated one way to find obstacles using infrared and sonar. The class created in this section was ObstacleNavigation, and it achieved obstacle avoidance by constructing a path around an obstacle.

In section 7.4, I showed you that by adding some structure to where you want your robot to travel, it can navigate any place you need it to indoors. The classes created in this section were

- Region: An idealized coordinate system using a 100 × 100 grid

- Room: A room consisting of many regions connected by DistanceVectors

- Dijkstra: An algorithm for finding the shortest path through a weighted graph between vertices

- IndoorNavigation: A navigation program using regions and rooms for moving to any named point

In section 7.5, I showed you how to get a NMEA reading from your BASIC Stamp and then send it to your Java program. By converting that reading to a coordinate system, you can perform various calculations with it (for example, get a DistanceVector), allowing you to pass it to a navigation class to move.

The classes created in this section were

- GPSReading: A data structure to hold the data from the BASIC Stamp

- OutdoorNavigation: A navigational class that converts between longitude and latitude to get my robot from the house to the mailbox and back again

This concludes the core functionality for programming your robot with Java. In the next chapter, we'll cover some advanced topics, such as database connectivity and having our robot figure out its own path through a maze.

■ ■ ■

CHAPTER 8

Other Topics

Sufficiently advanced technology is indistinguishable from magic.

— Arthur C. Clarke

8.0 Introduction

This is a catchall section. Here I'll discuss things that will make your Java robotics experience easier and more robust. The first topic we'll cover will be on executing programs outside of an IDE. For this, I'll talk briefly about creating batch files or shell scripts, and then scheduling those on their own via a schedule.

To assist in building and moving code to your robot, I'll also provide you with an overview of Ant. Ant is an Apache project that can be found at http://ant.apache.org, and though it was originally designed as just a build tool, it can do a whole lot more.

After that, we'll tackle the MySQL database, which is located at www.mysql.com. I'll also describe an example class that can be used to create, read, update, and delete data from your database using JDBC and SQL during robot navigation.

Another Apache project I'll discuss is Tomcat, located at http://jakarta.apache.org/tomcat. Tomcat is a servlet engine that allows your robot to run Java servlets or JavaServer Pages (JSP) pages. Both the servlets and the JSP pages can access the Java API you created (or the Java API from this book) to create a web client that you can use to access your robot.

Finally, the last item we'll cover concerns teaching your robot to create a map of regions on its own by running a program that navigates a robot out of a maze.

8.1 Running Your Java Programs

One of the things I've never liked about executing Java programs is the execution syntax. If you go to your command or shell prompt and type **java –?**, you'll be presented with a list of parameters you can use when executing your Java program. See Figure 8-1.

Figure 8-1. *Results from typing **java –?** at the command prompt in Windows XP*

Here you can see all of the different options you can run when executing your program. The most important one is the –cp or –classpath option, because this is where you have to specify your classpath of all the libraries your class will require when executing.

If you're executing the sound API or a vision API, then your classpath will be very large and difficult to type, so I recommend placing this entire string in a .bat or .cmd or .sh file that can be edited with a text editor. By renaming your file as something like foo.bat or foo.sh, you can execute your Java code without having to type the entire classpath.

You can also run several programs at the same time by just opening another window and executing your shell script. By doing this, you'll create another instance of the JVM with its own memory space and port allocation.

■**Note** If you're accessing your serial port in both programs, you'll get a port-in-use exception while the other program is running. To get around this, use the WebSerialPort.

Note the following batch file (or shell script). I've also made sure all the JARs were in this same directory.

```
java -classpath java_robot_book.jar;comm.jar;freetts.jarljai_codec.jar;jai_core.➥
jar; jmf.jar;jspapi.jar;mail.jar;servlet-api.jar;sphinx4.jar;WSJ_8gau_13dCep_8kHz_➥
31mel_200Hz_3500Hz.jar com.scottpreston.javarobot.chapter7. Navigation
```

This batch (or shell script) isn't the nicest way to execute your Java program, but unless you can convert your Java executable to an EXE or it has a UNIX equivalent, this is what you're left with.

8.2 Scheduling Your Programs

To give your robot a true sense of autonomy is to schedule certain programs to run at scheduled times. In Windows, you can use the "at" command or the Scheduled Task Wizard. In UNIX, you can use CRON.

I schedule diagnostic events, sleep events, database backup events—things that should run in the background just to make sure everything keeps running. One example is a localization routine that e-mails me my position once an hour. The second is a startup diagnostic routine that e-mails me those details.

To use the schedule command in Windows XP, go to Programs ➤ Accessories ➤ System Tools ➤ Scheduled Task. In the Scheduled Task window, click the Add Scheduled Task button, and then click Next (see Figure 8-2).

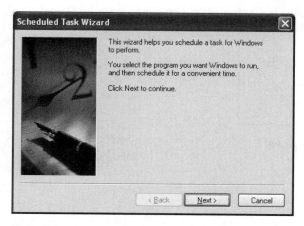

Figure 8-2. *The Scheduled Task Wizard, page 1 of 6*

Click Browse, and then navigate to your Java batch file (see Figure 8-3).

Figure 8-3. *The Scheduled Task Wizard, page 2 of 6*

Select a name then chose the schedule you would like (see Figure 8-4).

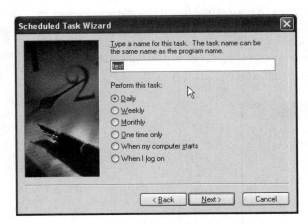

Figure 8-4. *The Scheduled Task Wizard, page 3 of 6*

Enter a time, as shown in Figure 8-5.

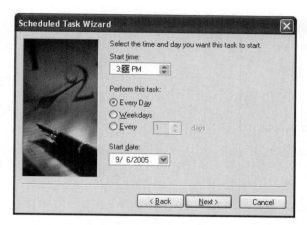

Figure 8-5. *The Scheduled Task Wizard, page 4 of 6*

Enter the username and password, as shown in Figure 8-6.

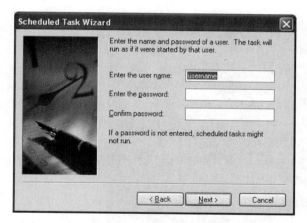

Figure 8-6. *The Scheduled Task Wizard, page 5 of 6*

Click Finish (see Figure 8-7).

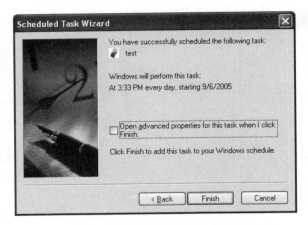

Figure 8-7. *The Scheduled Task Wizard, page 6 of 6*

You can also run the "at" command at the command prompt by typing **at/?** (see Figure 8-8).

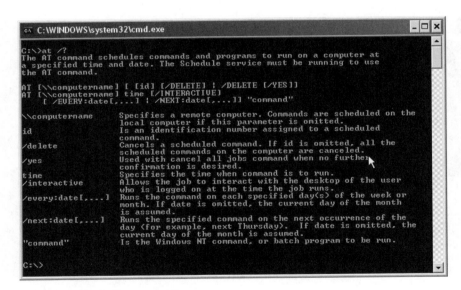

Figure 8-8. *The "at" command*

A sample command for our test.bat file that will run every day at 3:33 p.m. might look like the following:

```
At 15:33 c:\test.bat /every:M,T,W.Th,F,S,Su.
```

To run the same thing with UNIX, you can use the CRONTAB command or just edit the CRON files in your /var/spool/cron directory, as opposed to using the "at" command.

```
crontab -e
0    15:33    *    *    *    /home/scott/test.sh
```

This concludes the scheduling section of the chapter. I recommend you use the scheduling for diagnostic or cleanup activities like restarting your robot, putting it into standby mode, and so on.

8.3 Ant Building and More

Ant is a Java-based build tool, but it's also a whole lot more. Not only can you build all your Java programs with Ant, but you can also JAR them, and you can copy them to other places or other servers. You can even execute Java programs from within an Ant build file. Many excellent publications exist about Ant, and you can find all the information you need on the Web at http://ant.apache.org.

We'll now go over three aspects of Ant. They're the ones I use most with my robotics projects. They are

- Building and deploying

- Executing Java programs

- Sending notifications via e-mail

To install Ant, you need to download the latest version from http://ant.apache.org/bindownload.cgi and follow the instructions included with the download. Basically, unzip the binary distribution to your machine, and then add the following code from Examples 8-1 and 8-2 to your environment variables.

Example 8-1. *Windows*

```
set ANT_HOME = c:\ant_1_6_5
set JAVA_HOME=c:\jsdk_1_4_2
set PATH = %PATH%;%ANT_HOME%/bin
```

Example 8-2. *UNIX (bash)*

```
export ANT_HOME=/usr/local/ant_1_6_5
setenv JAVA_HOME /usr/local/jsdk_1_4_2
set path=( $path $ANT_HOME/bin )
```

Then, to execute Ant, make sure you have a build.xml file in your directory, and just type **ant**. The build file will then run. To illustrate an example, I'll show you the build file I use to distribute the source of this book.

Setup

First I created the following directories in my workspace /src for the source files, /bin for the binary compiled class files, and /dist for the output JAR files. Because I'm using the Eclipse IDE (www.eclipse.org), I can double-click the build.xml file and it will launch Ant to build my project.

Code Objective

The objective here is to create an Ant build script for the source files of this book.

Code Discussion

Here's an explanation of the code in Example 8-3:

Line 1: This is the project name or root element for the build file. It has a name and a default target. The target is the place Ant will go to begin working.

Lines 2–4: This is where I declare some project-level properties. These enable me to write them here as constants to be reused elsewhere in the build file.

Lines 5–8: This is where I declare the classpath. You can see from the syntax that inputting the classpath for a large collection of JARs is much nicer to write in XML format as opposed to a command-line syntax separated by a semicolon.

Line 10: This is the compile target. Note that the package target is dependent on this target. Thus, what happens soon after Ant loads the properties is it begins to execute this target. Once complete, it will move back to the package target.

Line 11: This is a write to the System.out.

Line 12: This is the standard javac command packaged with your JDK. I've included some sample options in Figure 8-9. You can refer to the Ant manual for the Ant syntax of such options.

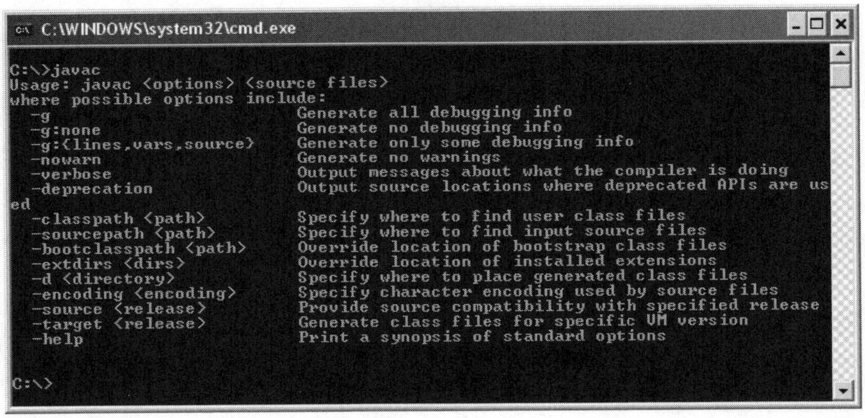

Figure 8-9. *javac help*

Line 13: This is where Ant will deposit all class files.

Line 14: This is the reference to the classpath.

Line 15: This is another echo to the System.out.

Line 17: This is the beginning of the package target.

Line 18: This is another echo to the System.out.

Line 19: This is the jar command, which is similar to the jar command packaged with the JDK. Some sample options can be found in Figure 8-10. Refer to the Ant manual for the Ant syntax of such options.

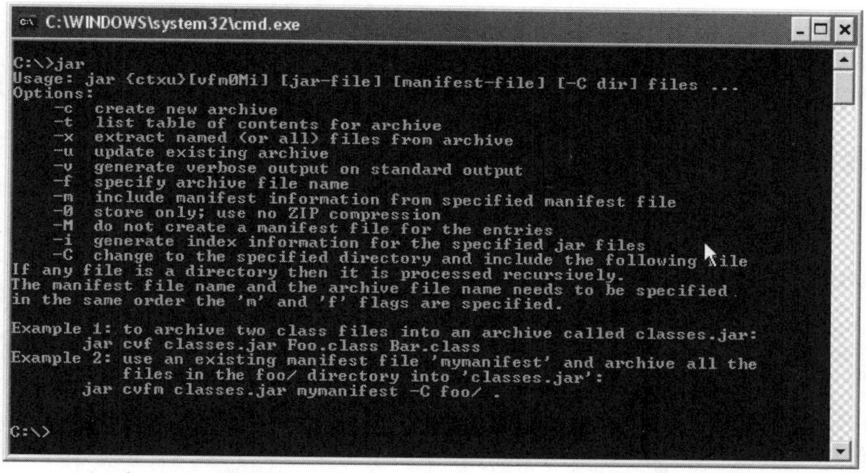

Figure 8-10. *jar command usage*

Example 8-3. *build.xml for JavaRobotBook*

```
1: <project name="JavaRobotBook" default="package">
2:     <property name="build.dir" value="bin"/>
3:     <property name="source.dir" value="src"/>
4:     <property name="this.jar.file" value="dist/java_robot_book.jar" />
5:     <path id="this.classpath">
6:         <pathelement location="${global.lib.dir}/comm.jar"/>
7:         <pathelement location="${global.lib.dir}/mail.jar"/>
8:     </path>
9:
```

```
10:     <target name="compile">
11:         <echo>Compiling ${ant.project.name}</echo>
12:         <javac srcdir="${source.dir}"
13:                destdir="${build.dir}"
14:                classpathref="this.classpath" />
15:         <echo>Finished compiling ${ant.project.name}</echo>
16:     </target>
17:     <target name="package" depends="compile">
18:         <echo>Packaging ${ant.project.name}...</echo>
19:         <jar destfile="${this.jar.file}" basedir="${build.dir}" />
20:         <echo>Done Packaging ${this.jar.file}...</echo>
21:     </target>
22:
23: </project>
```

Now I'll launch the same program via Ant.

Code Objective

The objective here is to create a sample Ant build script that executes a Java program.

Code Discussion

Here's an explanation of the code in Example 8-4:

Line 1: This is again the project name and the default target that's run.

Lines 2–4: This is the classpath, which will be the JAR of the distribution I created in the previous example.

Line 6: This is the default target.

Lines 7–11: This is the Java command included with any JRE or JDK. I've shown some sample options in Figure 8-1. Please refer to the Ant manual for the Ant syntax of such options.

Line 12: This is the ant task, which allows Ant to send e-mail.

Line 13: This determines the mail host. It should be either your current mail host or a local host on your LAN or PC. If you need a mail server, I'd recommend Apache James, a free Java Mail Server, at http://james.apache.org. If you can use your local server, you'll need to put in your SMTP user ID and password into the Ant script so you can log in.

Line 14: This is the list of "to" addresses.

Line 15: This is the "from" address. I put the robot name here.

Line 16: This is the subject line of the mail message.

Line 17: This will be the SMTP mail server port, which is usually port 25.

Line 18: This allows you to attach a file. Here, I've attached the output of the Java program we ran from the Java task in line 7.

Line 19: This is the message of the e-mail outside of the file and the subject.

Example 8-4. *Sample Client Build File: test.xml*

```
1: <project name="Client Demo" default="run">
2: <path id="run.classpath">
3:    <pathelement location="java_robot_book.jar" />
3:    <pathelement location="mail.jar" />
4: </path>
5:
6: <target name="run">
7:    <java
8:        classname="com.scottpreston.javarobot.chapter2.StampSerialTest"
9:        classpathref="run.classpath"
10:        output="test.log"
11:        />
12:    <mail
13:        mailhost="10.10.10.10"
14:        tolist="you@emailaddress.com"
15:        from="feynman@emailaddress.com"
16:        subject="status from feynman"
17:        mailport="25"
18:        files="test.log"
19:        message="please read log" />
20: </target>
21: </project>
```

The simple, one-line batch file previously shown uses the –f flag to identify the build file and the –l flag to log the Ant output into the ant.log file.

```
ant -f test.xml -l ant.log
```

This concludes our discussion of Ant. You can find many more tasks and details about the project on the web site mentioned earlier. I recommend you check out the manual since the number of customized tasks that have been created for Ant will add richly to your Java robotic building experience. The best part is, it's all free!

8.4   Database Access with JDBC and MySQL

JDBC stands for Java Database Connectivity. MySQL is the database I'll use for these examples. This section will show you how to use both of these to give your robot memory about what it's done and use that memory to help it calculate what to do next.

Each time we use data structures with our robots, whether they are the room layouts, images for vision, or grammar files for sound, it would be nice if we could get this data each time the program loaded. It would be even nicer if the robot could remember actions that were productive so it could avoid those things that were not.

I'll cover three things throughout the rest of this chapter:

- The MySQL open source database

- How to manage your data and database with Standard Query Language (SQL)

- How to create, read, update, and delete records in the database using JDBC

MySQL

MySQL is the most popular open source database server in the world. It's free to use and can be downloaded from www.mysql.com. (The exact URL will depend on your operating system.) The database comes with an install program that automatically configures the installation.

Once you download the software, you'll get a typical installation wizard like that shown in Figure 8-11.

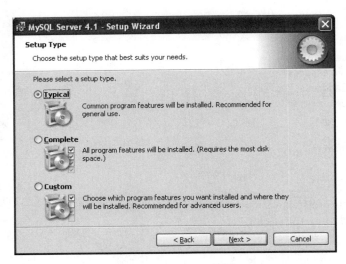

Figure 8-11. *The Windows XP version of MySQL 4.1*

Follow the instructions and you'll have a database installed in a matter of minutes.

Upon completing the installation of MySQL, you'll need a management console for your database. The one I use is SQLyog, which can be downloaded from www.webyog.com. A free version is available for both UNIX and Windows.

Once you install the management console, you can manage your databases from it to connect to your MySQL database, as shown in Figure 8-12.

Once you connect to your database, you'll see the screen similar to that in Figure 8-13, where you can create, update, and delete tables, and perform SQL operations.

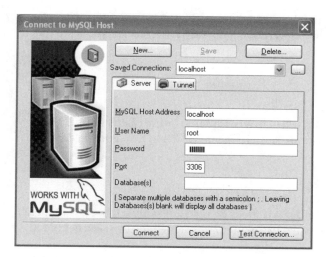

Figure 8-12. *The SQLyog console connect window*

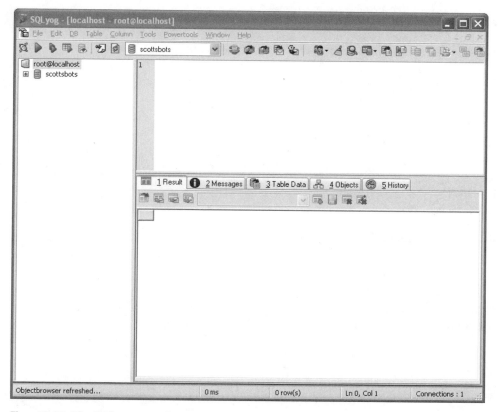

Figure 8-13. *The SQLyog console*

Let's say that we want to create a database table to log our navigation vectors. If you look at our data structure for com.scottpreston.javarobot.chapter8.MotionVector, you'll see that it contains the following fields:

- heading

- magnitude

However, it's missing two fields that will help us with some future calculations. So we'll have to create a new structure called MotionEpisode, where we'll add two more fields:

- motion_id

- name

This structure is called MotionEpisode.java and is defined in Example 8-5. For simplicity, I just extended the MotionVector we created in Chapter 7 and added the two new fields and some constructors.

Example 8-5. *MotionEpisode.java*

```
package com.scottpreston.javarobot.chapter8;

import com.scottpreston.javarobot.chapter7.DistanceVector;

public class MotionEpisode extends DistanceVector {

    public int motion_id = 0;

    public MotionEpisode() {
        super(0,0);
    }
    public MotionEpisode(int h, double m) {
        super(h, m);
    }
    public MotionEpisode(String h, String m) throws Exception {
        super(h, m);
    }
}
```

Now that we have data structures in Java, we can create the structures in MySQL with the SQLyog editor. You can see the example in Figure 8-14.

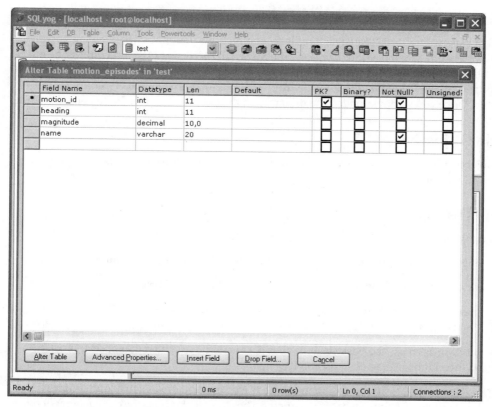

Figure 8-14. *SQLyog motion_episode table create/alter*

Or if you want, you can use SQL to create your table, where the SQL script in Example 8-6 is standard ANSI SQL.

Example 8-6. *motion_episodes Table Creation*

```
CREATE TABLE `motion_episodes` (
  `motion_id` int(11) NOT NULL auto_increment,
  `heading` int(11) default NULL,
  `magnitude` decimal(10,0) default NULL,
  `name` varchar(20) NOT NULL default '',
  PRIMARY KEY  (`motion_id`)
) TYPE=MyISAM AUTO_INCREMENT=1 ;
```

Now that our database is created and we have a data structure in Java, we're ready to start building our classes to perform our create, read, update, and delete operations.

Setup

The first class we need to create will handle all connections to our MySQL database server. Before you begin, you'll need to download the MySQL JDBC driver JARs. I recommend getting the 3.2 drivers, since that way you won't have any problems with MySQL and Java character set mappings. You can download them from http://dev.mysql.com/downloads/connector/j/ 3.2.html. Once you've downloaded the drivers, add the Connector/J JAR file to your classpath.

Code Objective

The objective here is to create a base class that can open and return java.sql.Connections to our MySQL database.

Code Discussion

The first thing I did was make the constructor take the following default parameters:

- host: This will be an IP address or a host name. Here, I'm using "localhost".

- database: This will be the database name. Here, I'm using "test".

- user: This is the username that has access to the specified database. For our example, I'm using "root".

- password: This is the password that has access to the specified database and corresponds to the user specified earlier.

Once I set these, I can call the open method. This method creates the connection string using the parameters in the database constructor. The close method sets the connection reference to null, potentially releasing resources.

Finally, in the main method I test this class to make sure it opens and closes the connection to the database. See Example 8-7.

Example 8-7. *MySQL.java*

```java
package com.scottpreston.javarobot.chapter8;

import java.sql.Connection;
import java.sql.DriverManager;

public class MySQL {

    private Connection conn;
    private String host;
    private String user;
    private String password;
    private String database;
```

```java
    public MySQL(String h, String d, String u, String p) {
        host = h;
        user = u;
        password = p;
        database  = d;
    }

    public void open() {
        try {
            Class.forName("com.mysql.jdbc.Driver").newInstance();
            conn = DriverManager
                    .getConnection("jdbc:mysql://" + host
                            + "/" + database
                            + "?user=" + user
                            + "&password=" + password);

        } catch (Exception e) {
            e.printStackTrace();
        }

    }
    public void close() {
        conn = null;
    }


    public Connection getConn() {
        return conn;
    }
    public void setConn(Connection conn) {
        this.conn = conn;
    }

    public static java.sql.Date toSqlDate(java.util.Date utilDate) {
        return new java.sql.Date(utilDate.getTime());
    }

    public static void main(String[] args) {
        MySQL test = new MySQL("localhost", "test" , "root","password");
        test.open();
        test.close();
        System.out.println("done" + new java.util.Date());
    }
}
```

Now, I'm ready to create a database access class for my motion episodes.

Code Objective

The objective here is to write the database access class for the motion_episodes table.

Code Discussion

This code uses the MySQL class to get connections to our MySQL database. It will use our MotionEpisode data structure as an input parameter and return types.

The first two methods are private methods that give the class connection the ability to manage connections to the database. The task of creating and returning the connection is given by getConn. Inside, I've hard-coded the host, database, userid, and password. The second method calls close on the mysql object, which in turn closes the connection and sets it to null.

The first data access method is Create. This will insert a record into the database. It's accomplished by creating a SQL string in PreparedStatement format. A PreparedStatement gives it the ability to parameterize the input of our SQL with a question mark and then replace those question marks later with Java objects like Strings, ints, doubles, dates, and so on. This is nice because your SQL statement won't break with special characters. The method then calls the sqlExecute method, which I created to save some space.

In sqlExecute, I take two parameters: one is the SQL string, while the second is the MotionEpisode object. From this, I create the prepared statement from my SQL string and insert the parameters from my MotionEpisode object. Notice I use the finally block in this method. This is so that even if the prepared statement throws an exception, I can still close the MySQL connection.

In the subsequent methods to update and delete, I call the same sqlExecute methods with the appropriate SQL statements.

The next set of methods returns a MotionEpisode or an ArrayList of MotionEpisodes. By passing the first method, readMotionEpisodeById(), the ID key of the motion_episodes table, you can get an individual record. You can repeat this for any of the fields in the table; however, you will need to return ArrayList versus a single MotionEpisode.

In the readAllMotionEpisodes method, we do just that. Here, besides adding individual MotionEpisode objects to an ArrayList, I show you how you close your Java database classes so you can be sure all the resources are closed. First, close your ResultSet if it's not equal to null. Second, catch and print your exception. Third, in the final block, close out your ResultSet (again, since an exception could have happened before closure). Fourth, close your statement, and last, close your MySQL connection. See Example 8-8.

■**Note** For more complicated object-to-relational mapping, check out Hibernate at www.hibernate.org.

Example 8-8. *DBMotion.java*

```java
package com.scottpreston.javarobot.chapter8;

import java.sql.Connection;
import java.sql.PreparedStatement;
import java.sql.ResultSet;
import java.sql.SQLException;
import java.sql.Statement;
import java.util.ArrayList;

public class DBMotion {

    private MySQL mysql;

    private Connection getConn() {
        mysql = new MySQL("localhost", "test", "root", "password");
        mysql.open();
        return mysql.getConn();
    }

    private void close() {
        mysql.close();
    }

    public void createMotionEpisode(MotionEpisode me) {
        String sql = "insert into motion_episodes (heading,magnitude,name)"
                + "vector_magnitude,obstacle) values(?,?,?)";
        sqlExecute(sql, me);
    }


    public void updateMotionEpisode(MotionEpisode me) {
        String sql = "insert into motion_episodes set heading=?,magnitude=?,name=?"
                + "where motion_id = "
                + me.motion_id;
        sqlExecute(sql, me);
    }
```

```java
    public void deleteMotionEpisode(MotionEpisode me) {
        // don't need just to reuse sqlExecute
        String sql = "delete from motion_episodes where heading=?" +
            " and magnitude=? and name=? and motion_id = " + me.motion_id;
        sqlExecute(sql, me);


    }

    private void sqlExecute(String sql, MotionEpisode me) {
        try {
            PreparedStatement ps = mysql.getConn().prepareStatement(sql);
            ps.setInt(0, me.heading);
            ps.setDouble(1, me.magnitude);
            ps.setString(2, me.name);
            ps.executeUpdate();
            ps.close();
        } catch (SQLException sqlEx) {
            sqlEx.printStackTrace();
        } finally {
            mysql.close();
        }
    }


    public MotionEpisode readMotionEpisodeById(int id) throws SQLException{

        Statement statement = getConn().createStatement();
        ResultSet rs = statement
                .executeQuery("SELECT heading,magnitude,name from ➥
    motion_episodes where motion_id = " + id);
        MotionEpisode ep = null;
        while (rs.next()) {
            ep.motion_id = id;
            ep.heading = rs.getInt("heading");
            ep.magnitude = rs.getDouble("manitude");
            ep.name = rs.getString("name");
        }
        return ep;
    }

    public ArrayList readAllMotionEpisodes() {

        ArrayList navEvents = new ArrayList();
        Statement statement = null;
        ResultSet rs = null;
```

```
        try {
            statement = getConn().createStatement();
            rs = statement
                    .executeQuery("SELECT motion_id,heading,magnitude,➥
name from motion_episodes");
            while (rs.next()) {
                int id = rs.getInt("motion_id"); // getInt(0);
                int h = rs.getInt("heading");
                double m = rs.getDouble("manitude");
                String n = rs.getString("name");
                MotionEpisode me = new MotionEpisode(h, m);
                me.motion_id = id;
                me.name = n;
                navEvents.add(me);
            }

            if (rs != null) {
                rs.close();
            }
        } catch (SQLException sqlE) {
            sqlE.printStackTrace();
        } finally {
            if (rs != null) {
                try {
                    rs.close();
                } catch (SQLException sqlEx) {
                    // do nothing
                }
                rs = null;
            }
            if (statement != null) {
                try {
                    statement.close();
                } catch (SQLException sqlEx) {
                    // do nothing
                }
                statement = null;
            }
            mysql.close();
        }

        return navEvents;
    }


}
```

Section Summary

Using a database with your robotics opens a lot of potential. You can store images in a database; you can store your room and region mappings; you can store just about anything you want. There are also many ways to put data in and get data out of your database. Here are just a few things to remember when working with them:

- KISS (Keep It Simple, Stupid) and don't try to do too much or overcomplicate your database classes. Use flat files when they make sense, or for performance reasons.

- Close your resources. Depending on the server you have or how much access you create to and from your database, remember to close your resources so you don't consume too much memory that could be used for speech or vision processing.

- Use a database external to your robot. By storing information on a separate machine, you can access it while your robot is charging, and if you get a failure you won't lose what may have caused it.

8.5   Using and Installing Tomcat

Tomcat is a servlet container that allows you to execute Java servlets or JSP pages. To install Tomcat, download the latest version that works with your installed Java runtime. Detailed instructions are available at http://jakarta.apache.org/tomcat/. The definitions of servlets and JSP can be quite daunting if you choose to look at the specification; however, the definitions that I find the easiest to remember are as follows:

- JavaServer Pages (JSP) pages: These are dynamic web pages that execute Java code. You can code them as HTML files or as you would any Java class's main method.

- Java servlets: One way to look at these are as compiled JSP pages, but if you aren't dealing with text (say, image data), servlets provide a convenient way to stream this binary output through HTTP.

For the formal definitions, you can refer to http://java.sun.com/products/servlets/index.jsp and http://java.sun.com/products/jsp.

One important thing to remember with web servers is that even though you are executing Java, your web server (Tomcat) is nothing more than a file server. Except, rather than opening a file from your file system (for example, c:\test.txt), you would open it via a URL (http://localhost/text.txt; or for a JSP it would be http://localhost/test.jsp). The URL is prefixed with a protocol called Hypertext Transfer Protocol (HTTP). You can look up the specification at www.w3.org/Protocols. HTTP has two main components: a request and a response. The request sends information from the client to the web server, and the response is the information sent from the web server to the requesting client. See Figure 8-15.

Note In communication between our PC's serial port and BASIC Stamp 2, you can think of the Stamp as a web server and our Java class as a web client.

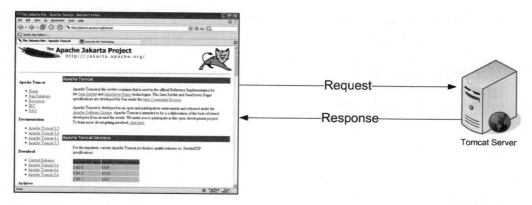

Figure 8-15. *A request/response diagram*

Code Objective

The objective here is to explain simple JSP syntax.

Code Discussion

In Example 8-9, you can see a very simple JSP page. I used something like line 2 to test and make sure things are installed and working correctly.

You can see the URL in Example 8-9 specifies the page and after the page name you see a question mark. This denotes the QUERY_STRING part of the URL. The QUERY_STRING allows the requestee (web browser or other client) to send name/value pairs to the web server for processing.

In the case of line 5 in Example 8-9, we can get these values from the URL and use them for processing by using the request object's getParameter method.

```
http://localhost/index.jsp?test=Hello%20World!
```

From the preceding URL the next example will run on the server. Each line is essentially as follows:

Line 1: This is the import declaration. Here you can import anything you would normally import in your Java class.

Line 2: This is embedded HTML with the start of a scriptlet tag (<%). This less-than-percent symbol tells Tomcat that it's time to look for Java syntax.

Line 3: This will write to your client. While you can still use System.out, this output will be in the Tomcat logs, not in the browser.

Line 4: This is just HTML syntax and is a line break. I could have also ended the scriptlet %>
<% and started it again before line 5.

Line 5: This line outputs the request parameter "test" back to the screen via out.println.

Line 6: This line closes the scriptlet marker.

Example 8-9. *index.jsp*

```
1: <%@ page import="java.util.Date" %>
2: Time Time Is: <%
3: out.println(new Date());
4: out.println("<br>");
5: out.println(request.getParameter("test"));
6: %>
```

Output is

```
The Time Is: Fri Jul 15 17:32:19 EDT 2005
Hello World!
```

What the servlet engine does for you is actually take your JSP or the code in Example 8-9 and convert it to a Java class that can be executed. You can find this in the following directory [TOMCAT INSTALL]/work/Catalina/localhost/_/org/apache/jsp as index_jsp.java.

The highlighted import that follows is listed in line 1 earlier. The carriage return new line is also printed, followed by new Date(), "<br>", and getParameter("test"), a carriage return, and a new line. The rest of the code not in bold is generated by Catalina, the JSP compiler. All of this happens automatically so the class that follows is only for informational purposes. Thus, you can see that the JSP you write is, at heart, a Java class. See Example 8-10.

Example 8-10. *A Compiled Version of index.jsp*

```
package org.apache.jsp;

import javax.servlet.*;
import javax.servlet.http.*;
import javax.servlet.jsp.*;
import java.util.Date;

public final class index_jsp extends org.apache.jasper.runtime.HttpJspBase
    implements org.apache.jasper.runtime.JspSourceDependent {

  private static java.util.Vector _jspx_dependents;

  public java.util.List getDependents() {
    return _jspx_dependents;
  }

  public void _jspService(HttpServletRequest request, HttpServletResponse response)
      throws java.io.IOException, ServletException {

    JspFactory _jspxFactory = null;
    PageContext pageContext = null;
    HttpSession session = null;
    ServletContext application = null;
```

```
    ServletConfig config = null;
    JspWriter out = null;
    Object page = this;
    JspWriter _jspx_out = null;
    PageContext _jspx_page_context = null;


    try {
      _jspxFactory = JspFactory.getDefaultFactory();
      response.setContentType("text/html");
      pageContext = _jspxFactory.getPageContext(this, request, response,
                null, true, 8192, true);
      _jspx_page_context = pageContext;
      application = pageContext.getServletContext();
      config = pageContext.getServletConfig();
      session = pageContext.getSession();
      out = pageContext.getOut();
      _jspx_out = out;

      out.write("\r\n");
      out.write("Time Time Is: ");

out.println(new Date());
out.println("<br>");
out.println(request.getParameter("test"));

      out.write('\r');
      out.write('\n');
    } catch (Throwable t) {
      if (!(t instanceof SkipPageException)){
        out = _jspx_out;
        if (out != null && out.getBufferSize() != 0)
          out.clearBuffer();
        if (_jspx_page_context != null) _jspx_page_context.handlePageException(t);
      }
    } finally {
      if (_jspxFactory != null) _jspxFactory.releasePageContext(_jspx_page_context);
    }
  }
}
```

The nice thing about having a Tomcat installed is that all of the code we have written can now be accessed via the web browser. More important, you and I can write remote control clients via HTML and JSP, and we can access them from anyplace in the world. Last year while traveling to South Africa, I was able to log into Feynman5 and have it navigate around my house. Accessing the classes we created in the previous chapters is easy. In Example 8-11, I created a simple JSP such that when the user clicks the link "move now" the robot will move. More complex examples of this will appear in Chapter 9.

Example 8-11. *move.jsp*

```
<%@ page import="com.scottpreston.javarobot.chapter2.*%>
<%@ page import="com.scottpreston.javarobot.chapter7.*>
<html>
<head><title>Simple Move</title></head>
<body>
<%
If (request.getParameter("move") != null) {
WebSerialClient com = new WebSerialClient("10.10.10.99", "8080",
                "1");
        Navigation nav = new Navigation(com);
        // move east 3 feet
        nav.move(new DistanceVector(90,36);
        out.println("success");
} else { %>
<a href="move.jsp?move=now">move now</a>
<%
}
%>

</body>
</html>
```

Section Summary

Like working with databases, using web pages for your clients can also be abused. Personally, I like to use web clients for remote control, speech, and data collection. In the next chapter, I'll use JSP pages for remote control clients and servlets to send images.

Here are a few pointers that should help:

- If your web server is on your robot, then use the SingleSerialPort rather than the WebSerialPort.

- Use JSP pages for robot clients over Swing clients if possible, so you can access them anywhere in the world.

- Download and install a JSP editor for use with your IDE. The color coding and code assist should help in creating your HTML clients.

8.6   Java Scripting Languages

You can choose from a number of available Java scripting languages. Don't be confused by the web-based scripting language of the same name, JavaScript. No, these scripting languages allow you to use Java classes just as you would in a typical Java class, but with the simplicity of a scripting language. The language I'll next talk about is Groovy.

Groovy is a dynamic scripting language for the Java 2 Platform. Groovy's home page is http://groovy.codehaus.org. There you can find the language guide, how to use Groovy, and plenty of features and examples. You can think of Groovy as Ruby or Python for a Java person. You get the benefits of these languages with the power and APIs of Java.

What I like about Groovy is its simplicity. By adding to your environment the Groovy install directory and adding the %GROOVY_HOME%/bin to your path, you can execute Java without having to compile, or specify a classpath. These are basically all the things that make Java more difficult to use than typical scripting languages.

Some of the added features of Groovy make it worth considering when programming your robotics, including the following:

- It's dynamically typed. An example of a variable that is dynamically typed means you can set a variable to an int or a string so var `x = 1`, and then in the following line `x = "foo"`.

- It simplifies unit testing. Because JUnit is built into the Groovy runtime, you can script a JUnit test for your test classes.

- It has a simplified syntax. For printing something to the console, you can just have `println "foo"`—there's no need for a semicolon or System.out.

- It has dynamic lists. For example, you can define a list via the following syntax: `def mylist = [1,2,'this is cool',new java.util.Date()]`.

- It has an easy syntax for maps—for example, `def mymap ['author':'scott preston', 'title':'the definitive guide to java robots','publisher':'apress']`.

- It includes helper methods such as each, collect, find, findAll, inject, every, any, min/max, join, and more.

Using Groovy gives you another option to execute your Java programs with your robot to batch files, shell scripts, Ant scripts, or within your IDE.

For example, I use Groovy scripts to help me with diagnostics. In Example 8-12, I include a main program I use to execute all my diagnostics. I can edit this with Notepad, which means that I don't need to copy new libraries to the robot, and I don't need an IDE there. All I need is my command prompt and Notepad, or in the case of a UNIX box, I can use VI or EMACs and a terminal window.

The first thing you might notice is that there are no semicolons. These are optional in Groovy. Second, the System.out.println statements are reduced to just println. Finally, I can call other Groovy scripts via the GroovyShell object.

Example 8-12. *diagnostic.groovy*

```
import java.io.File

println("Diagnostic Script for robot")

script = new GroovyShell()
script.run(new File("facenorth.groovy"), [])
script.run(new File("moveforward.groovy"), [])

println("Done")
```

Next, in the facenorth.groovy script, we must import some classes just like we do in normal Java, except that we don't need the semicolons. Second, we do want to trap our exception just like regular Java, so we add a try-catch block.

Inside the try-catch block, we create the serial port and a SimpleNavigation object. We can also create a voice object so that we can have the robot tell us when it's done moving north. See Example 8-13.

Example 8-13. *facenorth.groovy*

```
import com.scottpreston.javarobot.chapter2.WebSerialClient
import com.scottpreston.javarobot.chapter6.MicrosoftVoice
import com.scottpreston.javarobot.chapter7.Navigation
try {
    WebSerialClient com = new WebSerialClient("10.10.10.99", "8080","1")
    Navigation nav = new Navigation(com)
    nav.changeHeading(0)
    MicrosoftVoice voice = MicrosoftVoice.getInstance()
    voice.speak("I am facing north now.")
    println("done")
} catch (Exception e) {
    e.printStackTrace()
    System.exit(1)
}
```

Because you'll be spending more time in front of your robot debugging and testing code rather than behind your IDE, I recommend you pick up a scripting language. It will speed things up, and the flexibility it gives you will save time and, more important, battery life.

If you don't choose Groovy for your Java scripting language, there are some others to take a look at:

- Jython: Java Python (www.jython.org)

- JRuby: Java Ruby (http://jruby.sourceforge.net)

- BSF: Bean Scripting Framework (http://jakarta.apache.org/bsf)

8.7   Chapter Summary

In this chapter, I summarized a few things that could help you with your robotics programming.

In section 8.1, I discussed how to create batch files or shell scripts to simplify execution of your Java program outside of an IDE.

In section 8.2, I talked about scheduling your Java programs to show you how to give your robot some autonomy. In the next chapter, I'll show an example of a startup diagnostics that uses scheduling.

In section 8.3, I gave a brief overview about using Ant. I only showed a few things in this section: executing your Java programs, building your API, and using it to send e-mail; however, Ant has many other applications and uses. Make sure you learn Ant; it will save you time and effort in the future.

In section 8.4, I discussed the installation of MySQL and how to create and use Java and JDBC to create, read, update, and delete data from a database. I just barely scratched the surface of database access with robotics. The real value of the database comes into play during prolonged training and learning periods with your robot.

In section 8.5, I provided a light overview to Tomcat, as well as an explanation of how to install and use the robotics API with it. In the next chapter, I'll build some JSP pages and a servlet to operate the robot by remote control, and provide access to its web cameras.

Finally, in the last section I touched on using Groovy as a Java scripting language. Scripting languages give you some flexibility, while adding all the strength of Java.

In the next chapter, I'll create several sample programs from the functionality of the last eight chapters.

CHAPTER 9

Sample Programs

The first principle is that you must not fool yourself—and you are the easiest person—to fool.

— Richard Feynman

9.0 Introduction

Over the last eight chapters, I've covered the basics of robotics. In this chapter, however, I'll combine the functionalities presented in the previous chapters.

First, I'll show some miscellaneous utilities that can be used on their own. While there is nothing special about them, they show how to do some things you may, or may not, know how to do with Java.

Second, I'll cover some sample remote control programs. Remote control programs will get you access to your robot when it's not functioning autonomously. Or if you want to send your robot into a defined autonomous algorithm, you can control it via this mechanism. The first will utilize a Tomcat web server and JavaServer Pages (JSP). This has the benefit of allowing you to control your robot from any place in the world. The second will be voice command, and while this will only work when you're standing in front of your robot, it's still really cool to be able to tell your robot to fetch you a cold drink. The third will be a Swing client for controlling servos. For things like testing the positions of your robot arms or pan and tilt mechanisms, it's nice to use this to uncover the limits of those servos.

After that, I'll demonstrate some more webcam examples. The first will show how to get an image from Tomcat so you can view it in your browser. This is nice because you may want to connect your webcam to the Internet or move your robot around the house if you're away. Then you can log into your web site and see what your robot is seeing. Second, I'll show you how to follow a ColorGram or some motion with your robot's web camera connected to a pan and tilt mechanism. This is a great ability, since maybe you want your robot to follow you or a red shirt you're wearing. (My plan this winter is to have my robot help me with some Christmas shopping.) Third, I'll demonstrate how to have your robot speak to some items it recognizes. This is yet another very cool aspect of your robot—just imagine it greeting you or your dog by name. Even by recognition alone, you could tell your robot to do all kinds of things.

Following that, I'll go over some diagnostic programs (after all, you'll want to write more programs to assist you when troubleshooting your robot):

- The first one will calibrate the distance depending on what surface the robot is on.

- The second example will test four directions and speak them so you can watch the robot perform these actions without having to sit at your PC.

- The third example will have the robot read sensor data to you. This is helpful when moving the robot around or when you need to test sensor dead spots.

- The fourth example will include a sample diagnostic that is scheduled to run when the computer starts. It sends the startup status via e-mail so you have a record of all the information about the robot, and you'll know that if it gets through this diagnostic, it will be able to do anything else you ask of it.

The last program in this chapter (and this book, incidentally) will allow your robot to navigate its way out of a maze. It will build a map of its position, and then be able to follow that map the next time to get out.

Getting Started

To get started, we'll need the following acquired or taken care of:

- Tomcat installed

- Webcam installed

- A working robot with pan and tilt mechanism

9.1 Miscellaneous Utilities

In this section, I'll show you some of the ways you can get access to other programs or machines using Java. The first way will utilize HTTP to get text of images over the Internet. The second will show you how to send e-mail messages from your robot, and the third will show you how to invoke a separate process from within Java.

The following list describes some useful things you can do with it:

- Get the status of your robot via HTTP or e-mail.

- Have your robot read Real Simple Syndication (RSS) news feeds to you in the morning.

- Have your robot read your e-mail.

- Have your robot send information via HTTP to another robot.

- Have your robot or a client program get images from your robot's web camera.

Code Objective

The first set of utilities will show you some ways to get HTTP by way of the Internet.

Code Discussion

There are no fields in this class, nor a constructor. It has two methods: getImage() for getting an image from a URL and getText() for getting text from a URL. In getImage(), I converted the result to a BufferedImage since we could process it via some of our classes in Chapter 7. See Example 9-1.

Example 9-1. *HttpGet.java*

```
package com.scottpreston.javarobot.chapter9;

import java.awt.Image;
import java.awt.Toolkit;
import java.awt.image.BufferedImage;
import java.io.BufferedReader;
import java.io.InputStreamReader;
import java.net.URL;

public class HttpGet {

    // get image from Internet via URL
    public static BufferedImage getImage(String urlString)throws Exception {
        // construct URL
        URL url = new URL(urlString);
        // get AWT image
        Image image = Toolkit.getDefaultToolkit().getImage(url);
        // cast to BufferedImage
        return (BufferedImage)image;
    }

    // get text from Internet via URL
    public static String getText(String urlString) throws Exception {
        // construct url
        URL url = new URL(urlString);
        // create input buffer for reading
        BufferedReader in = new BufferedReader(new InputStreamReader(url
                .openStream()));
        // temp string
        String str;
        // create buffer to put information in
        StringBuffer buffer = new StringBuffer();
        // read until end of file
        while ((str = in.readLine()) != null) {
            // since reading line add line feed.
            buffer.append(str+"\n");
        }
        // close buffer
        in.close();
```

```
        // return as string
        return buffer.toString();
    }

    public static void main(String[] args) {

        try {
            // open my publisher's web site.
            System.out.println(HttpGet.getText("http://www.apress.com"));
        } catch (Exception e) {
            // print exception and exit
            e.printStackTrace();
            System.exit(1);
        }
    }
}
```

Code Objective

The objective here is to send e-mail from your Java program.

Code Discussion

While you can also use Ant to send e-mail via Simple Mail Transfer Protocol (SMTP), I thought it would be nice to have a special class you could use to send mail messages from your robot. For this to work, you will need a local mail server with a relay enabled, or you will need to use authentication for your normal SMTP mail server. Since I have an Apache James mail server installed locally with no relay, I can use the class that follows without any problems.

Some ways you can use the SendMailClient include

- Send status reports of key systems via e-mail.

- Send diagnostic information on certain events, like startup or before shutdown.

- By using this with other programs, like motion capture or navigation, you can send out e-mail events to users with URLs for action.

In SendMailClient.java, I have three fields: host for the hostname or host IP address of the mail server; port for the mail server port (most of the time this is set to 25, but because of relay concerns [viruses], I changed my port to 2525). The latter can be configured via your mail server and mailSession, which is just used to collect and store properties for the Java Mail API.

The constructor takes host and port. I set these in the javax.mail.Session, along with the property mail.smtp.auth to false since I'm using an anonymous relay.

In the only method of the class, send(), the arguments are to (for the e-mail address of the recipient), subj (for the subject of the mail message), and msg (for the actual body content of the mail message). Next, in a try-catch block I instantiate the MimeMessage via the mailSession created in the constructor. In the message, I set the "from," "to," "subj," and "msg." Notice the content type is set to "text/plain." If you want to send HTML or an image via this mechanism, you have to change it to the appropriate MIME type.

What is MIME? Its full name is Multipurpose Internet Mail Extension, and it's used with SMTP to identify what content your e-mail will contain. So, you can send more than just plain text. Some common ones used are text/html, text/xml, image/jpeg, and so on. Later, I'll use the MIME type in the web server header file to tell a browser I'm sending an image versus text.

Finally, the send() method calls sendMessage and close(). See Example 9-2.

Example 9-2. *SendMailClient.java*

```java
package com.scottpreston.javarobot.chapter9;

import java.util.Properties;

import javax.mail.Message;
import javax.mail.Session;
import javax.mail.Transport;
import javax.mail.internet.InternetAddress;
import javax.mail.internet.MimeMessage;

// requires mail.jar & activation .jar
public class SendMailClient {

    private String host = null;
    private String port = null;
    private Session mailSession;

    public SendMailClient(String host, String port) {
        Properties properties = System.getProperties();
        properties.put("mail.smtp.host", host);
        properties.put("mail.smtp.auth", "false");
        properties.put("mail.smtp.port", port);
        mailSession = Session.getInstance(properties, null);
    }

    public void send(String to, String from, String subj, String msg) {
        try {
            MimeMessage message = new MimeMessage(mailSession);
            message.setFrom(new InternetAddress(from));
            message.addRecipient(Message.RecipientType.TO,
                    new InternetAddress(to));
            message.setSubject(subj);
            message.setContent(msg, "text/plain");
            message.saveChanges();
            Transport transport = mailSession.getTransport("smtp");
            transport.connect();
            transport.sendMessage(message, message.getAllRecipients());
            transport.close();
```

```
        } catch (Exception e) {
            e.printStackTrace();
        }
    }

    public static void main(String[] args) {

        try {
            SendMailClient sendMail = new SendMailClient("localhost","25");
            String from = "feynman@scottsbots.com";
            String to = "info@scottsbots.com";
            String host = "127.0.0.1";
            String subj = "Test E-Mail";
            String msg = "Java Robots Are Cool!";
            sendMail.send(to,from,subj,msg);
            System.out.println("Email Message Sent");
        } catch (Exception e) {
            e.printStackTrace();

        }

    }
}
```

Code Objective

The objective here is to open an external Java or non-Java program from within a Java class.

Code Discussion

There may come a time when you want to execute a non-Java program from Java. So I'll show you how to do this from Windows via the Process class. While you can call Runtime.exec() to find native programs, the processing of the OutputStream, InputStream, and ErrorStream are handled via the java.lang.Process class. You can also kill the process via the destroy() method.

Some examples in which you could use the CmdExec are

- Calling another program without writing a Native extension

- Telling the machine to shut down or restart

- Calling Groovy or other shell scripts from within a Java program

- Creating another JVM to execute an additional Java program

In the class CmdExec, I have a single field, p, for Process. The constructor is empty and the exe() method actually does the work.

In exe(), I create the process from the Runtime.getRuntime().exec() method via some command line. This command line must either be in the PATH or explicitly defined from the file system. I then handle the OutputStream only via the BufferedReader and by reading each line of the input stream as it arrives.

In kill(), I provide a way for the invoking class to kill the process. See Example 9-3.

Example 9-3. *CmdExec.java*

```java
package com.scottpreston.javarobot.chapter9;

import java.io.BufferedReader;
import java.io.InputStreamReader;

public class CmdExec {

    // process invoking program will call
    private Process p;

    // empty constructor
    public CmdExec() {  }

    // execute command
    public void exe(String cmdline) {
        try {
            // string for system out
            String line;
            // create process
            p = Runtime.getRuntime().exec(cmdline);
            // capture output stream of program
            BufferedReader input = new BufferedReader(new InputStreamReader(p
                    .getInputStream()));
            // get all lines of output
            while ((line = input.readLine()) != null) {
                System.out.println(line);
            }
            // close input stream
            input.close();
        } catch (Exception e) {
            e.printStackTrace();
        }
    }
    // ability to kill process
    public void kill() {
        p.destroy();
    }
}
```

Section Summary

These miscellaneous utilities will help you connect your Java classes to other programs, other machines, other people, or other robots. While there are many more utilities out there, this section should give you a few to start with.

In this section, I created three classes:

- HttpGet.java: Shows how to get text and images from another web server

- SendMailClient.java: Shows how to send text or images to an e-mail address

- CmdExec.java: Shows how to let your Java programs call other programs or scripts outside of the current Java Runtime

One thing that might be of use to Windows users is to connect more than one webcam at a time to a single Java Runtime. Video for Windows (VFW) allows only one camera per JVM. So in order to use two at once, the method I've found most useful is to start two processes of the GetFrame class, and then save the images to a file on a web server that can be served and retrieved via HTTP. So that's what I'll talk about next.

9.2 Webcam Programs

This set of classes will show you how to combine some of the vision classes from Chapter 7 with some of the other chapters in this book. The first of these shows you a way to get dual input from web cameras with the CmdExec and HttpGet classes defined in the last section. Second, I'll show you how to create a servlet that gets a picture from your web camera. Finally, I'll combine speech and vision to have your robot identify colors, and follow colors and motion.

Setup

For this, you'll first need two web cameras. Because of image quality, I used two FireWire Pyro web cameras.

Second, you won't need to do this on UNIX systems. It's just VFW that seems to have a problem with two web cameras running in the same JVM.

Third, you'll need to be logged into Windows when the program starts, because it will prompt you to select a capture device (see Figure 9-1).

Fourth, depending on the speed of your machine, expect a minimum of 25-percent resource utilization while the cameras are running. If you have a slower single board machine, you might be at a higher percentage.

Figure 9-1. *The VFW selection dialog*

Code Objective

The objective here is to capture two frames of video from two cameras, save them to a web server directory, and get the images for processing.

Code Discussion

The first of the programs will be the ImageTimer class, which will be responsible for taking the picture and saving it to disk at a specified interval.

The fields in the class are getFrame from Chapter 7, which will be the worker class to get the frame from the webcam, and the Timer field, the timer in the class that will tell the getFrame class to snap a frame every 5 seconds, as defined by the Seconds field (it then saves it to the filename specified by the fileName field).

The constructor will take a single argument for the filename. This is because we'll use a command line to invoke these classes. The constructor also initializes the timer to call the savePic() method every 5 seconds.

In savePic(), we create a new file of the fileName specified in the constructor, and then save it as a JPG.

The main() method of this class tests the command line for a single argument, and then constructs the ImageTimer class. See Example 9-4.

Example 9-4. *ImageTimer.java*

```java
package com.scottpreston.javarobot.chapter9;

import java.awt.image.BufferedImage;
import java.io.File;
import java.io.IOException;
import java.util.Timer;
import java.util.TimerTask;

import javax.imageio.ImageIO;

import com.scottpreston.javarobot.chapter6.GetFrame;

public class ImageTimer {

    // image capture class
    public GetFrame getFrame;
    // timer class
    private Timer timer;
    // seconds to take pictures
    private int seconds = 5;
    // filename
    private String fileName;
    // url of camera
    private String url = "vfw://0";

    public ImageTimer(String fname) throws Exception {
        // init frame grabber
        getFrame = new GetFrame(url);
        // open it (takes 2500ms)
        //getFrame.open();
        // set filename
        fileName = fname;
        // schedule pictures every 5 seconds
        timer.schedule(new TimerTask() {
            public void run() {
                try {
                    savePic(getFrame.getBufferedImage());
                } catch (Exception e) {
                }
            }
        }, 1000, seconds * 1000);
    }
```

```java
    private void savePic(BufferedImage img) {
        try {
            // open file
            File file = new File(fileName);
            // write JPG
            ImageIO.write(img, "jpg", file);
        } catch (IOException ioe) {
            ioe.printStackTrace();
        }
    }

    public String getFileName() {
        return fileName;
    }

    public void setFileName(String fileName) {
        this.fileName = fileName;
    }

    public static void main(String[] args) {
        try {
            // since this takes a command argument, do some error handling
            if (args.length != 1) {
                System.out
                        .println("usage: java ImageTimer c://webroot/1.jpg");
                System.exit(1);
            }
            // create the class
            ImageTimer it = new ImageTimer(args[0]);
        } catch (Exception e) {
            // print stack trace and exit
            e.printStackTrace();
            System.exit(1);
        }
    }

}
```

The second class, StereoVision, will be the class calling ImageTimer.java. By having one Java Runtime controlling the other two instances of the Java runtime, we can bypass the bug with VFW and a single JVM.

This class has five fields. The first three—fname1, fname2, and path—are to define the filename for the image, while the remaining two are of type CmdExec to encapsulate the processes. The constructor sets the fields and initializes the CmdExec classes.

The two worker methods—openCamera1() and openCamera2()—invoke the actual processes via batch files. Here, I'm actually using these files to call batch scripts that will run the programs.

In the main() method, I pause 10 seconds between the opening of camera one and camera two, and then change the video device to VFW. To exit the program since it's a command line, I set the program to wait for a readLine(). This tells the program to wait until the Enter key is pressed. As soon as this happens, both camera processes are killed.

To process these images, just set the HttpGet.getImage() URL to the web server name, followed by the path and filenames of the two files. Depending on how often you have pictures being saved, you can process them as fast as once a second. See Example 9-5.

Example 9-5. *StereoVision.java*

```java
package com.scottpreston.javarobot.chapter9;

import java.io.BufferedReader;
import java.io.InputStreamReader;

import com.scottpreston.javarobot.chapter2.Utils;

public class StereoVision{

    private String fname1;
    private String fname2;
    private String path;
    private CmdExec cmd1;
    private CmdExec cmd2;
    private HttpGet http;

    public StereoVision(String fname1, String fname2, String path) {
        this.fname1 = fname1;
        this.fname2 = fname2;
        this.path = path;
        cmd1 = new CmdExec();
        cmd2 = new CmdExec();
        http = new HttpGet();
    }

    public void openCamera1() {
        // calls ant script to invoke since it requires large classpath
        cmd1.exe("c:/scripts/camera1.bat " + path + fname1);
    }

    public void openCamera2() {
        // calls ant script to invoke since it requires large classpath
        cmd2.exe("c:/scripts/camera2.bat " + path + fname2);
    }
```

```
    public void close() {
        // kills both processes
        cmd1.kill();
        cmd2.kill();
    }

    public static void main(String[] args) {
        try {
            // init class with two filenames and path
            StereoVision sv = new StereoVision("1.jpg", "2.jpg",
                    "c:\\wwwroot\\");
            System.out.println("opening camera one...");
            sv.openCamera1();
            // wait 10 seconds
            Utils.pause(10000);
            System.out.println("opening camera two...");
            sv.openCamera2();
            System.out.println("ready... press ENTER key to exit");
            // takes system in as a parameter and waits for ENTER key
            BufferedReader br = new BufferedReader(new InputStreamReader(
                    System.in));
            // reads new line
            String anyKey = br.readLine();
            // closes stereo vision killing processes
            sv.close();
        } catch (Exception e) {

        }
    }
}
```

Unless you're doing stereo vision testing, which I'd recommend with a native language or UNIX, getting a single image at a time from a web server is a lot simpler when you have a URL you can access any time you want for a live picture. For this, we can just create a servlet that runs in Tomcat to get a frame as the request happens.

To do so, we'll need to create two files: the servlet and the web.xml configuration file for the servlet.

First, we extend HttpServlet. For this to work with your IDE, you'll need to add servlet-api.jar from your Tomcat Roots /common/lib directory.

For servlets, the init() method acts to initialize the servlet. This is called when the servlet loads. The servlet can load either when requested or when the web server starts, as defined in the web.xml file. In this method, I create an instance of GetFrame.

The two other methods doGet() and doPost() give the servlet the ability to perform different processing for different types of requests. When the request method is a GET, like a URL request, the doGet() method is called. If the request method is a POST, like a form request, the doPost() method is called instead. Since I'm going to use the same functionality for both, I'll just put all the functionality in doPost().

The doPost() method gets the frame from the getFrame object. Then, because the requesting client (web browser) does not know what it's going to receive, I tell it to expect an image by setting the content type of the response to "image/jpeg". If you recall from the last section where I talked about MIME type, this is used to tell the browser an image is coming. Finally, the servlet gets the output stream and then encodes the BufferedImage from the webcam as a JPEG to the OutputStream, sending the image to your browser. See Example 9-6.

Example 9-6. *GetFrameServlet.java*

```java
package com.scottpreston.javarobot.chapter9;

import java.awt.image.BufferedImage;
import java.io.IOException;

import javax.servlet.ServletException;
import javax.servlet.ServletOutputStream;
import javax.servlet.http.HttpServlet;
import javax.servlet.http.HttpServletRequest;
import javax.servlet.http.HttpServletResponse;

import sun.awt.image.codec.JPEGImageEncoderImpl;

import com.scottpreston.javarobot.chapter6.GetFrame;

// requires servlet-api.jar
public class GetFrameServlet extends HttpServlet {

    private GetFrame getFrame;

    // happens when servlet loads
    public void init() {

        try {
            getFrame = new GetFrame("vfw://0");
        } catch (Exception e) {
            e.printStackTrace();
        }
    }

    // when there is a request via HTTP GET
    public void doGet(HttpServletRequest request, HttpServletResponse response)
            throws IOException, ServletException {
        /* Handle a GET in the same way as we handle a POST */
        doPost(request, response);
    }
```

```
      // when there is a request via HTTP POST
      public void doPost(HttpServletRequest request, HttpServletResponse response)
              throws IOException, ServletException {

          /* If there is no GetFrame do nothing */
          if (getFrame == null)
              return;

          BufferedImage bImage = null;
          try {// get frame
              if ((bImage = getFrame.getBufferedImage()) == null) {
                  return;
              }
              // set output MIME type
              response.setContentType("image/jpeg");
              // get output stream
              ServletOutputStream out = response.getOutputStream();
              // write image to stream
              JPEGImageEncoderImpl encoder = new JPEGImageEncoderImpl(out);
              // encode the image as a JPEG
              encoder.encode(bImage);
          } catch (Exception e) {
              e.printStackTrace();

          }
      }

}
```

Making modifications to the web.xml file in Example 9-7 it is really simple. The first tag <servlet-name> is for the name of the servlet. Here, I used the class name, which is fully qualified in the tag <servlet-class>. It's important that this class (or JAR containing this class) be placed either in the root lib of Tomcat, the JVM, or the WEB-INF/lib directory. Then I set the servlet to start up in order 1. If you have multiple servlets, the order of startup is determined by the number you place in this tag.

The next set of tags will map the servlet defined above to the URL. Here the servlet name GetFrameServlet will be mapped to the URL /getframe.

Example 9-7. *web.xml*

```
<servlet>
    <servlet-name>GetFrameServlet</servlet-name>
    <servlet-class>com.scottpreston.javarobot.chapter9.GetFrameServlet➥
</servlet-class>
    <load-on-startup>1</load-on-startup>
  </servlet>
```

```
<servlet-mapping>
  <servlet-name>GetFrameServlet</servlet-name>
  <url-pattern>/getframe</url-pattern>
</servlet-mapping>
```

After I started up Tomcat, I was then able to type in the URL—http://localhost:8080/getframe—to get the image from my web camera (see Figure 9-2).

Figure 9-2. *A sample URL from http://localhost:8080/getframe*

The next thing I want to show you is how to follow something with your web camera. For this, you'll need a camera hooked up to a pan and tilt mechanism as defined in Chapter 4. Also, if you have a robot hooked to the pan and tilt mechanism, the robot will turn when it's out of range of the camera.

Code Objective

The objective of the code here is to follow an object in the webcam's field of view.

Code Discussion

One field in the Follow class is for image processing, while the other moves a pan and tilt camera. Then there are two state fields keeping track of the current horizontal and vertical positions of the pan and tilt system, one for vertical and another for horizontal.

The constructor takes a JSerialPort, which is used to instantiate the variable head, and drive. Also, because I want to view this live, I extended the WebCamViewer class from Chapter 7.

The second method, doProcessing(), is overridden from DoubleWebCamViewer.doProcessing(). Since this method will always be called for processing the camera's output, this is where I put my logic to generate a point. But before I generate a point from the image, I need to process it. So, in Example 9-8 I choose to process a can of Coke, and since I already have a ColorGram for this object I'll set the bimg parameter to the colorRatio() from that can. Now I'm ready to generate a point from this image.

To generate it, I call the getAvgPoint() method from ImageProcessor, which returns a point of MEAN pixilation. In this method, shown in Example 9-8, I first calculate the mean X, and then calculate the mean Y. This point is going to be the average position of all the pixels in the sent image.

The moveHead() method looks at the current position of the head and tries to center it on the motion. For a 320 × 240 image, the midpoint is 160,120. So if the point of average motion is greater than 120, it moves the head up. If it's greater than 160, it moves the camera right. Also, depending on how far away the point of average motion is, the camera steps in larger or smaller increments until it's centered. Finally, if it's at its maximum left or right positions, the robot will turn to find the object. See Example 9-9.

Example 9-8. *ImageProcessor.getAvgPoint()*

```
public Point getAvgPoint(BufferedImage srcImg) {

        int h = srcImg.getHeight();
        int w = srcImg.getWidth();
        // difference image

        int meanX = 0;
        int meanY = 0;
        int meanThresh = 100;
        int count = 0;

        for (int y = 0; y < h; ++y) {
            int rowY = 0;
            for (int x = 0; x < w; ++x) {
                int srcPixel = getGrey(srcImg.getRGB(x, y));
                if (srcPixel > meanThresh) {
                    rowY = rowY + srcPixel;
                    meanY = meanY + y;
                    count++;
                }
            }
        }
        if (count > 0) {
            meanY = meanY / count;
        }
        count = 0;
        for (int x = 0; x < w; ++x) {
            int rowX = 0;
            for (int y = 0; y < h; ++y) {
                int srcPixel = getGrey(srcImg.getRGB(x, y));
```

```
                    if (srcPixel > meanThresh) {
                        rowX = rowX + srcPixel;
                        meanX = meanX + x;
                        count++;
                    }
                }
            }

        if (count > 0) {
            meanX = meanX / count;
        }
        return new Point(meanX, meanY);
    }
```

Example 9-9. *Follow.java*

```java
package com.scottpreston.javarobot.chapter9;

import java.awt.Point;
import java.awt.image.BufferedImage;

import com.scottpreston.javarobot.chapter2.JSerialPort;
import com.scottpreston.javarobot.chapter2.SingleSerialPort;
import com.scottpreston.javarobot.chapter2.Utils;
import com.scottpreston.javarobot.chapter3.PanTilt;
import com.scottpreston.javarobot.chapter6.ColorGram;
import com.scottpreston.javarobot.chapter6.DoubleWebCamViewer;
import com.scottpreston.javarobot.chapter6.ImageProcessor;

public class Follow extends DoubleWebCamViewer {

    private PanTilt head;
    private int hPos = PanTilt.HORZ_NEUTRAL;
    private int vPos = PanTilt.VERT_NEUTRAL;
    private ImageProcessor imageProcessor = new ImageProcessor();

    public Follow(JSerialPort sPort) throws Exception {
        super();
        head = new PanTilt(sPort);
        setTitle("Follow Color");
    }
```

```java
public BufferedImage doProcessing(BufferedImage bimg) {
    // get ColorGram of Coke
    bimg = imageProcessor.colorRatio(bimg,ColorGram.COKE);
    // get avg point of Coke
    Point pt = imageProcessor.getAvgPoint(bimg);
    // move head
    moveHead(pt);
    // display point to system.out
    Utils.log(pt.toString());
    return bimg;
}

private void moveHead(Point pt) {

    double x = pt.x;
    double y = pt.y;
    double xMax = 320;
    double yMax = 240;
    //x
    if (x < 50) {
        hPos = hPos - 5;
    }
    if (x > 270) {
        hPos = hPos + 5;
    }
    if (x < 100 && x >= 50) {
        hPos = hPos - 3;
    }
    if (x > 220 && x <= 270) {
        hPos = hPos + 3;
    }
    if (x < 220 && x > 190) {
        hPos = hPos + 1;
    }
    if (x > 100 && x < 130) {
        hPos = hPos - 1;
    }
    // y
    if (y < 30) {
        vPos = vPos + 5;
    }
    if (y > 210) {
        vPos = vPos - 5;
    }
    if (y < 60 && y >= 30) {
        vPos = vPos + 3;
    }
```

```
        if (y > 180 && y <= 210) {
            vPos = vPos - 3;
        }
        if (y < 180 && y > 150) {
            vPos = vPos - 1;
        }
        if (y > 60 && y < 90) {
            vPos = vPos + 1;
        }

        // this is where robot will turn
        if (hPos > 255) {
            hPos = 255;
        }
        if (hPos < 0) {
            hPos = 0;
        }
        if (vPos > 255) {
            vPos = 255;
        }
        if (vPos < 0) {
            vPos = 0;
        }
        try {
            head.moveBoth(hPos, vPos);
        } catch (Exception e) {
            // don't do anything since it could just move out of bounds
            System.out.println(e);
        }
    }

    public static void main(String[] args) {
        try {
            Follow fc = new Follow(SingleSerialPort.getInstance(1));
            fc.setFps(5);
            fc.start();
        } catch (Exception e) {
            e.printStackTrace();
        }
    }
}
```

To follow other objects or motion, just replace the doProcessing() with the desired filter. To follow your face or skin tone, create a ColorGram of your skin from a picture taken with your webcam, calibrate it, and then add this ColorGram to the doProcessing() method.

Code Objective

The code objective here is to recognize one of three things: Coke, 7-Up, or Pepsi.

Code Discussion

The first thing I'll need to do for recognizing is create an object that holds ColorGrams and names for these objects. This class is called ColorObject. See Example 9-10.

Example 9-10. *ColorObject.java*

```
package com.scottpreston.javarobot.chapter9;

import com.scottpreston.javarobot.chapter6.ColorGram;

public class ColorObject {

    public ColorGram colorGram;
    public String name;

    public ColorObject(){
        // default
    }
    public ColorObject(String nm ,ColorGram cg) {
        name = nm;
        colorGram = cg;
    }

}
```

The fields in this class are voice, to speak the colors it sees; the colorList, which will be an ArrayList of ColorObjects, holding a string for the description and the ColorGram of the object I want to recognize; and an ImageProcessor class for the image processing.

I have two constructors that initialize the voice. The first takes a pathname as a parameter. By including a pathname, you can add as many JPEGs as you want to the path. The method will look at all the JPEG files in this directory and then optimize these JPEGs for ColorGrams before adding them to the list of ColorObjects. The second constructor adds three ColorObjects of type "Coke", "7-Up", and "Pepsi".

The worker method doProcessing() compares the current frame to the ColorGram I get back, as well as a pixel count of all the hits of pixels that fall within this range. The item in the list with the highest count will be the winner, which is then spoken as the recognized item.

I've found that some additional processing to remove the background is helpful in reducing false readings; however, that takes more time to process than one frame per second. See Example 9-11.

Example 9-11. *RecognizeColor.java*

```java
package com.scottpreston.javarobot.chapter9;

import java.awt.image.BufferedImage;
import java.io.File;
import java.util.ArrayList;

import com.scottpreston.javarobot.chapter2.Utils;
import com.scottpreston.javarobot.chapter5.MicrosoftVoice;
import com.scottpreston.javarobot.chapter6.ColorGram;
import com.scottpreston.javarobot.chapter6.ColorGramCalibration;
import com.scottpreston.javarobot.chapter6.DoubleWebCamViewer;
import com.scottpreston.javarobot.chapter6.ImageProcessor;

public class RecognizeColor extends DoubleWebCamViewer {

    private MicrosoftVoice voice;
    private ArrayList colorObjects = new ArrayList();
    private ImageProcessor imageProcessor = new ImageProcessor();

    public RecognizeColor() throws Exception {
        init();
        colorObjects.add(new ColorObject("coke", ColorGram.COKE));
        colorObjects.add(new ColorObject("7up", ColorGram.SEVEN_UP));
        colorObjects.add(new ColorObject("pepsi", ColorGram.PEPSI));
    }

    public RecognizeColor(String path) throws Exception {
        super();
        init();
        voice.speak("opening directory");
        // gets images from directory
        File dir = new File(path);
        File[] files = dir.listFiles();
        for (int f = 0; f < files.length; f++) {
            // create object
            ColorObject co = new ColorObject();
            String file = files[f].getName();
            if (file.endsWith(".jpg")) {
                // calibrate for image
                ColorGramCalibration cgc = new ColorGramCalibration(path + file,
                        false);
                voice.speak("ColorGram optimization for " + file);
                // optimize
                cgc.optimize();
```

```java
            // set to ColorObject
            co.colorGram = cgc.getBestColorGram();
            // get rid of extension
            co.name = file.substring(0, file.length() - 4);
            // add to list
            colorObjects.add(co);
        }
    }
    voice.speak("done optimizing colors");
}

private void init() throws Exception {
    setFps(1);
    voice = MicrosoftVoice.getInstance();

}

public BufferedImage doProcessing(BufferedImage src) {
    BufferedImage dstImage = null;
    String winner = "";
    int maxCount = 0;
    ColorGram cg = null;
    //while (colorMaps.)
    for (int i = 0; i < colorObjects.size(); i++) {
        // get Object[] from list
        ColorObject cObj = (ColorObject) colorObjects.get(i);
        // get pixel count
        int tmpCount = imageProcessor.colorRatioCount(src, cObj.colorGram);
        // get maximum
        if (tmpCount > maxCount) {
            maxCount = tmpCount;
            winner = cObj.name;
            cg = cObj.colorGram;
        }
        Utils.log(cObj.name + " = " + tmpCount);
    }

    dstImage = imageProcessor.colorRatio(src, cg);
    try {
        // speak the winner
        voice.speak(winner);
    } catch (Exception e) {
    }
    return dstImage;
}
```

```
public static void main(String[] args) {
    try {
        RecognizeColor rc = new RecognizeColor();
        //RecognizeColor rc = new RecognizeColor("sample_images//cans//");
        rc.start();
    } catch (Exception e) {
        e.printStackTrace();
        System.exit(1);
    }
}
}
```

Section Summary

The webcam programs defined in this section should show you how to access, even if basically, the other classes we've created so you can use movement and speech with your camera.

The following classes created in this section are:

- ImageTimer.java: This program saves a file to your hard disk at a certain interval.

- StereoVision.java: This program helps if you have Windows and want to do stereo vision via VFW.

- GetFrameServlet.java: This program, along with modifications to the web.xml file, allows you to view images from a web server via a URL, and is processed in real time.

- Follow.java: This program, when used with a differential drive and a pan and tilt camera, allows your robot to follow motion with its head and body if needed.

- ColorObject.java: This is an object that stores a name and ColorGram for processing in RecognizeColor.

- RecognizeColor.java: This class is used with a voice to notify you if it sees things of a certain ColorGram.

Many more programs of this nature are available that can really add value to your robot and give it a sense of autonomy. There are times, though, when you need to intervene and tell your robot what to do, using your voice or a user interface. We'll discuss this in the next section.

9.3 Remote Control Programs

So far, we've talked about some basic utilities that allow your robot to communicate with other programs, as well as over the Internet via HTTP (Web) or SMTP (e-mail). We have even given your robot some sense of autonomy by including some vision algorithms. There are many times, however, when you just want to tell your robot what to do.

In this section, I'll start off by showing you how you can remotely control your robot over the Internet via a web browser. For example, if you have your robot at home and you're at work, you could have your robot check on the dog, or move around the house to make sure things are okay. I also provided a remote speech JSP so you can make your robot talk from anywhere.

After the web clients, I'll show you how to command your robot with your voice to perform some simple navigation steps. For example, let's say you're at a party and have your robot moving around with appetizers. When it runs out of food, someone could tell it to "get more food" and the robot would be able to find its way back to the serving area, and then once refilled, someone could tell it to "wander" again.

Finally, I'll end the chapter with a Swing client that gives you GUI access to a MiniSSC servo controller. It's a nice tool to debug positions for your robot's arms, or for pan and tilt cameras.

Code Objective

The objective here is to create a remote control program that can be accessed over the Internet with a browser.

Code Discussion

The first JSP I created was speech.jsp. In this JSP, the code that does the work is at the top of the page; this is where the voice object is instantiated. Then, if the parameter is not null, it speaks the parameter.

In the HTML half of the page, I display the spoken text, and then I create a form that sends the output of the button click back to the same page. The form has a single text field and a button labeled "Talk." See Example 9-12.

Example 9-12. *speech.jsp*

```
<%@ page import="com.scottpreston.javarobot.chapter6.*" %>
<%
MicrosoftVoice voice = MicrosoftVoice.getInstance();
String s = "";
if (request.getParameter("s") != null) {
                s = request.getParameter("s");
                voice.speak(s);
}
%>
<!DOCTYPE HTML PUBLIC "-//W3C//DTD HTML 4.01 Transitional//EN">

<html>
<head>
                <title>Speech</title>
</head>
<body>
Spoken '<%=s%>'.
<hr>
<form action="speech.jsp" method="get" name="myform">
<input type="text" name="s" size="50">
<input type="submit" value="Talk">
</form>
<script>
document.myform.s.focus();
</script>
```

Next, I'm ready to show you a remote control interface that will allow you to get sensor data and move your robot. The first set of pages will be simple ones that have a single purpose. I'll call these from a master remote page individually so that performance is faster and the interface is more robust.

Code Objective

The objective in this instance is to create four small JSP pages that will be called by a master remote control program.

Code Discussion

The first page is heading.jsp, which will instantiate the current local port and return as a string the output of the compass reading. See Example 9-13.

Example 9-13. *heading.jsp*

```
<%@ page import="com.scottpreston.javarobot.chapter2.*"
%><%@ page import="com.scottpreston.javarobot.chapter8.*"
%><%
JSerialPort sPort = SingleSerialPort.getInstance(1);
NavStamp stamp = new NavStamp(sPort);
out.println(stamp.getCompass());
%>
```

The second page is motion.jsp, which has two required parameters, "m" for magnitude, and "h" for heading, and one optional parameter, "stop", to stop the robot.

The parameters for magnitude and heading are used to construct a motion vector, and upon construction the move command is sent to a SimpleNavigation class. See Example 9-14.

Example 9-14. *motion.jsp*

```
<%@ page import="com.scottpreston.javarobot.chapter2.*"
%><%@ page import="com.scottpreston.javarobot.chapter8.*"
%><%
try {
JSerialPort sPort = SingleSerialPort.getInstance(1);
SimpleNavigation nav = new SimpleNavigation(sPort);
int m = new Integer(request.getParameter("m")).intValue();
int h = new Integer(request.getParameter("h")).intValue();
if (request.getParameter("stop") == null) {
        nav.move(new MotionVector(m,h));
} else {
        nav.stop();
}
} catch (Exception e) {
        e.printStackTrace(out);
}
%>
```

The third page is sonar.jsp. This page functions just like the heading.jsp except that instead of returning the heading, it returns the sonar output. See Example 9-15.

Example 9-15. *sonar.jsp*

```
<%@ page import="com.scottpreston.javarobot.chapter2.*"
%><%@ page import="com.scottpreston.javarobot.chapter8.*"
%><%try {
JSerialPort sPort = SingleSerialPort.getInstance(1);
NavStamp stamp = new NavStamp(sPort);
out.println(stamp.getSonar().toString());
} catch (Exception e) {
        e.printStackTrace(out);
}
%>
```

The fourth page is ir.jsp. This page functions just like heading.jsp and sonar.jsp, except it returns the output from the two infrared modules. See Example 9-16.

Example 9-16. *ir.jsp*

```
<%@ page import="com.scottpreston.javarobot.chapter2.*"
%><%@ page import="com.scottpreston.javarobot.chapter8.*"
%><%try {
JSerialPort sPort = SingleSerialPort.getInstance(1);
NavStamp stamp = new NavStamp(sPort);
out.println(stamp.getIr().toString());
} catch (Exception e) {
        e.printStackTrace(out);
}
%>
```

The next page is called remote.jsp. Notice there isn't any JSP syntax in the page. The only Java evident is JavaScript, which is not really Java but a web scripting language that gives the web client we're creating some nice features.

As I create the page, I add styles to the page to make it pretty. The styles I'm using are called Cascading Style Sheets, or CSS for short. You can reference them at www.w3.org/Style/CSS.

The second part of the page shows a picture from the web camera, followed by an empty tag that acts as a placeholder for the heading.

The third part of the page is a form that contains the elements required to make the robot move.

The fourth part of the page is the JavaScript that makes the calls to the four components we spoke of earlier. The function moveRobot() takes the values from the form and sends them to move.jsp. The function stopRobot() sends the stop parameter to move.jsp. The three populate functions—populateHeading(), populateIR, and populateSonar()—all make calls to their respective JSP pages for insertion into the placeholders via the [*tagname*].innerHTML property. See Example 9-17.

Example 9-17. *remote.jsp*

```
<!DOCTYPE HTML PUBLIC "-//W3C//DTD HTML 4.01 Transitional//EN">
<html>
<head>
     <title>Remote Control</title>
    <style>
    body {font-family:arial;font-size:.9em}
    caption{background-color:navy;color:white;font-weight:bold;}
    input{background-color:#e2e2e2;}
    </style>
</head>
<body>
<div align="center"><img src="/getimage" width="320" height="240"><br>
<div id="heading"></div>
<hr>
<form name="remoteForm">
<table>
    <caption>Navigation</caption>
    <tr>
        <td align="right">heading:</td>
        <td><input type="text" name="heading" size="3"></td>
    </tr>
    <tr>
        <td align="right">magnitude:</td>
        <td><input type="text" name="magnitude" size="5"></td>
    </tr>

</table>
<button onclick="move()">Move</button> <button onclick="stop()">Stop</button>
</form>
</div>
</body>
</html>
<script>

var req;
var reqText;

function moveRobot() {
    var url = "move.jsp?h=" + document.remoteForm.heading.value
    + "m=" + document.remoteForm.heading.value;
    loadDoc(url);
}
```

```
function stopRobot() {
    var url = "move.jsp?stop=true";
    loadDoc(url);
}

function populateHeading() {
    var headingDiv=document.getElementById("heading");
    loadDoc("heading.jsp");
    headingDiv.innerHTML = "heading: " + reqText;
}

function populateIR() {
    var irDiv=document.getElementById("ir");
    loadDoc("ir.jsp");
    headingDiv.innerHTML = "ir: " + reqText;
}

function populateSonar() {
var sonarDiv=document.getElementById("sonar");
    loadDoc("sonar.jsp");
    headingDiv.innerHTML = "sonar: " + reqText;
}

function loadDoc(url) {
    // branch for native XMLHttpRequest object
    if (window.XMLHttpRequest) {
        req = new XMLHttpRequest();
        req.onreadystatechange = doRequest;
        req.open("GET", url, true);
        req.send(null);
    // branch for IE/Windows ActiveX version
    } else if (window.ActiveXObject) {
        req = new ActiveXObject("Microsoft.XMLHTTP");
        if (req) {
            req.onreadystatechange = doRequest;
            req.open("GET", url, true);
            req.send();
        }
    }
}

function doRequest() {
    if (req.readyState==4)  {
        if (req.status==200) {
        reqText = req.responseText;
```

```
    } else {
        alert("Problem retrieving XML data");
    }
  }
 }
}

</script>
```

■**Note** It's always a good idea to put your JavaScript at the bottom of the page so that all the elements load before anything is called.

Let's say that rather than being behind a PC or laptop and commanding your robot about what to do, you are in a location where you just want to tell it what to do with your voice.

Code Objective

The objective this time is to control the actions of your robot with your voice.

Code Discussion

This class has three fields, one for the ear (the SphinxSR class from Chapter 5), one for the voice (MicrosoftVoice), and one to launch an external program.

■**Tip** Before running this class, I had to increase the memory of my Java program. Thus, you might need to use the JVM arguments –Xms and –Xmx to increase the memory size before launch.

The constructor for this class is empty but goes through the process of loading the commands.config.xml file and commands.gram file for the SphinxSR class, as well as instantiating the voice object. I also created a reference to CmdExec() and told the robot to start listening.

The listen() method listens for the command "move." Once it hears this, it will then prompt the speaker to enter three heading values and one magnitude value in seconds. While not the most efficient in coding or using the Sphinx Speech API, it does provide a simple means of explanation for how to get your robot to understand the sentence.

The beginning of the method waits until a word is passed back from the recognizer. I then parse through those words and set certain variables representing states for the command sequence (see Example 9-18). The sequence of language is

1. Robot hears "move."

2. Robot prompts user to enter heading.

3. User enters one, two, three.

4. Robot prompts user to enter magnitude in seconds.

5. Robot calls move command, converting the numbers to integers for use in the SimpleNavigation class's move() method.

Example 9-18. *VoiceControl.java*

```java
package com.scottpreston.javarobot.chapter9;

import java.net.URL;

import com.scottpreston.javarobot.chapter6.MicrosoftVoice;
import com.scottpreston.javarobot.chapter6.SphinxSR;

public class VoiceControl{

    private SphinxSR ear;
    private MicrosoftVoice voice;
    private CmdExec cmd;

    public VoiceControl() throws Exception {
        URL url = VoiceControl.class.getResource("commands.config.xml");
        ear = new SphinxSR(url);
        System.out.println("Opening...");
        ear.open();
        System.out.println("Starting...");
        ear.start();
        voice = MicrosoftVoice.getInstance();
        System.out.println("speak");
        voice.speak("ready to listen");
        cmd = new CmdExec();
        listen();
    }

    public void listen() throws Exception {
        String words;
        boolean heading = false;
        boolean time = false;
        boolean cmdDone = false;
        StringBuffer headingString = new StringBuffer();
        String timeString = null;
        while (true) {
            words = ear.listen();
            System.out.println("words="+words);
            if (words.indexOf("move") >= 0) {
                voice.speak("enter direction");
                heading = true;
                words = null;
            }
```

```java
            // expect heading
            if (heading && words != null) {
                voice.speak(words);
                headingString.append(wordsToNumber(words));
            }
            if (heading && headingString.length() == 3) {
                voice.speak("heading is, " + headingString.toString());
                heading = false;
                time = true;
                voice.speak("enter seconds");
                words = null;
            }
            if (time && words != null) {
                timeString = wordsToNumber(words);
                time = false;
                cmdDone = true;
            }
            if (cmdDone) {
                move(headingString.toString(),timeString);
            }
            if (words != null && words.indexOf("exit") >= 0) {
                break;
            }
        }
        ear.stop();
        ear.close();

    }

    private void move(String heading, String time) throws Exception{
        voice.speak("moving direction equal to " + heading
                + " degrees. time will be  " + time + " seconds.");
        // need on new thread
        //cmd.exe("c:\\commands\\move.bat " + heading + " " + time);
    }

    private String wordsToNumber(String word) {
        String out = "";
        if (word.equalsIgnoreCase("zero")) {
            out = "0";
        }
        if (word.equalsIgnoreCase("one")) {
            out = "1";
        }
        if (word.equalsIgnoreCase("two")) {
            out = "2";
        }
```

```java
            if (word.equalsIgnoreCase("three")) {
                out = "3";
            }
            if (word.equalsIgnoreCase("four")) {
                out = "4";
            }
            if (word.equalsIgnoreCase("five")) {
                out = "5";
            }
            if (word.equalsIgnoreCase("six")) {
                out = "6";
            }
            if (word.equalsIgnoreCase("seven")) {
                out = "7";
            }
            if (word.equalsIgnoreCase("eight")) {
                out = "8";
            }
            if (word.equalsIgnoreCase("nine")) {
                out = "9";
            }
            return out;
        }

    public static void main(String[] args) {
        try {
            VoiceControl vc = new VoiceControl();
            System.out.println("done!");
        } catch (Exception e) {
            e.printStackTrace();
            System.exit(1);
        }
    }
}
```

The commands.gram file is shown in Example 9-19. I only have three types of commands: a command to move, numbers, and a command to exit.

Example 9-19. *commands.gram*

```
grammar commands;

public <move> = move;
public <numbers> = zero | one | two | three | four | five | six | seven | ➡
eight | nine | ten;
public <exit> = exit;
```

The final class in the remote control section is the servo control client. This is a Swing client that gives you the ability to control your servos with sliders, and is good for setting the limits of things like your pan and tilt or robotic arms. You can see in Figure 9-3 that it has sliders and text boxes to move your servo to the position you need.

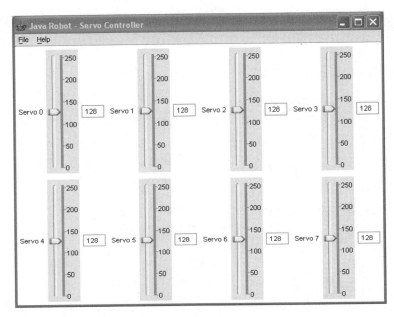

Figure 9-3. *ServoControlClient*

To create this application required the creation of five separate Java classes. The first main class is ServoControlClient, which extends the JFrame and is the container you see in Figure 9-3.

The second class is the SscPanel, which holds the MinSsc classes and will actually make the calls to the servo controller.

The third class is the SliderFieldCombo, which contains both the slider and the text field.

The fourth class is the ServoSlider, which has a range from 0 to 255 with minor increments at every five positions and major ones at every 50.

The fifth and final class is the PrefFrame, which allows you to change both the serial port number and the baud, as shown in Figure 9-4.

Figure 9-4. *PrefFrame.java*

Code Objective

The objective here is to create a servo control Swing client.

Code Discussion

The first class to discuss will be the ServoControlClient. It has fields of JMenuBar for the menu bar of File and Help, the JSerialPort for construction of the MiniSsc, the PrefFrame to modify serial port properties, and two default values for the serial port id = 1 and baud = 9600.

The constructor lays out and creates the initial frame. The mainMenuBar() method creates the menu bar you see. The methods showAbout() and showHelp() pop up dialogs with information in them, and showPrefs() makes visible the PrefFrame for setting the serial port parameters. See Examples 9-20 and 9-21.

Example 9-20. *ServoControlClient.java*

```
package com.scottpreston.javarobot.chapter9;

import java.awt.Color;
import java.awt.GridLayout;
import java.awt.event.ActionEvent;
import java.awt.event.ActionListener;
import java.awt.event.WindowEvent;

import javax.swing.JFrame;
import javax.swing.JMenu;
import javax.swing.JMenuBar;
import javax.swing.JMenuItem;
import javax.swing.JOptionPane;

import com.scottpreston.javarobot.chapter2.JSerialPort;
import com.scottpreston.javarobot.chapter2.SingleSerialPort;
import com.scottpreston.javarobot.chapter6.ExitListener;
import com.scottpreston.javarobot.chapter6.WindowUtilities;

public class ServoControlClient extends JFrame {

    private JMenuBar myMenuBar;
    private JSerialPort sPort;
    private PrefFrame prefFrame;
    private int id = 1;
    private int baud = 9600;

    public ServoControlClient() {
        // set caption
        super("Java Robot - Servo Controller");
        // get current look and feel
        WindowUtilities.setNativeLookAndFeel();
```

```
        // set size
        setSize(640, 480);
        // create panel
        SscPanel content = null;
        // add serial port to panel
        try {
            // sets the serial port
            setSerialPort();
            // adds to panel
            content = new SscPanel(sPort);
        } catch (Exception e) {
            e.printStackTrace();
            System.exit(1);
        }
        // sets panel as content pane
        setContentPane(content);
        // set background color
        content.setBackground(Color.white);
        // set grid layout as 2 rows, 4 columns
        content.setLayout(new GridLayout(2, 4));
        // create new combos with loop
        for (int x = 0; x < 8; x++) {
            SliderFieldCombo slider = new SliderFieldCombo(x);
            content.add(slider);
        }
        // create menu bar
        makeMenuBar();
        // set menu bar
        setJMenuBar(myMenuBar);
        // set frame
        prefFrame = new PrefFrame(this);
        // set visible = false
        prefFrame.setVisible(false);
        // add exit listener
        addWindowListener(new ExitListener());
        // pack this for display
        pack();
        // display frame
        setVisible(true);

    }

    public void makeMenuBar() {
        myMenuBar = new JMenuBar();
        // creates first one
        JMenu fileMenu = new JMenu("File");
```

```java
// adds items
String[] fileItems = new String[] { "Preferences", "Exit" };
// create shortcut
char[] fileShortcuts = { 'P', 'X' };

ActionListener printListener = new ActionListener() {
    public void actionPerformed(ActionEvent event) {
        actionFactory(event.getActionCommand());
    }
};

for (int i = 0; i < fileItems.length; i++) {
    JMenuItem item = new JMenuItem(fileItems[i], fileShortcuts[i]);
    item.addActionListener(printListener);
    fileMenu.add(item);
    // add separator between preferences and exit
    if (fileItems[i].equalsIgnoreCase("Preferences")) {
        fileMenu.addSeparator();
    }
}
// add shortcut key
fileMenu.setMnemonic('F');
// add to menu bar
myMenuBar.add(fileMenu);
// help
JMenu helpMenu = new JMenu("Help");
String[] fileItems2 = new String[] { "Help Contents", "About" };
char[] fileShortcuts2 = { 'C', 'A' };

ActionListener printListener2 = new ActionListener() {
    public void actionPerformed(ActionEvent event) {
        actionFactory(event.getActionCommand());
    }

};

for (int i = 0; i < fileItems.length; i++) {
    JMenuItem item = new JMenuItem(fileItems2[i], fileShortcuts2[i]);
    item.addActionListener(printListener);
    helpMenu.add(item);
    if (fileItems[i].equalsIgnoreCase("Help Contents")) {
        helpMenu.addSeparator();
    }
}
```

```java
        helpMenu.setMnemonic('H');
        myMenuBar.add(helpMenu);

    }
    // shows about dialog
    private void showAbout() {
        String msg = "Simple Servo Controller\n" + "Version 1.0\n"
                + "Updates can be found at www.scottsbots.com";
        JOptionPane.showMessageDialog(null, msg,
                "About - Simple Servo Controller",
                JOptionPane.INFORMATION_MESSAGE, null);
    }

    // shows pref frame
    private void showPrefs() {

        ExitListener closeListener = new ExitListener() {
            public void windowClosing(WindowEvent event) {
                prefFrame.setVisible(false);
            }
        };

        prefFrame.setVisible(true);
        prefFrame.addWindowListener(closeListener);

    }
    // shows different dialogs
    private void actionFactory(String s) {

        if (s.equalsIgnoreCase("preferences")) {
            showPrefs();
        }

        if (s.equalsIgnoreCase("about")) {
            showAbout();
        }
        if (s.equalsIgnoreCase("exit")) {
            System.exit(0);
        }
    }
    // called from child
    public void setSerialPort() throws Exception {
        sPort = SingleSerialPort.getInstance(id, baud);
        System.out.println("serial port id is " + id);
    }
```

```java
    public int getBaud() {
        return baud;
    }

    public void setBaud(int baud) throws Exception {
        this.baud = baud;
        setSerialPort();
    }

    public int getId() {
        return id;
    }

    public void setId(int id) throws Exception {
        this.id = id;
        setSerialPort();
    }

    public void setSerialPort(int id, int baud) throws Exception {
        this.id = id;
        this.baud = baud;
        setSerialPort();
    }

    public static void main(String[] args) {
        ServoControlClient scc = new ServoControlClient();
    }

}
```

Example 9-21. *SscPanel.java*

```java
package com.scottpreston.javarobot.chapter9;

import javax.swing.JPanel;

import com.scottpreston.javarobot.chapter2.JSerialPort;
import com.scottpreston.javarobot.chapter3.MiniSsc;

public class SscPanel extends JPanel {

    private MiniSsc ssc;

    public SscPanel(JSerialPort sPort) throws Exception{
        ssc = new MiniSsc(sPort);
    }
```

```
    public void moveServo(int pin, int pos) {
        try {
            ssc.move(pin, pos);
        } catch (Exception e) {
            e.printStackTrace();
        }
    }

}
```

The ServoSlider class is important for knowing that the initial values and size of the slider is set to the minimum servo position, maximum servo position, and neutral positions. The constructor also contains a ChangeListener, which calls the parent class of the JSlider SliderFieldCombo to send the new value of the slider to it for propagation to the SscPanel to actually move the servo to a new position. See Example 9-22.

Example 9-22. *ServoSlider.java*

```
package com.scottpreston.javarobot.chapter9;

import javax.swing.JSlider;
import javax.swing.JTextField;
import javax.swing.event.ChangeEvent;
import javax.swing.event.ChangeListener;

public class ServoSlider extends JSlider {

    private JTextField textField;

    public ServoSlider() {
        super(JSlider.VERTICAL, 0, 255, 128);
        this.setMajorTickSpacing(50);
        this.setMinorTickSpacing(1);
        this.setPaintTicks(true);
        this.setPaintLabels(true);
        this.setLabelTable(this.createStandardLabels(50));
        this.addChangeListener(new ChangeListener() {
            // This method is called whenever the slider's value is changed
            public void stateChanged(ChangeEvent evt) {
                JSlider slider = (JSlider)evt.getSource();
                if (!slider.getValueIsAdjusting()) {
                    // Get new value
                    int value = slider.getValue();
                    textField.setText(value+"");
                    SliderFieldCombo sfc = (SliderFieldCombo)getParent();
                    sfc.moveServo(value);
                }
            }
        }
```

```
        });

    }

    public void bind(JTextField tf) {
        textField = tf;
        textField.setText(this.getValue()+"");
    }
}
```

In this combination class, the servo pin was set in the constructor. Because the event propagated from the ServoSlider class calls the moveServo() method, the ID of the current SliderFieldCombo can now be sent to its parent class, the SscPanel. See Example 9-23.

Example 9-23. *ServoFieldCombo.java*

```
package com.scottpreston.javarobot.chapter9;

import java.awt.Container;
import java.awt.FlowLayout;

import javax.swing.JLabel;
import javax.swing.JTextField;

public class SliderFieldCombo extends Container {

    private ServoSlider servoSlider;
    private JTextField jTextField;
    private int id;

    public SliderFieldCombo(int i) {
        id = i;
        servoSlider = new ServoSlider();
        jTextField = new JTextField(3);
        servoSlider.bind(jTextField);
        JLabel label = new  JLabel("Servo " + i);
        this.setLayout(new FlowLayout());
        this.add(label);
        this.add(servoSlider);
        this.add(jTextField);
    }

    public void moveServo(int value) {
        SscPanel sscPanel = (SscPanel)this.getParent();
        sscPanel.moveServo(id,value);
    }
```

```java
    public JTextField getJTextField() {
        return jTextField;
    }
    public void setJTextField(JTextField textField) {
        jTextField = textField;
    }
    public ServoSlider getServoSlider() {
        return servoSlider;
    }
    public void setServoSlider(ServoSlider servoSlider) {
        this.servoSlider = servoSlider;
    }
    public int getId() {
        return id;
    }
    public void setId(int id) {
        this.id = id;
    }
}
```

The SscPanel class contains the MinSsc class. It's constructed from the main frame Servo-ControlClient via the JSerialPort. The ServoFieldCombo class calls the moveServo method here to actually move the servo on the associated pin to the position defined by the slider that moved.

Finally, in the PrefFrame I construct this with a reference to the ServoControlClient. Here, when the serial port parameters change via the Save button click, I can call the parent class setSerialPort() method. Because this method uses the SingleSerialPort, it will just get another instance from the pool of serial ports so this way the servo controller can access multiple serial ports. See Example 9-24.

Example 9-24. *PrefFrame.java*

```java
package com.scottpreston.javarobot.chapter9;

import java.awt.Container;
import java.awt.GridLayout;
import java.awt.event.ActionEvent;
import java.awt.event.ActionListener;

import javax.swing.JButton;
import javax.swing.JFrame;
import javax.swing.JLabel;
import javax.swing.JPanel;
import javax.swing.JTextField;
```

```java
public class PrefFrame extends JFrame implements ActionListener {

    private JTextField comTxt;
    private JTextField baudTxt;
    private ServoControlClient scc;

    public PrefFrame(ServoControlClient parent) {
        super("Preferences");
        scc = parent;
        this.setSize(400, 400);
        Container content = this.getContentPane();
        content.setLayout(new GridLayout(3, 2));
        JPanel pan1 = new JPanel();
        pan1.add(new JLabel("Com :"));
        comTxt = new JTextField(2);
        comTxt.setText(scc.getId() + "");
        baudTxt = new JTextField(4);
        baudTxt.setText(scc.getBaud() + "");
        pan1.add(comTxt);
        JPanel pan2 = new JPanel();
        pan2.add(new JLabel("Baud :"));
        pan2.add(baudTxt);
        JPanel pan3 = new JPanel();
        JButton saveButton = new JButton("Save");
        pan3.add(saveButton);
        content.add(pan1);
        content.add(pan2);
        content.add(pan3);
        this.pack();
        saveButton.addActionListener(this);
    }

    public void actionPerformed(ActionEvent event) {
        //Object source = event.getSource();
        int id = new Integer(comTxt.getText()).intValue();
        int baud = new Integer(baudTxt.getText()).intValue();
        setVisible(false);
        try {
            scc.setSerialPort(id,baud);
        } catch (Exception e) {
            e.printStackTrace();}

    }
}
```

Section Summary

In this section, I talked about various types of remote control: control via the Internet over a browser, control with your voice, and control with a Swing client. The classes discussed were

- speech.jsp: For remotely making your robot talk
- ir.jsp, heading.jsp, sonar.jsp, motion.jsp, and remote.jsp: For creating a remote group of web pages that allow for remote control of your robot through the Internet
- VoiceControl.java: For controlling your Java programs with your voice
- ServoControlClient.java and supporting classes: For controlling the MiniSsc class with a Swing client

For those times when your robot is not functioning autonomously, you'll want to use a combination of programs like this to give you remote control over your robot. Other types of remote control allow you to debug your programs without having to power down, recharge your battery, or disassemble your robot. These are diagnostic programs and are the topic of the next section.

9.4 Diagnostic Programs

I wish diagnostic programs weren't needed. But things never seem to go according to plan. Maybe your robot isn't facing the direction you think it should because there's interference someplace with the compass (my speakers caused this at distances of over 10 feet). Other things you might want to work on are calibrating your robot when it travels on different surfaces, since we didn't talk about encoders. Finally, it's good to get health and status reports from your robot if it's running autonomously and not doing anything.

I encourage you to write your own diagnostic programs that test the various subsystems of your robot: vision, speech, navigation, and so on. When things go wrong, this data will help you fix the problem so you're not spending all your time recharging the batteries of your robot or writing test programs.

Code Objective

The objective in this case is to write a test program in which your robot can face four directions: north, east, south, and west.

Code Discussion

I find this useful when testing the robot's ability to find its start position. Also, because I'm watching the robot and I'm not planted in front of my PC, it's nice to have the robot talk to me to tell me what's going on.

The class in Example 9-25 is constructed with a JSerialPort, and then a SimpleNavigation class is instantiated to do the work necessary in facing four directions. I also instantiated the voice object so that the robot could tell me when it has reached the following directions.

Example 9-25. *FourDirections.java*

```java
package com.scottpreston.javarobot.chapter9;

import com.scottpreston.javarobot.chapter2.JSerialPort;
import com.scottpreston.javarobot.chapter2.Utils;
import com.scottpreston.javarobot.chapter2.WebSerialClient;
import com.scottpreston.javarobot.chapter5.MicrosoftVoice;
import com.scottpreston.javarobot.chapter7.Navigation;

public class FourDirections {

    private Navigation nav;
    private MicrosoftVoice voice;

    public FourDirections(JSerialPort sPort) throws Exception {
        nav = new Navigation(sPort);
        voice = MicrosoftVoice.getInstance();
        voice.speak("ready to move");
    }

    public void turn() throws Exception {
        nav.changeHeading(Navigation.REL_NORTH);
        voice.speak("facing north now");
        Utils.pause(3000);
        nav.changeHeading(Navigation.REL_EAST);
        voice.speak("facing east now");
        Utils.pause(3000);
        nav.changeHeading(Navigation.REL_SOUTH);
        voice.speak("facing south now");
        Utils.pause(3000);
        nav.changeHeading(Navigation.REL_WEST);
        voice.speak("facing west now");
        Utils.pause(3000);
        voice.speak("done");
    }

    public static void main(String[] args) {
        try {
            WebSerialClient sPort = new WebSerialClient("10.10.10.99", "8080", "1");
            FourDirections me = new FourDirections(sPort);
            me.turn();
        } catch (Exception e) {
            e.printStackTrace();
            System.exit(1);
        }
    }
}
```

Code Objective

The objective here is to calibrate the distance traveled.

Code Discussion

This next class, CalcDistance, will help you in defining the constants for the surface your robot travels on.

The fields used are of type SimpleNavigation and NavStamp. The constructor, as always, takes a JSerialPort that is used to construct sNav and stamp.

There are two calibrate() methods, one that takes the parameter for the number of times to test before an average is output, and the other that will just test three times. The algorithm works like this:

1. Take current sonar reading forward.

2. Move forward.

3. Take current sonar reading forward.

4. Compare the two readings and move in reverse.

5. Take another sonar reading.

6. Compare the two and repeat until the count is up.

7. At the end, count the average distance measured for the speed and then exit.

In Example 9-26, I am moving north, and then moving in reverse by changing the magnitude of the time to a negative number.

Example 9-26. *DistanceCalibration.java*

```java
package com.scottpreston.javarobot.chapter9;

import com.scottpreston.javarobot.chapter2.JSerialPort;
import com.scottpreston.javarobot.chapter2.Utils;
import com.scottpreston.javarobot.chapter2.WebSerialClient;
import com.scottpreston.javarobot.chapter7.NavStamp;
import com.scottpreston.javarobot.chapter7.Navigation;
import com.scottpreston.javarobot.chapter7.SonarReadings;

public class DistanceCalibration {

    // navigation class
    private Navigation sNav;
    // stamp class
    private NavStamp stamp;
```

```java
public DistanceCalibration(JSerialPort sPort) throws Exception{
    sNav = new Navigation(sPort);
    stamp = new NavStamp(sPort);
}

public void calibrate() throws Exception {
    // default 3 times
    calibrate(3);
}

public void calibrate(int times) throws Exception{
    // avg fwd dist per second
    int avgFWDperSec = 0;
    int avgREVperSec = 0;
    int count = 0;
    int interval = 1000;
    SonarReadings sr;
    int startDist;
    // total distance to summ
    int totalDistF = 0;
    int totalDistR = 0;
    int totalTime = 0;
    int dist;
    int speed  = 25;
    while (count < times) {
        // get forward readings & distance
        sr = stamp.getSonar();
        startDist = sr.center;
        Utils.pause(250);
        // face north
        sNav.changeHeading(0);
        sNav.setSpeed(speed);
        // move forward
        sNav.moveRaw(Navigation.RAW_FWD,count*interval);
        Utils.pause(250);
        // take new sonar reading
        sr = stamp.getSonar();
        dist = startDist - sr.center;
        totalDistF = totalDistF + dist;
        // get reverse readings & distance
        startDist = sr.center;
        Utils.pause(250);
        sNav.changeHeading(0);
        sNav.setSpeed(speed);
        // move reverse
        sNav.moveRaw(Navigation.RAW_REV,count*interval);
        Utils.pause(250);
```

```java
                // take sonar
                sr = stamp.getSonar();
                dist = sr.center - startDist ;
                totalDistR = totalDistR + dist;
                totalTime = totalTime + count*interval;
                count++;
            }
        System.out.println("avg fwd:" + totalDistF / (double)totalTime);
        System.out.println("avg rev:" + totalDistR / (double)totalTime);
    }

    public static void main(String[] args) {

        try {
            WebSerialClient com = new WebSerialClient("10.10.10.99", "8080",
                "1");
            DistanceCalibration cal = new DistanceCalibration(com);
            cal.calibrate();
        } catch (Exception e) {
            e.printStackTrace();
            System.exit(1);
        }

    }

}
}
```

Code Objective

The objective here is to speak sensor data.

Code Discussion

The next class will speak the sensor data continuously (see Example 9-27). I've found this useful when testing ranges of the robot's sensors and tweaking the constants used for obstacle avoidance.

This method uses a MicrosoftVoice and a NavStamp. Depending on the number of checks, it repeats reading the sensor data to me. I have it set to read for about 2 minutes.

Example 9-27. *SpeakSensors.java*

```java
package com.scottpreston.javarobot.chapter9;

import com.scottpreston.javarobot.chapter2.JSerialPort;
import com.scottpreston.javarobot.chapter2.Utils;
import com.scottpreston.javarobot.chapter2.WebSerialClient;
import com.scottpreston.javarobot.chapter5.MicrosoftVoice;
```

```java
import com.scottpreston.javarobot.chapter7.DistanceReadings;
import com.scottpreston.javarobot.chapter7.NavStamp;

public class SpeakSensors {

    private MicrosoftVoice voice;
    private NavStamp stamp;

    public SpeakSensors(JSerialPort sPort) throws Exception {
        stamp = new NavStamp(sPort);
        voice = MicrosoftVoice.getInstance();
    }

    public void readSensorData() throws Exception {
        int heading = stamp.getCompass();
        DistanceReadings readings = stamp.getSonarIR();
        voice.speak("heading is " + heading + " degrees.");
        voice.speak("left infrared is " + readings.ir.left + " degrees.");
        voice.speak("right infrared is " + readings.ir.right + " degrees.");
        voice.speak("left sonar is " + readings.sonar.left + " inches.");
        voice.speak("center sonar is " + readings.sonar.center + " inches.");
        voice.speak("right sonar is " + readings.sonar.right + " inches.");
    }

    public static void main(String[] args) {
        try {
            WebSerialClient sPort = new WebSerialClient("10.10.10.99",
                    "8080", "1");
            SpeakSensors ss = new SpeakSensors(sPort);
            int checks = 50;
            for (int x=0; x < checks; x++) {
                ss.readSensorData();
                Utils.pause(1000);
            }
        } catch (Exception e) {
            e.printStackTrace();
            System.exit(1);
        }
    }
}
```

Code Objective

The objective here is to create a startup diagnostic that provides information about the health of the robot.

Code Discussion

The final class discussed will be the first one that gets executed when the robot starts up.

There is just one field in the class of type MicrosoftVoice. Everything else is self-contained, because during troubleshooting I may not want to test things with serial connections.

I've created a helper method, speak(), which does two things: logs the output to the system out, and speaks. The output will later be captured and e-mailed.

The first diagnostic method, testInternet(), ensures that the network is working and that the robot can send e-mails out and accept commands from the Internet.

The second method is testTomcat(), which tests to see if Tomcat has started. On my single-processor machine, it takes about 11 seconds to fully start with the GetImageServlet, and about 8.5 seconds without it.

The third method is testStamp(), which tests connectivity to the microcontroller. Once connectivity is confirmed, I can call testHeading() and testSensors(), and the program will read off the values of everything.

The seventh method is testNavigation(). This method tells the robot to face north. It's followed by testMotion(), which moves the robot north for 1 second and tests the distance moved, if it is a positive distance, and then the robot reports the distance traveled.

Finally, the program tests the image from the web camera. Here, I'll make use of the Httpget.getImage() method defined in section 9.1 and the GetImageServlet in section 9.2. I'll save this to a temp folder that I'll later e-mail. See Example 9-28.

Example 9-28. *StartDiagnostic.java*

```java
package com.scottpreston.javarobot.chapter9;

import java.awt.image.BufferedImage;
import java.io.File;

import javax.imageio.ImageIO;

import com.scottpreston.javarobot.chapter2.JSerialPort;
import com.scottpreston.javarobot.chapter2.SingleSerialPort;
import com.scottpreston.javarobot.chapter2.Utils;
import com.scottpreston.javarobot.chapter5.MicrosoftVoice;
import com.scottpreston.javarobot.chapter7.DistanceReadings;
import com.scottpreston.javarobot.chapter7.MotionVector;
import com.scottpreston.javarobot.chapter7.NavStamp;
import com.scottpreston.javarobot.chapter7.Navigation;
import com.scottpreston.javarobot.chapter7.SonarReadings;

public class StartDiagnostic {

    private MicrosoftVoice voice;
```

```java
public StartDiagnostic() throws Exception {
    voice = MicrosoftVoice.getInstance();
    speak("starting diagnostic");
}

public void speak(String txt) {
    Utils.log(txt);
    try {
        voice.speak(txt);
    } catch (Exception e) {
        Utils.log(e.getMessage());
    }
}

public void testInternet() throws Exception {
    speak("testing internet connection");
    testUrl("http://www.apress.com");
    speak("connected to internet");
}

public void testTomcat() throws Exception {
    speak("testing tom cat");
    testUrl("http://localhost:8080/test.txt");
    speak("connected to tom cat");
}

private void testUrl(String url) throws Exception {

    int i = 0;
    while (HttpGet.getText(url) != null && i < 10) {
        speak("testing");
        Utils.pause(1000);
        i++;
    }

}

public void testStamp(JSerialPort sPort) throws Exception {
    speak("testing stamp connection");
    NavStamp stamp = new NavStamp(sPort);
    if (stamp.diagnostic()) {
        speak("stamp return is good");
    } else {
        speak("stamp return is bad");
        throw new Exception("unable to connect to stamp");
    }
}
```

```java
public void testHeading(JSerialPort sPort) throws Exception {
    speak("heading is " + new NavStamp(sPort).getCompass());
}

public void testSensors(JSerialPort sPort) throws Exception {
    speak("testing sensors");
    DistanceReadings readings = new NavStamp(sPort).getSonarIR();
    speak("left infrared sensor is " + readings.ir.left);
    speak("right infrared sensor is " + readings.ir.right);
    speak("left sonar is " + readings.sonar.left + " inches");
    speak("center sonar is " + readings.sonar.center + " inches");
    speak("right sonar is " + readings.sonar.right + " inches");
}

public void testNavigation(JSerialPort sPort) throws Exception {
    speak("testing navigation, facing north");
    Navigation simpleNav = new Navigation(sPort);
    simpleNav.changeHeading(Navigation.REL_NORTH);
    speak("facing north now");
}

public void testMotion(JSerialPort sPort) throws Exception {
    speak("testing navigation, moving north");
    Navigation simpleNav = new Navigation(sPort);
    NavStamp stamp = new NavStamp(sPort);
    SonarReadings readings = stamp.getSonar();
    Utils.pause(250);
    int startReading = readings.center;
    simpleNav.move(new MotionVector(Navigation.REL_NORTH, 1000));
    Utils.pause(250);
    readings = stamp.getSonar();
    int endReading = readings.center;
    if (endReading < startReading) {
        speak("moved north " + (startReading - endReading) + " inches");
    } else {
        speak("did not move north");
        throw new Exception("unable to move north");
    }
}

public void testCamera() {
    try {
        BufferedImage img = HttpGet.getImage("http://localhost:8080/getimage");
        // open file
        File file = new File("%temp%//start.jpg");
        ImageIO.write(img, "jpg", file);
```

```
        } catch (Exception e) {
            e.printStackTrace();
        }
    }

    public void testAll(JSerialPort sPort) {
        try {
            testInternet();
            testTomcat();
            testStamp(sPort);
            testHeading(sPort);
            testSensors(sPort);
            testHeading(sPort);
            testNavigation(sPort);
            testMotion(sPort);
            testCamera();
            speak("completed diagnostic successfully");
        } catch (Exception e) {
            speak("error occurred during diagnostic");
        }
    }

    public static void main(String[] args) {
        try {
            StartDiagnostic diagnostic = new StartDiagnostic();
            diagnostic.testAll(SingleSerialPort.getInstance(1));
            SingleSerialPort.close(1);
        } catch (Exception e) {
            e.printStackTrace();
        }

    }
}
```

The Ant script in Example 9-29 calls the Diagnostic class and utilizes two calls: the ANT:Mail task to first send the diagnostic.log file; and GetImageServlet, to send the image it captured from the webcam.

Example 9-29. *diagnostic.xml (Ant Script)*

```
<project name="diagnostic.xml" default="run">

<path id="run.classpath">
    <pathelement location="dist/java_robot_book.jar" />
</path>
```

```
<target name="run">
    <java
        classname="com.scottpreston.javarobot.chapter9.StartDiagnostic"
        classpathref="run.classpath"
        output="diagnostic.log"
        />
    <mail
        mailhost="9.9.9.1"
        tolist="me@scottsbots.com"
        from="feynman5@scottsbots.com"
        subject="diagnostic log"
        mailport="25"
        files="diagnostic.log"
        message="please read log" />
    <mail
        mailhost="9.9.9.1"
        tolist="me@scottsbots.com"
        from="feynman5@scottsbots.com"
        subject="diagnostic image"
        mailport="25"
        files="%temp%/start.jpg"
        message="image facing forward" />
</target>
</project>
```

The actual diagnostic script that I scheduled contains only one line (see Example 9-30).

Example 9-30. *diagnostic.bat*

```
ant -f diagnostic.xml -l ant.log
```

I've also included a Groovy script that allows me to debug while logged into the console of the application or via telnet. The contents of this script should be the contents of the Diagnostic.main() method. See Example 9-31.

Example 9-31. *diagnostic.groovy*

```
import com.scottpreston.javarobot.chapter2.*;
import com.scottpreston.javarobot.chapter9.*;

println("diagnostic script for robot")

Diagnostic diagnostic = new StartDiagnostic()
//diagnostic.testAll(SingleSerialPort.getInstance(1))
diagnostic.speak("this is a test")
diagnostic.testInternet()
SingleSerialPort.close(1)

println("done")
```

Section Summary

This concludes our discussion on various robotic diagnostic programs. It's important to have good troubleshooting skills and for you to write diagnostic software for your robotics programs. They'll save you a lot of time in the long run.

The classes I talked about in this section were

- FourDirections.java: This program is good for debugging directional problems with your robot. Because it also calls the directions out, you can monitor what your robot's actions are while standing next to it.

- CalcDistance.java: This program is good for determining how far your robot travels in certain directions. By adding a compass reading to this, it could also be used to see how straight your robot travels.

- SpeakSensors.java: This program calls out sensor readings from your robot. You use it to assist in obstacle avoidance.

- StartDiagnostic.java: This program will give you your robot's status during startup.

9.5   Navigation Programs

As you saw in Chapter 7, I generated a static method that created the regions and DistanceVectors, and then connected these regions together in a graph so that the robot could navigate. What if I did not have to input that information and instead let the robot learn it, store it, and use that information in a way that lets the robot navigate the room without any operator intervention?

To illustrate how the robot can start to build its own map, I'm going to put Feynman5 in a maze and have it construct a room while it navigates its way out.

Setup

First, create a maze for your robot. I used a previously created space of a 100-inch × 100-inch grid and modified it to be a simple maze of three walls, one on the top and two on the bottom. I will make this room perpendicular with the four coordinate axes: north, east, south, and west. I'll start the robot in the lower-left corner and have it figure out on its own when it's come to an exit. It will determine this when one of its four coordinate axes has a sonar reading of greater than 4 feet, which will be on the lower left.

Travel Algorithm

How is the robot going to figure out how it needs to move? First, I'll explain the algorithm, and then I'll explain how it works in code.

1. The robot calculates its current region.

2. The robot calculates the characteristics of this region—in other words, is there a wall to the north, to the east, to the south, and to the west?

3. Based on these characteristics, the robot creates adjacent regions, where there is room to move (as shown in Figure 9-5).

4. The robot finds the region with the smallest edge weight (or times traveled) and then moves in that direction.

5. The robot moves, sets the current region to be 1 at the end of the edge where it traveled, and then updates the weight of the edge traveled between regions 0 and 1.

6. Is the robot out of the maze? If not, repeat.

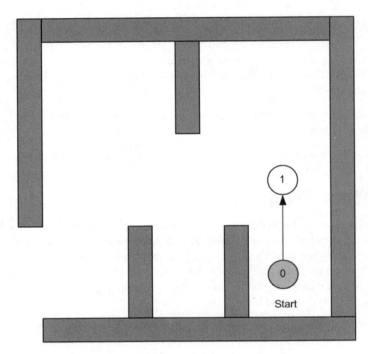

Figure 9-5. *The robot at its start position in a simple maze.*

On the second iteration through the algorithm, the robot moves to 1. It then calculates adjacent regions 2 and 3 before moving to the region of smallest weight, either 2 or 3. See Figure 9-6.

At the end of the loop, the total regions number from 0 to 8. The robot may have not traveled to all the regions, but they are mapped and have a weight depending on the number of times traveled. See Figure 9-7.

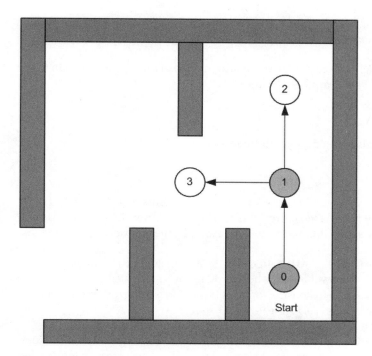

Figure 9-6. *The robot after the first iteration movement.*

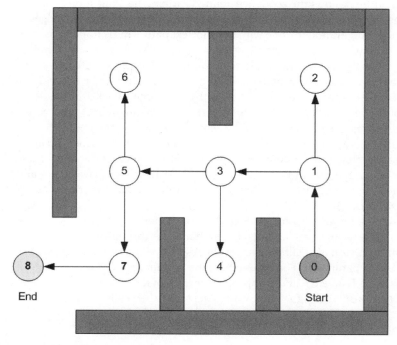

Figure 9-7. *N-iterations through the loop until the end*

Because the diagram in Figure 9-7 is just a graph of edges and vertices, in order to optimize a path through this maze of the shortest distance, I can use the Dijkstra Algorithm and the IndoorNavigation class.

Here it would be best to add this map of the room to a database where the robot can then pull the map so it does not have to learn it each time.

Code Objective

The objective in this instance is to build a map through a maze.

Code Discussion

Two of the fields in this class—edges and regions—are the components required to build a room object. The room built will be called currentRoom. The field, currentRegion, is to keep track of how far along the robot is in building its map (for example, the grey dots in the previous figures).

The constant in this class is the DEFAULT_REGION_SIZE, which I have set to be the minimum size the robot can navigate within—in other words, its the robot's diameter + 1 foot.

This class extends Localization so its constructor takes JSerialPort, setting the currentRegion and adding the initial adjacent regions (see Figure 9-7).

The two public methods are findExit(), which allow the robot to find its exit, and getFourCoordinates(). getFourCoordinates() overrides the parents method from Localization so that the robot does not have to move north to get the four coordinates. Instead, it looks at its closest angle to the four coordinate axes, and then turns in that direction to take the four.

In findExit(), the algorithm follows the sequence defined earlier. The while loop contains the conditional to let the robot know it's at the exit. The next loop iterates through all edges, leaving the current vertices and finding the one with the shortest path. This is important because let's say the robot chooses to go to vertex 2 instead of vertex 3, since both have a weight of 0. As the robot moves to vertex 2, along the way it increases the weight of the path between 1 and 2 to 1. While at vertex 2, the robot's only path out is the edge it came from, so it moves back down that edge, and increases its weight from 1 to 2. Now that the robot's back at vertex 1, it compares the weights between vertex 1 and 2. This time, vertex 1 has a weight of 2, while vertex 2 has a weight of 0. The robot chooses the minimum weight path and continues.

The last step in findExit() is a call to the method addAdjacentRegions(). This method looks at all the edges, leaving the region based on the characteristic of the region. The characteristic will be populated with either a 1 or a 0. A 1 in the characteristic means there is a wall there and a reading can be taken for a position. A 0 means that there is nothing in that direction that's at least the length of the DEFAULT_REGION_SIZE.

To prevent edges from being added twice, I added the helper method isValidEdge(). This method takes the heading of the edge as a parameter, and then looks through the list of edges. For edges where the current region is the first vertex, it checks to see if there is an edge with a heading equal to the heading parameter. For edges where the current region is the second vertex, it checks to see if there is an edge in the opposite direction of the parameter heading.

Finally, the test method just creates the navigation object, and then calls findExit(). See Example 9-32.

Example 9-32. *MazeNavigation.java*

```java
package com.scottpreston.javarobot.chapter8;

import java.util.ArrayList;
import java.util.Arrays;

import com.scottpreston.javarobot.chapter2.JSerialPort;
import com.scottpreston.javarobot.chapter2.Utils;
import com.scottpreston.javarobot.chapter2.WebSerialClient;
import com.scottpreston.javarobot.chapter7.DistanceVector;
import com.scottpreston.javarobot.chapter7.Localization;
import com.scottpreston.javarobot.chapter7.Region;
import com.scottpreston.javarobot.chapter7.SonarReadings;

public class MazeNavigation extends Localization {

    private static final int DEFAULT_REGION_SIZE = (ROBOT_RADIUS * 2) + 12;

    // this will be list of all edges
    private ArrayList edges = new ArrayList();
    private ArrayList regions = new ArrayList();
    private Region currentRegion = null;

    public MazeNavigation(JSerialPort serialPort) throws Exception {
        super(serialPort);
        // creates 1st region robot is in
        currentRegion = new Region(regions.size() + "", DEFAULT_REGION_SIZE);
        currentRegion.setCharacteristic(toCharacteristic(getFourCoordinates()));
        // add first region to list of regions
        regions.add(currentRegion);
        // add adjacent regions & edges
        addAdjacentRegions();
    }

    public void findExit() throws Exception {

        // number of inches until out of maze
        int target = 84;
        // current max size of all sonar readings
        int maxSize = 0;
        // loop until robot is out of maze
        while (maxSize < target) {
            // get four corners readings
            int[] nesw = getFourCoordinates();
            // init minimum vector found for all 4 coordinate vectors
            DistanceVector minVector = null;
```

```java
            // set min weight to high number
            int minWeight = Integer.MAX_VALUE;
            // loop through edges
            for (int i = 0; i < edges.size(); i++) {
                // get temp vector
                DistanceVector tmpVector = (DistanceVector) edges.get(i);
                // only get vectors with first vertex as current region
                if (tmpVector.v1.name.equals(currentRegion + "")) {
                    // get smallest weighted
                    if (tmpVector.weight < minWeight) {
                        minWeight = tmpVector.weight;
                        minVector = tmpVector;
                    }
                }
            }
            // increase size so less likely next time to go through it.
            minVector.magintude = minVector.magintude + 1;
            // create a motion vector of region size
            DistanceVector currentVector = new DistanceVector(minVector.heading,
                    DEFAULT_REGION_SIZE);
            // move
            move(currentVector);
            // sets current name to next vertex
            for (int x = 0; x < regions.size(); x++) {
                Region tmp = (Region) regions.get(x);
                if (tmp.name.equalsIgnoreCase(minVector.v2.name)) {
                    currentRegion = tmp;
                    break;
                }
            }

            // update characteristic of this region since it was not set
            // when adjacent regions were added
            currentRegion.setCharacteristic(toCharacteristic(getFourCoordinates()));
            // sort all values
            Arrays.sort(nesw);
            // set largest sonar to maxSize
            maxSize = nesw[3];
            // now update adjacent regions to this one based on characteristic
            addAdjacentRegions();
        }
    }
    // override so don't have to face just north.
    public int[] getFourCoordinates() throws Exception {
        getSonarServos().lookSide();
        Utils.pause(500);
        int heading = getNavStamp().getCompass();
```

```java
        // straighten robot up
        int newHeading = 0;
        if (heading > 315 && heading < 45) {
            newHeading = 0;
        }
        if (heading > 45 && heading < 135) {
            newHeading = 90;
        }
        if (heading > 135 && heading < 225) {
            newHeading = 180;
        }
        if (heading > 225 && heading < 315) {
            newHeading = 270;
        }
        changeHeading(newHeading);
        Utils.pause(500);
        // take new readings
        SonarReadings sonarReadings = getNavStamp().getSonar();
        int front = sonarReadings.center;
        int left = sonarReadings.left + ROBOT_RADIUS;
        int right = sonarReadings.right - ROBOT_RADIUS;
        getSonarServos().lookAft();
        Utils.pause(500);
        sonarReadings = getNavStamp().getSonar();
        // average of two readings
        int back = (int) ((sonarReadings.left + sonarReadings.right) / 2.0);
        int[] nesw = null;
        // send array based on new Heading
        switch (newHeading) {
            case 0:
                nesw = new int[] {front,right,back,left};
                break;
            case 90:
                nesw = new int[] {left,front,right,back};
                break;
            case 180:
                nesw = new int[] {back,left,front,right};
                break;
            case 270:
                nesw = new int[] {right,back,left,front};
                break;
        }
        return nesw;
    }
```

```java
    private void addAdjacentRegions() {
        //       gets possible regions by looking at edges
        int[] c = currentRegion.getCharacteristic();
        // iterate through four coordinate axes
        for (int i = 0; i < 4; i++) {
            // if c=0, which means greater than the default region size"
            if (c[i] == 0) {
                // create the region
                Region nextRegion = new Region(regions.size() + "",
                        DEFAULT_REGION_SIZE);
                // create the DistanceVector / edge
                DistanceVector vect = new DistanceVector(i * 90, 0);
                // set current region as source vertex
                vect.v1 = currentRegion;
                // set next region as end vertex
                vect.v2 = nextRegion;
                // checks to see if already a vertex
                // if false already a vertex so skip.
                if (isValidEdge(vect.heading)) {
                    edges.add(vect);
                    regions.add(nextRegion);
                }
            }
        }
    }

    private boolean isValidEdge(int heading) {

        // get all edges since it contains all regions
        for (int i = 0; i < edges.size(); i++) {
            // look through each edge
            DistanceVector edge = (DistanceVector) edges.get(i);
            // if edge already exist with the same heading then not valid
            if (edge.v1 == currentRegion && edge.heading == heading) {
                return false;
            }

            // adjust heading so that it can see edge from opposite end.
            int tempHeading = edge.heading + 180;
            if (tempHeading > 360) {
                tempHeading = tempHeading - 360;
            }
            // if current region is already the target vertex
            // at angle opposite, then there is already an edge for this direction
            /// with a vertex pointing to current region.
```

```java
                if (edge.v2 == currentRegion && tempHeading == heading) {
                    return false;
                }
        }
        // if did not return by now, heading must be valid from current region
        return true;
    }

    private int[] toCharacteristic(int[] nesw) {
        int[] characteristic = new int[4];
        for (int i = 0; i < 4; i++) {
            // 4 feet determines characteristic
            if (nesw[i] > DEFAULT_REGION_SIZE) {
                // greater
                characteristic[i] = 0;
            } else {
                // less than
                characteristic[i] = 1;
            }
        }
        return characteristic;
    }

    public static void main(String[] args) {

        WebSerialClient com = new WebSerialClient("9.9.9.99", "8080", "1");
        try {
            MazeNavigation nav = new MazeNavigation(com);
            nav.findExit();
        } catch (Exception e) {
            e.printStackTrace();
            System.exit(1);
        }
        System.out.println("done");
    }

}
```

This section created an algorithm that builds maps of rooms in a maze. This can be extended to any room by adjusting the angles in which potential regions are calculated and adjusting the region size.

I recommend combining this method of room creation with database access to then store and retrieve rooms for later use.

9.6 Chapter Summary

This concludes the example programs chapter, but there's much more to explore using these building blocks.

In section 9.1, I showed you a few ways to communicate with external systems or people with the HttpGet and SendMailClient. I also showed you how to invoke external programs via the CmdExec.

In section 9.2, we worked more with the webcam to implement stereo vision on Windows and get live images from your webcam via a servlet. We also discussed how to process an image to follow motion or color with a camera or your whole robot, or recognize and speak about those colors the robot recognized.

In section 9.3, we talked about three types of remote control interfaces. The first was a web-based client, so you could communicate with your robot over the Internet. The second was voice control, and the third was a servo control program Java Swing client for testing and controlling up to eight servos with a MiniSsc class.

In section 9.4, we covered some diagnostic programs that help debug navigation or provide calibration. The first program moved to the four coordinate axes. The second calibrated distance by moving forward and backward a specific number of times. The third program gave voice readings of sensor data that are really useful while debugging obstacle avoidance algorithms. Finally, the last program was a diagnostic used when the robot started up. It tested all major functionalities and then sent us an e-mail about its status and a picture of what's currently in front of it.

Finally, in section 9.5, we discussed how to extend some of the navigation classes to have your robot build a map on its own and navigate its way out of a maze.

This concludes *The Definitive Guide to Building Java Robots*. In the appendixes at the end of the book, I include the following:

- An API description for every class in this book, as well as every dependent Java class or package.

- A microcontroller program reference as it relates to the BASIC Stamp programs in this book. I'll also list the Javelin Stamp counterparts so you can use both.

- A robotic parts reference where you can download and purchase all of the products and parts in this book, as well as some others I've used in the past.

Thanks for reading. I hope I've shown you some new ways to have fun with robotics and Java. I'll post updates and more sample programs as they become available on my web site at www.scottsbots.com/definitiveguide.

The Definitive Guide API

All Chapters

Software Prerequisites

- Java 1.4.2: http://java.sun.com/j2se/1.4.2/download.html

- Eclipse IDE: www.eclipse.org

- All software for *The Definitive Guide to Building Java Robots* can be downloaded from www.scottsbots.com/definitiveguide

- All JavaDocs for *The Definitive Guide to Building Java Robots* can be downloaded from www.scottsbots.com/definitiveguide/javadoc

Chapter 2: Serial Communications

Software Prerequisites

- Java Communications API: http://java.sun.com/products/javacomm/index.jsp

- Apache Tomcat: http://jakarta.apache.org/tomcat

com.scottpreston.javarobot.chapter2

Controller

Controller is a superclass for all controllers implementing the JController interface. Example controllers are the MiniSSC-II and the Parallax BASIC Stamp.

JController

JController is the interface for all controller classes. This interface will enforce common behavior between all implementing classes.

JSerialPort

JSerialPort is the interface for all serial port classes, and it enforces a common behavior among all implementing classes.

ListOpenPorts

ListOpenPorts is a diagnostic class to test the installation of the Java Communications API.

SimpleStamp

SimpleStamp is an example class for communicating to the BASIC Stamp using the Controller superclass.

SingleSerialPort

SingleSerialPort is a class that ensures thread-safe concurrent access to a serial port.

StampSerialTest

StampSerialTest is an example class for communicating to the BASIC Stamp without usage of the Controller superclass.

StandardSerialPort

StandardSerialPort is a simpler-to-use serial port wrapping the Java SerialPort class.

Utils

Utils is a utility class used for pausing and other common functionalities.

WebSerialClient

WebSerialClient is an implementation of the JSerialPort for serial communications over the Web via HTTP.

WebSerialPort

WebSerialPort is a class used with a JSP page called webcom.jsp to listen and to transfer strings to and from the JSP page to the StandardSerialPort.

Chapter 3: Motion

Software Prerequisites

None.

com.scottpreston.javarobot.chapter3

ArmTest1

ArmTest1 is a sample arm motion class using the BasicArm class.

BasicArm

The BasicArm class uses the MiniSSC to position and move an arm with two joints, a shoulder, and an elbow.

BasicDiffDrive

The BasicDiffDrive class uses the MiniSSC to move a robot in four directions: forward, reverse, right, and left. It is also the parent class to TimedDiffDrive and SpeedDiffDrive.

BasicLeg

The BasicLeg class represents a single leg for a Hexapod robot. Similar to the BasicArm, it acts more as a data structure than a movement class.

ComplexArm

The ComplexArm class uses the Lynxmotion SSC-32 to move a complex arm with five joints, two shoulder joints, an elbow, a wrist, and two grippers.

GroupMoveProtocol

GroupMoveProtocol is an interface that enforces the group move communications protocol with the Lynxmotion SSC-32.

Hexapod

Hexapod is a robot class that implements the JMotion interface using the Lynxmotion SSC-32 and the Extreme Hexapod 2 robot from Lynxmotion.

JMotion

JMotion is a motion interface that standardizes motion behavior between walking or differential drive robots.

LM32

The LM32 class extends the SSC class and implements both GroupMoveProtocol and SSCProtocol. It is used with the Lynxmotion SSC-32.

MiniSsc

The MiniSsc class extends the Ssc class and implements the SSCProtocol. It is used with the Scott Edwards MiniSSC-II.

MiniSscGM

The MiniSscGM class extends the Ssc class and implements the GroupMoveProtocol. It is used with the Scott Edwards MiniSSC-II.

PanTilt

The PanTilt class uses the MiniSsc to control the movement of a pan and tilt camera system.

PanTiltSpeed

The PanTiltSpeed class extends PanTilt to provide for speed control of the pan and tilt camera system.

SerialSsc

SerialSsc is an example class that communicates using the SSCProtocol but without using the Controller class.

ServoPosition

ServoPosition is a data structure holding servo positions.

ServoPosition2

ServoPosition2 is another data structure holding more complicated servo positions.

SpeedDiffDrive

The SpeedDiffDrive class extends TimedDiffDrive and allows for speed control of the differential drive. It also implements the JMotion interface.

Ssc

Ssc is the parent class to the MiniSsc and the LM32. It shares some functionality in common with both and is responsible for implementing the SSCProtocol in both classes.

SSCProtocol

SSCProtocol is the protocol for the Scott Edwards MiniSSC-II controller.

TimedDiffDrive

The TimedDiffDrive class extends BasicDiffDrive and allows for timed movements of a differential drive.

Chapter 4: Sensors

Software Prerequisites

None.

com.scottpreston.javarobot.chapter4

Compass

Compass is a class representing the compass attached to a BASIC Stamp containing the code for commutating with a digital compass.

CompassStamp

CompassStamp is the stamp class that contains the logic and timing required to get information from the BASIC Stamp for the digital compass.

DistanceStamp

DistanceStamp is the stamp class that contains the logic and timing required to get information from the BASIC Stamp for the distance sensors.

SwitchStamp

SwitchStamp is the stamp class that contains the logic and timing required to get information from the BASIC Stamp for the switch sensors.

Chapter 5: Speech

Software Prerequisites

- Microsoft Speech SDK 5.1: www.microsoft.com/speech/download/sdk51

- QuadmoreTTS.dll: www.quadmore.com

- QuadmoreSR.dll: www.quadmore.com

- Sphinx-4: http://cmusphinx.sourceforge.net/sphinx4

- FreeTTS 1.2: http://freetts.sourceforge.net/docs/index.php

- JSAPI: http://java.sun.com/products/java-media/speech

com.scottpreston.javarobot.chapter5

EchoTalk

The EchoTalk class repeats what it hears you say by using MicrosoftSR and MicrosoftVoice.

FreeTTSVoice

The FreeTTSVoice class uses the FreeTTS text-to-speech engine.

JavaVoice

The JavaVoice class uses JSAPI for text-to-speech synthesis.

JRecognizer

JRecognizer is an interface that standardizes speech recognition for the different implementations of speech recognition classes.

JVoice

JVoice is an interface standardizing text to speech for the different implementations of the text-to-speech classes.

MicrosoftSR

MicrosoftSR is the Microsoft speech recognition class using QuadmoreSR and is an example of dictation speech recognition.

MicrosoftVoice

MicrosoftVoice is the Microsoft text-to-speech class using QuadmoreTTS.

QuadmoreSR

QuadmoreSR is a JNI to the QuadmoreSR.dll, which uses the Microsoft Speech SDK.

QuadmoreTTS

QuadmoreTTS is a JNI to QuadmoreTTS.dll, which uses the Microsoft Speech SDK.

SphinxSR

SphinxSR is a speech recognition class written entirely in Java and is an example of command and control speech recognition.

TempConvert

TempConvert is an example class that uses the JNI to connect to a C++ program.

TTSCompare

TTSCompare is an example class that compares all the text-to-speech engines: JavaVoice, FreeTTSVoice, and MicrosoftVoice.

Chapter 6: Vision

Software Prerequisites

- Java Media Framework: http://java.sun.com/products/java-media/jmf/index.jsp

- Java Advanced Imaging API: http://java.sun.com/products/java-media/jai

com.scottpreston.javarobot.chapter6

ColorGram

The ColorGram class is a data structure used to calculate the ratios of color in an object to assist in identification and image processing.

ColorGramCalibration

ColorGramCalibration is a class that autocalibrates for a specific ColorGram based on a sample image.

DoubleWebCamViewer

DoubleWebCamViewer is a webcam viewer class that allows you to view the original webcam image on one side and the processed image on the other.

ExitListener

ExitListener is a utility class that's used to reduce some code in Swing-based classes.

FilterParameters

FilterParameters is a class used to simplify adding image processing filters for the DoubleWebCamViewer.

FindCamera

FindCamera is a diagnostic class used to validate the installation of the Java Media Framework.

GetFrame

The GetFrame class gets a single frame from the webcam.

ImagePanel

ImagePanel is a panel used to hold the image captured from a webcam.

ImageProcessor

ImageProcessor is the image processing class.

ImageViewer

ImageViewer is a simple class used to display an image.

SimpleSwing

SimpleSwing is a simple Swing class.

WebCamViewer

WebCamViewer is a class used to display the image streams from a webcam at a specified frame rate.

WindowUtilities

WindowUtilities is another utility class used to set look and feel and reduce code in other Swing classes.

Chapter 7: Navigation

Software Prerequisites

None.

com.scottpreston.javarobot.chapter7

Dijkstra

Dijkstra is an implementation of the shortest path algorithm created by Edsger Dijkstra.

DistanceReadings

DistanceReadings is a data structure used to hold information from both sonar and infrared sensors.

DistanceVector

DistanceVector is a data structure representing a vector of distance.

Edge

Edge is a data structure used to represent the edge connecting two vertices and is taken from Graph Theory.

GpsReading

GpsReading is the data structure used to hold information taken from GPS sensors and will represent longitude and latitude.

IndoorNavigation

IndoorNavigation is a navigational class used to navigate the robot indoors.

IRReadings

IRReadings is the data structure used to hold information taken from infrared sensors.

Localization

Localization is a navigational class used to localize the robot.

MotionVector

MotionVector is a data structure representing the vector of time.

Navigation

Navigation is a navigational class used for simple navigation such as changing headings and basic movements.

NavPoint

NavPoint is a data structure that represents a named point.

NavStamp

NavStamp is the class used to communicate to the microcontroller and get sensor data from the compass, sonar, and infrared sensors.

ObstacleNavigation

ObstacleNavigation is a navigation class used to avoid obstacles by calculating a bypass vector.

OutdoorNavigation

OutdoorNavigation is a navigational class that uses GPS to navigate.

Region

Region is a data structure representing an idealized space in which to navigate.

Room

Room is a data structure holding many regions connected via edges of distance vectors.

SonarReadings

SonarReadings is the data structure used to hold information taken from the robot's sonar.

SonarServos

SonarServos is the class used to move the top sonar aboard the Feyman5 robot.

Vertex

Vertex is a data structure used to represent a region or a point and is taken from Graph Theory.

Chapter 8: Other Topics

Software Prerequisites

- Apache Ant: http://ant.apache.org
- Groovy: http://groovy.codehaus.org
- MySQL: www.mysql.com
- SQLyog: www.webyog.com

com.scottpreston.javarobot.chapter8

DBMotion

DBMotion is a data access class used to create, read, update, and delete data from a database using SQL and JDBC.

MotionEpisode

MotionEpisode is a data structure used to encapsulate information representing a unit of motion from a navigation class.

MySQL

The MySQL class is used to connect to a MySQL database using JDBC and Connector/J.

Chapter 9: Sample Programs

Software Prerequisites

None.

com.scottpreston.javarobot.chapter9

CmdExec

The CmdExec class is used to encapsulate a command normally used via the command line.

ColorObject

ColorObject is a data structure used to hold the name of an object and its sample image.

DistanceCalibration

DistanceCalibration is a diagnostic class used to calibrate the distance a robot travels for a given unit of time.

Follow

The Follow class controls the movements of a pan and tilt camera to follow a specific color or motion.

FourDirections

FourDirections is a diagnostic class used to move the robot in the four coordinate directions.

GetFrameServlet

GetFrameServlet is a servlet that sends an image taken from a webcam to a browser.

HttpGet

HttpGet is a utility class used to get text or images from the Internet via HTTP.

ImageTimer

The ImageTimer class captures images at specified intervals and saves them to a particular location.

MazeNavigation

MazeNavigation is a navigational class that allows a robot to build its own map of an environment, and then stores that map in a Room data structure.

PrefFrame

PrefFrame is the preferences frame for setting the communications port and baud rate for the ServoControlClient.

RecognizeColor

The RecognizeColor class recognizes specific items based on a ColorGram taken from a directory of sample images.

SendMailClient

The SendMailClient class sends out e-mail.

ServoControlClient

ServoControlClient is a servo control client.

ServoSlider

ServoSlider is a component of the ServoControlClient that represents the slider for a specific servo.

SliderFieldCombo

SliderFieldCombo is a component of the ServoControlClient that represents the field value and slider for a specific servo.

SpeakSensors

SpeakSensors is a diagnostic class used to speak the sensor readings out loud.

SSCPanel

SSCPanel is a component of the ServoControlClient that's used to hold an instance of the MiniSsc.

StartDiagnostic

StartDiagnostic is a diagnostic program used during the startup of Feynman5.

StereoVision

StereoVision is a sample class that used an example of CmdExec and ImageTimer to allow for processing the two images running in two separate virtual machines.

VoiceControl

VoiceControl is a navigation program that allows a robot to navigate through voice commands.

Microcontroller Reference

All Chapters

Software Prerequisites

- Parallax BASIC Stamp Editor: www.parallax.com/html_pages/downloads/software/software_basic_stamp.asp

- Parallax Javelin Stamp IDE: www.parallax.com/javelin/downloads.asp

BASIC Stamp Commands

Command Reference obtained from the help file located in BASIC Stamp Editor.

SERIN

SERIN is used for serial input.

```
Syntax: SERIN Rpin {\Fpin}, Baudmode, {Plabel,} {Timeout, Tlabel,} [InputData]
```

SEROUT

SEROUT is used for serial output.

```
Syntax: SEROUT Tpin {\Fpin}, Baudmode, {Pace,} {Timeout, Tlabel,} [OutputData]
```

BRANCH

BRANCH goes to a specific address specified by an offset.

```
Syntax: BRANCH Offset, [Address1, Address2, ...AddressN]
```

LOOKDOWN

LOOKDOWN compares the target to a list of values.

```
Syntax: LOOKDOWN Target, {ComparisonOp} [Value0, Value1, ...ValueN], Variable
```

PAUSE

PAUSE is used to pause a program.

Syntax: `PAUSE Duration`

GOTO

GOTO is used to jump ahead in the program to a point specified by an address label.

Syntax: `GOTO Address`

PULSOUT

PULSOUT generates a pulse on Pin with a width of Duration.

Syntax: `PULSOUT Pin, Duration`

PULSIN

PULSIN measures the width of a pulse on Pin described by State and stores the result in Variable.

Syntax: `PULSIN Pin, State, Variable`

SHIFTIN

SHIFTIN shifts data in from a synchronous serial device.

Syntax: `SHIFTIN Dpin, Cpin, Mode, [Variable {\Bits} {, Variable {\Bits}...}]`

RCTIME

RCTIME measures time while Pin remains in State. It's usually used to measure the charge/discharge time of a resistor/capacitor (RC) circuit.

Syntax: `RCTIME Pin, State, Variable`

IN

IN reads the logic value on a defined pin.

Syntax: `INx where x is the Pin`

LOW

LOW sends logic low to a pin.

Syntax: `LOW Pin`

HIGH

HIGH sends logic high to a pin.

Syntax: HIGH Pin

Equivalent Javelin Stamp Commands

All JavaDocs are located at the following URL: www.parallax.com/javelin/doc/index.html.

SEROUT

```
Uart xmit = new Uart(Uart.dirTransmit, CPU.Pin0,Uart.invert,
Uart.speed9600, Uart.stop1);
xmit.sendByte(); // sends byte
```

SERIN

```
Uart rcv = new Uart(Uart.dirRecive, CPU.Pin0,Uart.invert,
Uart.speed9600, Uart.stop1);
rcv.byteAvailable(); // waits for byte
rcv.receiveByte(); // gets byte
```

LOOKDOWN / BRANCH

If-Then-Else Syntax

PAUSE

CPU.delay() each int = 95.48 Microseconds.

GOTO

N/A

PULSOUT

CPU.pulseOut (int length, int portPin)

PULSIN

CPU.pulseIn(int timeout, int portPin, boolean pinState)

SHIFTIN

CPU.shiftIn(int dataPortPin, int clockPortPin, int bitCount, int mode)

RCTIME

```
CPU.rcTime(int timeout, int portPin, boolean pinState)
```

IN

```
readPort(int portPin)
```

LOW

```
writePort(int portPin)
```

HIGH

```
writePort(int PortPin)
```

Class for SRF04

```
stamp.peripheral.sensor.range.SRF04
```

■ ■ ■

Robot Parts Reference

General

The following entries denote web sites where various parts for your robot can be found.

General Electronics

Jameco Electronics: www.jameco.com

Mouser Electronics: www.mouser.com

Allied Electronics: www.alliedelec.com

Digikey Electronics: www.digikey.com

MicroControllers

Parallax, Inc.: www.parallax.com

Fasteners

McMaster Supply: www.mcmaster.com

Micro Fasteners: www.microfasteners.com

Connectors

Keystone Electronics Corporation: www.keyelco.com

McMaster Supply: www.mcmaster.com

PC Equipment

NewEgg.com: www.newegg.com

Amazon.com: www.amazon.com

Printed Circuit Boards

PCBExpress: www.pcbexpress.com

Robots

Parallax, Inc.: www.parallax.com

Lynxmotion, Inc.: www.lynxmotion.com

Chapter 2: Serial Communications

Parallax BASIC Stamp: www.parallax.com

Parallax Javelin Stamp: www.parallax.com

Parallax Board of Education: www.parallax.com

Parallax EB500 Bluetooth Transceiver Module: www.parallax.com

D-Link DBT-120 Bluetooth USB Adapter: www.dlink.com

Chapter 3: Motion

Hitec HS-422 Standard Servo: www.lynxmotion.com

Hitec HS-1422 Continuous Rotation Servo: www.lynxmotion.com

CubeBot—CubeBot Standard: www.prestonresearch.com

MiniSSC-II—Scott Edwards' MiniSSC-II: www.lynxmotion.com

SSC-32—Lynxmotion 32 Channel Servo Controller: www.lynxmotion.com

LynxB PanTilt Kit—Lynxmotion Pan and Tilt Camera Kit: www.lynxmotion.com

Robot Arm—Offers a wide variety of robotic arms: www.lynxmotion.com

Extreme Hexapod 2—This is a 12-servo walker: www.lynxmotion.com

Victor 883 Electronic Speed Controller—IFI Robotics: www.ifirobotics.com

Chapter 4: Sensors

CMPS03 Electronic Compass—Devantech Ltd.: www.robot-electronics.co.uk

Vector 2x Electronic Compass—Jameco Electronics: www.jameco.com

Dinsmore 1490 Compass: www.dinsmoresensors.com

Sharp GP2D15 Proximity Sensors: www.lynxmotion.com

Devantech SRF04 Ultrasonic Ranging Module: www.hobbyengineering.com

Single Line Detector: www.lynxmotion.com

BumperSwitch Assembly Kit: www.lynxmotion.com

Sharp GP2D02—Infrared Distance Sensor: www.hobbyengineering.com

Chapter 5: Speech

None.

Chapter 6: Vision

None.

Chapter 7: Navigation

Garmin eTrex GPS Unit: www.walmart.com

Sonar Distribution Board: www.prestonresearch.com

CMPS03 Carrier Board: www.prestonresearch.com

80-20 Aluminum Extrusion: www.mcmaster.com

Black PVC Sheeting: www.mcmaster.com

NPC WheelChairMotors: www.npcrobotics.com

Chapter 8: Other Topics

None.

Chapter 9: Sample Programs

None.

Index

▉Y

forums.apress.com
FOR PROFESSIONALS BY PROFESSIONALS™

JOIN THE APRESS FORUMS AND BE PART OF OUR COMMUNITY. You'll find discussions that cover topics of interest to IT professionals, programmers, and enthusiasts just like you. If you post a query to one of our forums, you can expect that some of the best minds in the business—especially Apress authors, who all write with *The Expert's Voice*™—will chime in to help you. Why not aim to become one of our most valuable participants (MVPs) and win cool stuff? Here's a sampling of what you'll find:

DATABASES
Data drives everything.

Share information, exchange ideas, and discuss any database programming or administration issues.

INTERNET TECHNOLOGIES AND NETWORKING
Try living without plumbing (and eventually IPv6).

Talk about networking topics including protocols, design, administration, wireless, wired, storage, backup, certifications, trends, and new technologies.

JAVA
We've come a long way from the old Oak tree.

Hang out and discuss Java in whatever flavor you choose: J2SE, J2EE, J2ME, Jakarta, and so on.

MAC OS X
All about the Zen of OS X.

OS X is both the present and the future for Mac apps. Make suggestions, offer up ideas, or boast about your new hardware.

OPEN SOURCE
Source code is good; understanding (open) source is better.

Discuss open source technologies and related topics such as PHP, MySQL, Linux, Perl, Apache, Python, and more.

PROGRAMMING/BUSINESS
Unfortunately, it is.

Talk about the Apress line of books that cover software methodology, best practices, and how programmers interact with the "suits."

WEB DEVELOPMENT/DESIGN
Ugly doesn't cut it anymore, and CGI is absurd.

Help is in sight for your site. Find design solutions for your projects and get ideas for building an interactive Web site.

SECURITY
Lots of bad guys out there—the good guys need help.

Discuss computer and network security issues here. Just don't let anyone else know the answers!

TECHNOLOGY IN ACTION
Cool things. Fun things.

It's after hours. It's time to play. Whether you're into LEGO® MINDSTORMS™ or turning an old PC into a DVR, this is where technology turns into fun.

WINDOWS
No defenestration here.

Ask questions about all aspects of Windows programming, get help on Microsoft technologies covered in Apress books, or provide feedback on any Apress Windows book.

HOW TO PARTICIPATE:
Go to the Apress Forums site at **http://forums.apress.com/**.
Click the New User link.